INVITATION TO
PHILOSOPHICAL
THINKING

ELIZABETH L. BEARDSLEY
Temple University

MONROE C. BEARDSLEY
Temple University

INVITATION TO PHILOSOPHICAL THINKING

HARCOURT BRACE JOVANOVICH, INC.
New York   Chicago   San Francisco   Atlanta

49321

FOREWORD

A beginning student of philosophy might well be grateful to the instructor who places in his hands one of the admirable collections of readings that are now available (even though it may weigh rather heavily, in both a physical and a mental sense). But he might also welcome a more continuous and organized account of at least a few of the main problems of philosophy, to help him see the intellectual gestalts that may be obscured by the variety of concerns and styles that a book of readings in philosophy inevitably presents. It is this second need that we hope to satisfy by offering this brief abridgment of our *Philosophical Thinking: An Introduction to Philosophy*. We have selected three very basic and central groups of problems—in theory of knowledge, philosophy of mind, and normative ethics—as samples of philosophical discussion. They are designed to open up thought rather than close it off, to suggest connections with ideas that turn up in widely used selections from philosophic writings, and to help the student toward a clear and coherent sense of what philosophers are up to when they question, analyze, theorize, offer refutations, and defend their views.

Since this short preface to philosophy is intended not as a finishing course but as a springboard for further thinking, we supply, at the end of the text, comprehensive reading lists on the main topics discussed. They will guide the reader to many interesting discussions which he will find helpful to his own thinking and writing.

E.L.B.   M.C.B.

CONTENTS

INVITATION TO PHILOSOPHICAL THINKING

CHAPTER ONE

❧

THE NATURE OF PHILOSOPHICAL THINKING

Philosophical questions grow out of a kind of thinking that is familiar to all of us: the thinking that we do when we ask ourselves whether something that we believe is reasonable to believe. "Reasonable" has a broad, but definite, meaning here: a reasonable belief is simply a belief for which a good reason can be given. Reasonable beliefs are logically justifiable. It would seem that a belief that is reasonable stands a better chance of being true than one that is not, so anyone who is interested in the truth of his beliefs should be concerned about their reasonableness.

All of us have known, long before we approached the systematic study of philosophy, what it is like to want to make a belief reasonable, and also what it is like not to care whether a belief is reasonable or not. We have all had the experience of accepting beliefs without worrying about their logical justification, for we have all been children. We absorbed the beliefs of our parents, or the opinions current in our society or culture, without thinking about them very much or looking at them with a critical eye. We may not even have been fully aware that we had them; we may have acted on them without ever having put them into words. As long as our own experience did not seem to conflict with those early beliefs, or those beliefs did not seem to clash with one another, it did not occur to us to question them or to inquire into the reasons that could be given for them.

But experience, if we pay heed to it, is bound to challenge some of our beliefs, even at an early age. The child who discovers the Christmas presents hidden away in a closet on December 24 may well begin to reconsider his cherished faith in Santa Claus. The junior high school student who begins to observe what is happening around him in his city or neighborhood may find that his city government doesn't seem to be working as well as the government ideally described in his school civics book. Of course there may be answers that satisfy them for a while: that Santa Claus has his "helpers"; that our city or our neighborhood is merely an unfortunate exception to what generally obtains. But still further experience —a better grip on the laws of nature, or travel to other cities—may undermine these answers, too. Many questions that are suggested by experience are answered by more experience, but some go deep and linger long. And at some stage of life and growth, we may even wonder whether there is anything we can be really sure of. Are any "authorities," no matter how eminent, really to be depended upon? Can we trust even the evidence of our own senses?

The search for good reasons for our beliefs, and for good reasons for the reasons, can be carried as far as we wish. If it is carried far enough, the searcher finds himself confronted by questions of a peculiar kind: the questions of philosophy. Among these questions you will find some that you have already thought about, as well as others that will be unfamiliar to you. Many of them, however, originally came to be asked because someone undertook a critical examination of his ordinary beliefs.

§ 1. • *Philosophical Questions*

As our first example, let us trace the origin of a few philosophical questions that arise out of the moral aspects of life. People say, "He ought to be put in jail for that." Sometimes this is only an exclamation of anger at some instance of meanness or brutality; sometimes it leads to action, however, for juries do put people in jail because (if the jurors are conscientious) they believe that this punishment is just. Suppose you hear a friend remark, about the recent conviction of someone who has violated the law—a holdup man, a venal judge, an industrialist who has conspired to fix prices, a civil rights demonstrator who has blocked a construction site—that the jail sentence is deserved. After you hear all the relevant details, you may agree with him. But even so, you might still wonder whether you are right, and—not because you plan to do anything about the case, but merely because you would like to be sure you *are* right—you may begin to ask further, more searching, questions.

Why does the man deserve to be sent to jail? Because he committed a crime, of course. Yes, but why should he be sent to jail for committing a crime? Because to disobey the laws of the state is wrong. But *why?* Just because certain people you don't even know, perhaps people who died years before you were born, passed a law against, let us say, spitting in the subway or disorderly conduct, how does that obligate you to obey the law?

This line of questioning, as we can foresee, will, if carried far, lead into some perplexing questions about the moral basis of the law, the tests of right and wrong, the purposes of government and society. For example, we may discover that in approving the jail sentence we are assuming that the existence of a government is so important to maintain that governments have the right, under certain conditions, to deprive any citizen of his liberties. This assumption is a philosophical belief. And when we ask whether or not it is true, we are asking a philosophical question.

Notice how our questions elicit not only the direct reasons that are actually given, or could sensibly be given, for a particular belief, but also certain underlying assumptions, of which, indeed, the believer may have been quite unaware until pressed. Suppose we ask someone why he says that X ought to be sent to jail, and he replies that X is criminally inclined and needs to be reformed by punishment. That is his reason. But the reason, so to speak, does not stand by itself; it only works if we assume that putting people in jail actually does reform them. Whether this proposition is true is a question of fact—a question for psychologists and sociologists to answer—though it, too, will yield philosophical puzzles if we examine the further assumptions that might be made in trying to test it. The underlying assumptions of a belief are not, in a strict sense, the reasons for it, but they are part of its logical justification, since they have to be true for the reasons to count. One of the most remarkable features of persistent philosophical questioning is the way it brings to light hidden or half-hidden assumptions, including some of the greatest importance.

Now consider how the questioning might turn into a different channel. Granted that the act was illegal, there still remains the question whether the man should be punished. Sometimes people do wrong things because they are feeble-minded or mentally ill, and we do not regard them as punishable. Well, in this case, it might be said, the man is responsible for his action. Why responsible? Because he was free when he committed it— free to commit the act or to refrain from committing it. He had, some would say, free will. Indeed, all men have free will—though they do not always exercise it. Then what reason is there to believe that this in turn, is true? How do we know there is such a thing as free will? Again, we seem to have uncovered an underlying belief that lies deeper than the lawyer's or the juror's immediate problems, something they do not themselves discuss, but (according to one theory) take for granted. We have reached another belief that can be called philosophical, and exposed another philosophical question: do human beings have free will?

Let us see what it is about these questions that makes them philosophical. One of the first things that might be noticed about them is that they are highly *general*. One question is more general than another if it is about a broader class of things: about brown cows rather than about Farmer Jones's brown cow Bossy, or about cows rather than about brown cows, or about animals rather than about cows. A question about everything there is would be the most general of all. Most philosophical questions are highly general: are all right actions those that promote human happiness? Is all knowledge based on sense-experience? Or—to recall those that turned up in our example—do all human beings have free will? Do all citizens owe certain obligations to their governments? Those who specialize in subjects other than philosophy may be interested in particular things or events, such as individual crimes or criminals. Or they may be interested in things or events of certain limited kinds, such as the psychological or sociological causes of crime. The philosopher goes into action when questions are raised about much larger classes, such as the class of human beings or of true propositions. Those who limit their investigations are entirely justified in doing so, for human knowledge could scarcely develop otherwise. Courts would never get their work done if every judge felt called upon to solve wide-ranging questions about guilt and responsibility before he could get down to the business of trying a particular case. But somebody, sometime, must ask those broad questions and try to answer them. That is the job of the philosopher.

Some questions count as philosophical because of a second, and even more important, quality: they are highly *fundamental*. The beliefs that a particular person has at a particular time constitute a more or less orderly system, depending on the extent to which they are logically interconnected, some being reasons for others, some of the others being in turn reasons for still others, etc. When you are pressed for your reason for predicting rain, if you reply that you observe dark clouds, then in your thinking at that time the second belief is more fundamental than the first. Of course a belief that is very fundamental in one person's thinking may not be at all fundamental in another's; that is one reason why each person comes at philosophy a little differently from everyone else. But there are some beliefs that are pretty sure to be fundamental in the thinking of anyone who holds them at all, and it is these that we have in mind when we speak of fundamental beliefs and fundamental questions without mentioning any particular believer.

When one belief supports another, but is not itself supported by it, it is logically more fundamental; there is more to it, so to speak, and therefore, in principle at least, it is capable of supporting a wider range of other beliefs. Thus, of two beliefs, the more fundamental one is probably the one that underlies and supports more of your other beliefs. If you should discover that you were mistaken about a particular fact, you would probably not have to revise many of your other beliefs to accommodate this change. But, for example, a belief in the immortality of the soul may be tied up with many other beliefs about morality, religion, education, and science. A highly fundamental question is a question about the truth of a highly fundamental belief. And such questions are philosophical ones. The more general a question is, the more fundamental it is likely to be, because it will range over a large area. But this is not necessarily true. For example, the question "Are all men selfish?" and the question "Do all men wear shoes?" are equally general, since they are about all men; but they are not equally fundamental, since the former has important consequences for our beliefs about the nature of moral obligation (which includes a host of beliefs about particular obligations), while little seems to depend upon the latter. On the other hand, the philosophical question "Does God exist?" does not seem to be general at all, for it is about a single being. Nevertheless, this question is fundamental for many people, since many other beliefs about human beings and the physical universe may depend upon the answer to it—and some of these beliefs are themselves highly general.

We do not know how to set up any rules telling exactly how general or how fundamental a question must be in order for it to be considered a philosophical one. Philosophers themselves might not all agree on the proper classification of every question you can think of. But if the demand for good reasons is pressed, beginning with any belief, it will gradually pass beyond the scope of various special fields of knowledge and investigation, and at some point it will bring to light a question that many philosophers would be interested in, and would recognize—perhaps with joy, and perhaps, if it is a very tough one, with uneasiness—as their very own.

§ 2. • *Philosophical Examination*

Any thinking that concerns the truth of a philosophical belief is *philosophical thinking*. It may take the form of accepting a belief as true and investigating its logical connections with other beliefs; this may be called *exploring* the belief. Or it may take the form of questioning the belief and attempting to determine whether it is based on good reasons; this may be called *examining* the belief. Professional philosophers are those who have made philosophical thinking their vocation; but they have no monopoly on that activity. It is pursued by specialists in other fields—by scientists, historians, literary critics—whenever they inquire into the fundamental questions about their own disciplines. And it is pursued by all intelligent human beings who want to understand themselves and their world. Professional philosophers who genuinely respect their subject do not erect "No Trespassing" signs around philosophical questions.

In order to illustrate a little more fully what is involved in the process of examining a belief philosophically, let us take an example from history —let us begin with the belief that such-and-such a culture flourished hundreds of years before the Christian era in Central Africa or Nigeria. When the historian tells us this, we believe him. But if we have some intellectual curiosity, we might wonder how he knows it. Since the culture had no written language, he cannot rely on documents. And since their thatched houses and all the organic materials they once used in their daily life (wood, hide, cloth) would long ago have disintegrated in the tropical climate, the African historian has less to go on than his colleagues in other areas.[1] The usual methods developed by archaeologists are seldom available to him. It is hard to find organic materials on which to use the carbon 14 dating method (based on the constant rate of decay of this isotope in living organisms), though some artifacts have been dated in this way. Because of the rapid decay of dead wood and the eccentricities of seasonal growth, he cannot make much use of dendrochronology (dating by tree rings). But suppose the historian answers our challenge by using another method, thermoluminescence. In pottery there are uranium impurities that radiate naturally, but this radiation is trapped until the pottery is heated to a very high temperature. When the radiation rate for a particular substance is known, it is possible to determine how long ago the pottery was baked by measuring the amount of radiation built up in it.

Now we began with a question asked by the historian, "When did this culture flourish?" and the historian gave his answer. But when we ask him for his reasons he appeals to principles of physics: for example, that the radiation rate of this kind of pottery is always such-and-such. If we ask him, "How do you know this?" he will, of course, conduct us to the physicist and advise us to direct our question to him—he is the expert on radiation. Suppose we do so. Presumably the physicist's answer will be something of this sort: "We have tested various samples in our laboratory under controlled conditions, and found that the radiation rate is constant." Now, "constant" here means that it holds not only for last week's laboratory samples, but for the same substance a thousand years ago and a thousand years hence.

Our historical curiosity is satisfied, and we would ordinarily be content to accept the physicist's conclusion, too. But, however irritating it may be, let us continue to press our question ruthlessly. "Why do you say," we ask the physicist, "that just because the radiation rate was constant all last week, it must have been the same thousands of years ago?" At first he may not quite know what we are after. "Well," he might say, hoping to appease us, "my experiments have shown that the radiation rate is independent of various environmental conditions, such as moisture, and I have reason to believe that the *relevant* conditions were the same in the past as they are now." If we are astute as well as doggedly persistent, we can point out something to him in return: "But you seem to be assuming a general proposition that whenever the same conditions exist, the same effects will occur—'like causes, like effects,' or something of the sort."

Granted that if this general principle holds true, the physicist's particular law about the constancy of radiation rate can be justified—but again we can ask, "How do we know that like causes produce like effects? How do we know that an event always has certain relevant causal conditions,

[1] For this example, and the details concerning it, we are indebted to Harrison M. Wright, "Tropical Africa: The Historian's Dilemma." *Swarthmore Alumni Magazine* (October, 1963).

and that whenever these conditions recur, the effect must recur, too?" Now we have left the physicist behind, too, and crossed over into the mysterious territory of philosophy. For we have asked a highly general question—since it is about all events, without exception, including everything that has happened or ever will happen. And it seems to be a highly fundamental question, since the assumption that every event has a cause, if it is true, must underlie an enormous number of other beliefs, not only in history and physics but in the common affairs of ordinary life.

Indeed, at this point we seem to have left everyone behind but the philosopher. And that is one of the peculiarities of this subject. When Harry Truman was President, he had a sign over his desk that said, "The buck stops here." The philosopher does his intellectual work under a similar sign, for there is no one to whom he can pass on a question with the plea that it is too general or too fundamental for him to deal with. The philosopher—and with him anyone else who is doing philosophical thinking—stands at the end of the line.

Here are two more samples of thinking that begins with a nonphilosophical belief but leads gradually but directly into philosophy. We present them in the form of brief dialogues.

Dialogue I

A: You ought to have written to your parents last Sunday.

B: Why?

A: Because you promised you would write every Sunday.

B: I know I did, but I've been awfully busy. Why was it so important to keep my promise?

A: Not just *that* promise—*any* promise. It's wrong ever to break a promise.

B: Well, I used to think that, but now I'm not sure. What makes you think it's always wrong to break promises?

A: My reason is simply that most people in our society disapprove of it. You know perfectly well that they do.

B: Of course I know that most people in our society disapprove of breaking promises, but does that prove it really is always wrong to do it? The majority opinion in our society could be mistaken, couldn't it? I don't see why it should be taken for granted that what most Americans *think* is wrong and what really *is* wrong should always coincide. What's the connection between the two?

Dialogue II

A: In my paper for political science I had to define "democracy." "Democracy" means "government by the people collectively."

B: What made you choose that definition?

A: I looked up the word in the dictionary, of course.

B: How do you know your dictionary is right? My dictionary doesn't always give the same definitions as yours.

A: Oh, but mine is larger and more recent, so it's bound to be more reliable.

B: Yes, but language is constantly changing, and words like "democracy" are used in lots of different ways. I think one shouldn't feel bound by any dictionary definition. Every writer should feel free to define any word as he wishes.

A: But that would be chaotic. Besides, you wouldn't really have definitions at all, in that case.

B: Why wouldn't you have definitions? There's no such thing as *the* "one true meaning" of a word, is there? Words mean whatever people make them mean, so why shouldn't I select my own meanings and put them in definitions of my own?

Very different topics are discussed in these brief conversations; but they follow a similar pattern. In each case, speaker A makes an opening remark of a fairly specific sort, speaker B asks A to give a good reason for his opening statement, and A does provide what, on the level of ordinary common-sense thinking, would be regarded as a satisfactory reason. Many conversations would end at this stage; but B is disposed to probe more deeply, to uncover the assumptions underlying A's reasons, and to ask whether these more basic assumptions, in turn, are reasonable. Notice how the beliefs being questioned become more general and more fundamental as the questioning goes on. In each of the little dialogues, B pushes A over the brink into philosophy. At the end of each, he raises a question concerning the truth of a philosophical belief—and there the matter is left, for the time being.

But you may not be content to leave it at that. If you feel some frustration or impatience with the way A and B are arguing, you are on the verge of doing some philosophical thinking yourself. Wouldn't you like to ask B some searching questions—for example, about the way in which he is using some of his key words? This would all be a lot clearer, you may have said to yourself while you were reading Dialogue I, if we were sure just what the word "wrong" means here. Maybe it means simply "disapproved by a majority of people in one's own society." In that case, what happens to B's final question? Isn't he confused? But *does* "wrong" mean only this? And take the term "free will," which was used in one of the other examples of philosophical thinking discussed above. How can we decide whether it is reasonable to believe that human beings have this mysterious thing without saying precisely what it is?

If you have been thinking for yourself along these lines, or (even if you haven't) if you can now see the sense in raising these questions about the meaning of key words, you will be able to sympathize with a good deal of what contemporary philosophers have been doing. Philosophers at all periods have been concerned to analyze the meaning of basic philosophical terms, but this task has received more attention from twentieth-century philosophers—or from many of them, at least—than ever before. By "key words" in philosophy we mean simply those words that are used in statements of beliefs that are highly general and fundamental, and in questions about these beliefs. A question about the meaning of such a word, such as the question "What does 'cause' mean?" is itself highly fundamental, since the notion of causality plays a pervasive part in our thinking, and much might depend upon being clear about it. And we can see how it is that questions about the meaning of particular terms have led philosophers very naturally to still more fundamental questions about meaning itself, along with other basic characteristics of language. This further stage of interest in language is displayed in Dialogue II, in which speaker B is not content to accept A's remarks about the definition of the word "democracy" without questioning his assumptions about the very process of definition itself. Here B reveals a conviction (which we all can share) that we ought to be as clear as possible about the words in which we express our beliefs.

Increased clearness in your own beliefs is, then, one of the three chief benefits you can derive from a study of philosophy—if, as we hope, you are not content merely to learn about the theories and arguments of the great philosophers (interesting and valuable as that is), but will make this study an active exercise in philosophical thinking.

The second benefit, partly dependent on the first, is increased assurance that your beliefs are reasonable. A belief whose reasons have been examined deeply enough to reach the level of philosophical questioning rests on a firmer foundation than one that has been examined less thoroughly. This does not mean that everyone should become a professional philosopher. Admittedly, the philosopher's desire to base his beliefs on good reasons is unusually persistent and intense: the philosopher would not only rather be right than President—he would rather be right than anything. But all of us who want assurance that our beliefs are well grounded should do some philosophical thinking about some of them, at least, in order to secure the firmest possible grounds.

The third benefit which the study of philosophy can confer upon our beliefs is increased consistency. For philosophical thinking forces each of us to see whether his fundamental beliefs in different areas of experience form a logically coherent whole. We have already encountered in this chapter a pair of philosophical beliefs that seem in danger of clashing head-on in a contradiction. You will recall how we found that the philosophical examination of a belief about an African culture seemed to uncover an underlying assumption that every event happens under such conditions that when they are repeated, the same sort of event must happen again—in other words, that every event happens in accordance with a law of nature. And when we examined the assumptions underlying punishment we found that these seem to include the assumption that human beings have free will. To have free will is to be able to act in two different ways under precisely the same conditions. But if it is ever true that a man could have acted differently under the same conditions—i.e., that the conditions did not completely determine his action—then there is *one event* (namely the action) that did *not* happen in accordance with any law of nature. Perhaps further examination would clear things up; but it looks as if we have here a contradiction in beliefs. Philosophical thinking has diagnosed it, and further philosophical thinking is the only thing that will provide a cure.

The three values we have cited—clarity, reasonableness, and consistency—are basic intellectual values. But perhaps you are saying to yourself something like this: "I can see that studying philosophy may help me improve my beliefs, but, after all, there is more to life than thinking and believing. What I most want from my education is to improve my *actions*. How can philosophical thinking help me to *live* better?"

Part of our answer here is that we must beware of drawing too sharp a line between beliefs and actions. Our beliefs—including philosophical beliefs—have a considerable influence on our actions. This influence can be seen most directly in one area of philosophy, where we are concerned with questions of value, but answers to some other basic philosophical questions may also possess some power to affect, however indirectly, the way we live. Although knowledge may be valuable for its own sake, as well as for its practical consequences, it is not wrong to expect philosophy to have its effects. It would be wrong, however, to ask every philosophical belief to show a direct and simple connection with human action. Perhaps the growing appreciation of the importance of basic research in science may foster an appreciation of the quest for answers to other highly fundamental questions, without insistence on immediate practical results.

In saying that beliefs influence actions, we do not mean to lose sight of the effect of emotions on human conduct. Temporary emotions, as well as more enduring emotional attitudes, are often powerful enough to make us behave in ways counter to what we believe intellectually. Philosophical thinking can do a great deal to clarify and harmonize our beliefs at all levels, and to strengthen their foundations. But the philosopher is no substitute for the psychiatrist, or for the parents and teachers of our early years who helped create our emotional make-up. Yet many philosophers have claimed that the experience of thinking about philosophical questions can affect our emotional attitudes as well as our beliefs.

When we detach our minds from immediate practical matters and from the limited boundaries of particular fields of specialization, we experience a kind of release from petty and provincial concerns. The experience of thinking as human beings who are trying to understand themselves and their universe may produce a serenity and breadth of mind that can in time become enduring attitudes. Bertrand Russell, whom many regard as a great philosopher, has expressed this claim in this way: "The mind which has become accustomed to the freedom and impartiality of philosophic contemplation will preserve something of the same freedom and impartiality in the world of action and emotion."[2] This is an important thing to say about philosophical thinking, if it is true. Whether it *is* true is something that each individual must discover for himself.

§ 3. • *The Divisions of Philosophy*

As will be evident later, the problems of philosophy are closely intertwined; the more you explore one problem, the more you see how it calls for a consideration of others. And to see such connections, to understand how a solution to one problem helps you with, or even commits you to, a solution to another is one of the interesting things about philosophy. But when you first come to study it systematically, you must find places to begin, and for this purpose it is convenient to sort out the problems into various groups.

One method of classification is to collect together all the philosophical questions that arise from examining beliefs in each recognized special field of human knowledge or experience. For example, we might gather all philosophical questions concerning our beliefs about the events and processes of history. If we did this, we would have to include some very broad questions, such as the question whether all events whatsoever are governed by law, which we have just encountered. There would be many others, not quite so general or so fundamental, but still sufficiently so to be considered philosophical: Are there repeated cyclical patterns in history? Can the historian be objective? Do the actions of individual great men, as opposed to the yearnings and discontents of ordinary men, determine historical change? Questions of this degree of generality and fundamentalness are sometimes dealt with by thinkers whose training and experience are those of the historian rather than those of the philosopher, for they lie near the borderline between history and philosophy. But since they arise out of reflection upon historical events and written history, they may be grouped together as the philosophy of history.

The phrase "philosophy of" is an important one for the philosopher, though there is a tendency for people who are not philosophers to cast it about rather loosely. Football coaches sometimes speak of their "philosophy of football," and no doubt there are philosophical questions that one can be led to by thinking seriously and deeply about football. Indeed, sometimes the views of football coaches—about the role of sports in the life of high school or college, in relation to other values—clearly verge upon the philosophy of education. Very often, however, one's "philosophy of X" is little more than one's vague convictions about X; but this usage is too loose to be helpful. If there is such a thing as the philosophy of football, it comprises beliefs more general and more fundamental than the view

[2] *The Problems of Philosophy* (London, Oxford University Press, 1912), p. 160.

that it is more effective strategy to run a small number of well-rehearsed plays than to have a variety of complicated ones.

But the phrase "philosophy of football" nevertheless reflects an important insight, for thinking about football, like thinking about anything else, becomes more nearly philosophical as it goes deeper and becomes broader. If philosophy departments do not (as far as we know) provide courses in this subject, it is because the scope of the inquiry is relatively restricted, and the philosophical problems that would arise are taken up in other courses. When we consider broader areas of knowledge or experience, however, and inquire into the foundations of beliefs in these areas, we get groups of philosophical problems that are separately investigated and written about. We get, in short, such branches of philosophy as these:

philosophy of science
philosophy of religion
philosophy of art (aesthetics)
philosophy of history
philosophy of education
philosophy of government (political philosophy)
philosophy of law
philosophy of mathematics
philosophy of language

These are distinguishable areas of philosophical interest, and they make a useful classification for some purposes. But the classification is not a very basic one, because the categories overlap. For example, some of the questions that arise from the philosophical examination of literature and literary criticism will turn out to be the same as those that arise out of social science or history. In fact, certain questions, such as those concerning the nature of sound reasoning in general (questions of logic), will arise in all of these areas. Therefore, it is useful to work out another classification, based upon more fundamental considerations.

If we were to make a list of words that commonly turn up in philosophical questions, or in questions that approach a philosophical level of generality and depth, these words would quite readily fall into three large groups. Each of these groups of words, and consequently each group of questions, might be said to reflect a fundamental direction of philosophical inquiry.

1. There is first a set of words—some of them technical and odd, some of them very common and familiar, though no less puzzling—that refer to the whole of reality or to some of its major divisions. Among such words are "thing," "event," "existence," "essence," "space," "time," "eternal," "substance," "cause," "mental," "physical," "God," "creation," "nature." The questions we ask by means of such words—"Does part of man exist eternally?" "Can all reality be regarded as physical?" "Does God exist?"—are called *metaphysical questions,* or reality-questions. And,

for convenience and simplification, let us say that all metaphysical questions are parts of, or preparations for, the central metaphysical question, "What is the nature of reality?"

This central metaphysical question is intended to have a certain scope. In one sense, of course, any branch of human knowledge tells us something about reality, in that it gives us information about the way things are. The same is true of ordinary experience. When you say, for example, that there were no empty seats in the motion picture theater last night, you are asserting that reality is such that on December 31 all the seats were occupied by human beings. Such an addition to the sum of our knowledge is pretty restricted; and even a great deal of what the sciences tell us about the world is not sufficiently general or fundamental to be considered an answer to the central question of metaphysics. Biology, for example, is not metaphysically interesting when it describes the nervous system of the dogfish. But when biologists tell us the distinctive criteria by which they distinguish living from nonliving things, metaphysicians prick up their ears. The question how living beings differ from nonliving ones is still not quite a full-fledged metaphysical question, but a question to which it leads— whether these apparent differences are ultimate and irreducible, or whether so-called living beings cannot satisfactorily be regarded as just enormously complicated machines—is metaphysical. This latter question might be asked in this way: "Are organisms really mechanisms?" That is to say, "Does reality include nonmechanical organisms?"

This metaphysical question arises from the examination of a scientific belief. Some arise in other ways. The question whether all human beings have free will grew out of a line of inquiry concerned with an ethical belief about the justifiability of punishment. The question whether all events have causes arose directly from a statement of physics (about radiation), but originally from examining a historical fact. These questions are about the nature of reality: is the universe such that all events in it are caused? that human beings have free will?

2. A second set of philosophically noteworthy words consists of those used in evaluating or appraising things, that is, rating them in accordance with some standard of value. Among such words we find "good," "valuable," "bad," "evil," "right," "wrong," "beautiful," "just," "ought," and hundreds of others. Such words are said to have a *normative* element in their meaning. The questions that we ask by means of such words—"What makes an action wrong?" "What is a just society?" "Are some works of art better than others?"—are called *normative questions,* or value-questions. And we may take as our central, or model, value-question, "What is valuable?"

We saw that some statements about what reality is like are too narrow and unfundamental to be considered answers to metaphysical questions. Similarly, a great many beliefs concerning the value or lack of value of particular things, or even limited classes of things, are not general or fundamental enough to raise normative questions. "That picture is beautiful," "Roast turkey is good," "It is right to be grateful to your parents" are not answers to the value-questions of philosophy, though each of them, if examined, could lead to such questions. A philosopher is concerned, not with examples of valuable things, but with theories of value itself or with the basic principles underlying the major kinds of normative judgment. What troubles him is not that we never discover or experience good things, but that we sometimes disagree about what is good, or right, or beautiful, and that even when we do not disagree we often do not have full assurance that our beliefs are reasonable, because we haven't examined them and their foundations very carefully. What speaker B was trying to do in Dialogue I in the preceding section was to examine the foundations of the belief that it is never right to break a promise.

3. The third set of words used in philosophical inquiry includes words like "true," "false," "probable," "logical," "certain," "proof," "reason," "faith," "intuition," "sense-experience," "knowledge," "opinion." These refer, not to what reality is like or what is valuable, but to our *knowledge* of reality or value. The questions we ask by means of such words—"What makes one proposition follow logically from another?" "Is religious belief based on faith?" "Is anything certain?" "Can we trust our sense-experience?"—are questions about logic and what is called "theory of knowledge." Questions of this kind may be called *epistemological questions,* or knowledge-questions. And as a central, or model, epistemological question, we may take the question "How do we know?"

This question, understood as expressing the epistemologist's special concern, is not simply a general demand for a reason. For his task is to inquire into the basic principles and methods of knowing—the rules of logical reasoning, the grounds of probable inference, the nature of observation, intuition, evidence, self-evidence. These principles and methods are often taken for granted or used with little awareness that they are being used, and the problems that may be prompted by the examination of them are among the most difficult and challenging that philosophers can face.

Perhaps a word should be said here about an epistemological problem of a different kind, one that may have occurred to you in connection with our discussion of fundamental questions in the preceding section. We said that some questions are more fundamental than others. Are there ultimate —that is, *most* fundamental—questions and answers? If we consider a belief to be justified only if we can give a good reason for it, and then we must give a good reason for that reason in turn, it would seem that we may be committed to a fatal choice. Either (1) this questioning goes on forever, in which case, apparently, no good reason is given for anything, since no reason stands on its own feet, or (2) we must hope in the end to get back to beliefs that require no further reasons, that are, so to speak, their own warrant, somehow self-evident or undeniable. But in that case, since we have to accept some propositions without reasons, why could we not save trouble and accept the ones we started with? The first alternative seems to deny that it is possible to have good reasons for one's belief; the second seems to deny that it is necessary to have good reasons for one's beliefs. Each alternative has been accepted by some philosophers; other philosophers have tried to find a way out. We shall return to this challenging epistemological problem later in this book.

There is still another set of words often used in philosophical inquiry, words such as "meaning," "reference," "definition," "meaningless," "emotive," "sign," "symbol," "poetic," and many others, all having to do with certain basic characteristics of language, including the symbolic language of logic and mathematics. Questions that are asked with the help of such terms may be grouped together as questions of *semiotic,* or meaning-questions. And these are often philosophical questions, too, which might indeed be counted as a fourth group.

It seems best to us, however, at least in this introductory account of philosophy, to distribute the meaning-questions among the three groups already distinguished, for these questions are of two different sorts. We ask philosophical meaning-questions about particular terms that belong to the vocabulary of the three basic groups, and these meaning-questions are best dealt with in close connection with the other questions in each group. When we think philosophically about reality, as we have seen, we may ask about the difference between the living and the nonliving, or about the universality of causality, but we shall also almost certainly want at some point to ask for a definition of "mechanism," or of "cause." When we raise the value-questions, we can ask what actions are right, but also what the word "right" means when applied to actions. These are different questions, but both are important and philosophical. And when we raise questions about knowledge, we may want to ask not only how we know what propositions are true or probable, but how the words "true" and "probable" are used, or should be used.

Because philosophy is one subject that is not exempt from its own scrutiny, we encounter another set of problems when we turn our attention to the fundamental features of language itself. Does every meaningful word (for example, "unicorn") refer to something that exists? What is the difference between the language of poetry and the language of science? Does every grammatically correct sentence (for example, "The square root of two has purple stripes") make sense? And meaning-questions like these—since they concern the nature of the language in which we refer to the world, conduct our investigations of it, and formulate our conclusions about it—may be put into the general category of knowledge-questions. To understand how knowledge is possible at all, what its types and limitations may be, we must understand how, and under what conditions, we can talk about reality, can think about it in signs and symbols.

Our second way of classifying the problems of philosophy—as meta-physical, normative, epistemological—provides the basic distinction among the following three chapters, though a different order is followed. We pro-ceed next to what is perhaps the most important epistemological problem: whether or not all our knowledge is empirical. Then we consider a very broad metaphysical problem that has a bearing on much of our life: whether there are characteristics of human beings that distinguish them radically from all other things. Finally we consider the most familiar and pressing problem of normative ethics: what makes an action right or wrong.

CHAPTER TWO

✿

EMPIRICAL KNOWLEDGE

Each of us has, at all times, a great many beliefs (of which most are temporarily below the level of consciousness), but not all of them constitute *knowledge*. We can believe that civil disobedience is sometimes morally acceptable, yet not be very sure of this. We can believe that someone will repay a loan, but discover later that what we believed is untrue. It is philosophically convenient to have a special term for what we believe when we believe something: let us use the term "proposition." We may believe, then, the proposition "Civil disobedience is sometimes morally permissible," or the proposition "The loan will be repaid." And the proposition believed is either true or false.

What must be added to belief in order for it to constitute knowledge? Two things, at least, philosophers would agree. The first is truth. We can *believe* a false proposition, but we cannot (strictly speaking) *know* it. We can know that it is false, to be sure, but we cannot know that it is true if it is not true. Knowing that pigs have wings is equivalent to knowing that the proposition "Pigs have wings" is true, but since pigs don't have wings, to believe that pigs have wings is to be mistaken, not to have knowledge. Second, even if the proposition we believe happens to be true, we cannot be said (strictly speaking) to know that it is true unless our belief is *justified*. A true belief may be a lucky guess or a mere prejudice; in either case, it does not amount to genuine knowledge. One way of justifying a belief is to give a good reason to support the proposition believed. Some philosophers hold that there is a second way—to show that the proposition believed can be accepted on its face, and does not require the support of any reason.

A great many of the propositions we believe are clearly supported by reasons, in the form of an appeal to sense-experience. How do we know that the moon has rocks? Because the astronauts have seen them and have brought some back for us to see. How do we know that lightning is often accompanied by thunder? Because we have heard that thunder. Let us introduce the term "empirical knowledge" for knowledge that is justified in this way. This is a very rough characterization of empirical knowledge; to refine and clarify it will be one of the main purposes of the present chapter. It is too simple to say that you know something empirically when your knowledge is justified in the last analysis by an appeal to sense-experience. In the first place, as we shall see, it is not only sense-experience that can be appealed to, but feelings and emotions—as when a person comes to realize how strongly attached he was to a friend by his sense of loss at her departure. But as we shall also see, feelings and emotions do not provide empirical knowledge unless they are reasoned about in certain ways—so that the kind of knowledge claimed, for example, by the mystic is not empirical knowledge, though it is supposed to come from immediate feelings.

SCIENTIFIC METHOD

Suppose you look out the window and report that it is raining. "Are you sure?" we might ask. (Sometimes it is hard to tell whether the rain has stopped, if the window is beaded and the ground is soaked.) You look again: "Yes, I am sure." Now if we ask how you know it is raining, the answer is short and simple: "I can see the rain falling." No more, for ordinary purposes, is required. If the rain is fine and sparse, you might want to check by opening the window and holding out your hand; you might even look up to make sure the water is not just dripping off a tree. But when the rain is pouring down, you are in no doubt. Nor, apparently, do you have to hesitate, or think about it, or go through a process of deliberation: you are quite certain, all at once, that it is raining as soon as you see the rain clearly. In this case your knowledge of the rain is *direct*. On the other hand, suppose you are driving along the highway and come to a village where the sun is shining but the grass glistens with wetness, the roadway is full of puddles, and people are walking about with damp raincoats. You may conclude that it has been raining there, and recently. And you may even claim to know that it has been raining there. But you don't see it raining; you have to infer that from what you see. You may hesitate before you believe it; you may even think momentarily of alternative possibilities (water-sprinklers; a Fourth of July water-battle between the rival volunteer fire companies). In this case your knowledge of the rain is *indirect*.

The things we know directly, in this sense, may be divided into two broad classes. First, there are physical objects, events and processes in the world about us: the grey squirrel, the doctor's voice, the reading of the thermostat, the smoke pouring out of the fireplace, the hurried driver backing into the fender of a parked car. Second, there are events and states within ourselves, which we are said to know by introspection: the pain in the side, the crick in the neck, the tickle in the nose, the pervasive feeling of grief, the satisfying sense of smoothly working muscles. These feelings, emotions, pleasures and pains, and other assorted mental and somatic states we are not acquainted with by means of the external senses; but they seem equally to be matters of direct experience. When your nose tickles, you do not have to make an inference that it is tickling; you know it just by feeling the tickle.

Propositions that are backed up immediately by direct experience may be called "observation-propositions." Perhaps in ordinary speech we would not be likely to call the introspective ones "observations" (a person does not strictly observe his own toothache, it might be said). Yet it will be handy to have a term that covers both sorts of directly obtained knowledge —that is, all propositions that are directly confirmed by experience. Other things, we shall say, are known, not by observation alone, but by inference from observations. And it is the nature of that inference that concerns us now.

Doubts may arise about the nature of the distinction between direct and indirect empirical knowledge, and it is puzzling to know exactly where the line should be drawn. When we see a goblet in a good light, we are certainly observing it; when we read about the Holy Grail, we are certainly not observing it. But suppose we see the goblet reflected in a mirror—are we observing it then? Suppose it is a distorting mirror? Does the astronomer strictly observe the moons of Jupiter through his telescope, or if they are photographed by an apparatus sent high up into the rarer atmosphere in a balloon? For our purposes it is not necessary to refine the distinction: we may speak of "observation" when the seeing is closely connected with what is observed. To look through the telescope or microscope is to observe; to see the object in a photograph or on TV is not to observe that object, though it is to observe something else: namely, the picture that is presented.

§ 1. • *Indirect Empirical Knowledge*

It follows from the way in which our distinction has been introduced that directness is sometimes relative to an individual person. What one knows directly is not exactly what another knows directly. Where their experience overlaps—where both have been to Spain or bird-watched in the same swamp—two people may both know the same things directly. If their lives are separated by many centuries, a great part of what one knows directly is either unknown to, or known only indirectly by, the other. Not quite all: the constellations in the night sky will be the same; A. E. Housman, in his poem "On Wenlock Edge," imagines the modern Englishman and the ancient Roman staring at the same wind-blown hilltop forest. If two people's paths never cross, they will know few of the same things directly. Of course, their experience may be similar, even closely similar, as when two people have both spent three years in the Peace Corps—but each knows his own career directly and the other's indirectly.

In one aspect, what you know directly is amazingly various and manifold, but fortunately much of it is quickly forgotten, because in another aspect it is rather limited. For most of the important and interesting things you know are matters of indirect knowledge, at least to you, and in the most important and interesting cases to all human beings. You know, for example, a great deal about the past, and though most of this was at one time directly known by someone who left a record (a memoir, a carved rock, a stamped coin), to you it is indirect. (Whether our own memories should be classified as direct or indirect knowledge is a hard question that we here leave open.) You know a great deal indirectly about distant places on the earth, though you have not visited them, and even about stars and galaxies enormous distances away.

One of the main philosophical questions of the present chapter can be raised about these two types of proposition—propositions about the past and propositions about distant objects. How do we know they are true? In every particular case the answer may be easy. You learned about the lamas of Tibet from a returned traveler or Cinerama. You learned about the unsavory activities of Caligula and Nero, perhaps, from reading Suetonius. But what we want is a general answer—what is the method, or principle, involved? In both cases, the general pattern is clear. To justify your indirect knowledge, when pressed, you fall back upon something you know directly: the motion picture, the voice of the traveler, the words on the printed page. What, then, gives you the right to say you know certain matters indirectly merely because you have certain direct knowledge? How does it come about that you manage to know anything at all indirectly— that you are not condemned to remain forever within the circle of your immediate experience?

These will be our leading questions, and they become even more difficult and far-reaching when we consider two other sorts of indirect empirical knowledge that are extremely important to us. The first is knowledge about matters that are not only beyond the range of one person's experience or the experience of human beings so far, but beyond any possible human experience. Some people have seen the sources of the Nile, some haven't; but nobody will ever know an electron directly, for it is just not the kind of thing that can be seen, touched, or smelled. An electron (and the same holds for other fundamental entities that are referred to in microphysics) is unobservable, not just in fact, but in principle; it is defined in such a way, or plays such a role in physical theory, that it would be nonsense to say, "Last night I saw an electron."

Our presumed knowledge of these (in principle) unobservable entities raises a special problem in the philosophy of science. It is too technical to deal with at all adequately in this book. But note what sort of problem it is. Suppose we could understand how one person knows indirectly about things that are directly known to others, or at least could be directly known to others. The astronomer's telescope brings him closer to Mars, and what he infers about snow or vegetation on Mars he imagines as being subject to further check if someone could get over there and look around. But the nuclear physicist who performs elaborate calculations and then experiments with a Wilson cloud chamber or cyclotron or linear accelerator can deal only indirectly with his diminutive particles, some of which last but the tiniest fraction of a second. There is no such thing as direct knowledge in this case; it is all indirect. But then how can this sort of knowledge be connected with the direct knowledge—the marks on the photograph taken in the cloud chamber, the readings of the instruments on the cyclotron control board?

The second kind of knowledge that goes beyond direct experience is problem-raising in another way. It is *general* knowledge: the kind of knowledge that is expressed in scientific laws. Newton's first law of motion states that "A body not acted on by an impressed force will continue in a state of rest or of uniform motion in a straight line," and, despite the corrections that would have to be introduced from relativity theory, it will serve as a good example of a law. It is universal in form: it covers *all* particles of matter, past, present, and future. And it states a correlation between two quantities, force and acceleration (or change of velocity).

Now consider the familiar law discovered by Georg Simon Ohm in 1827: that when an electric current passes through a solid metallic conductor that is inactive and electrolytic and is maintained at a constant temperature, the magnitude of the current is proportional to the total electromotive force, or

Under conditions C, $I \propto E$.

Another way of formulating this law is to say that under certain exactly specifiable conditions the relation of I to E is always the same:

Under conditions C, $\dfrac{I}{E}$ is constant.

The first point to notice about this law is that it is stated in a perfectly general way. It does not hold under all conditions, of course. When the circuit is raised to a very high temperature, the conductance—that is, the ratio I/E—generally decreases (this holds for most metals, but not carbon, for example). But what the physicist is after when he searches for a law is still universality. For when all the conditions that affect the conductance of the conductor are known, the law can be made quite general: under such-and-such conditions, a certain quantity holds constant, whatever (say) the weather or the humor of the laboratory assistant or the pollen count of the atmosphere may be. Thus to discover a constant relationship among certain physical quantities is at one and the same time to discover that a certain quantity depends upon others and that it is *independent* of still others. For example, the conductance is not affected by the magnitude of the current, from extremely weak currents to currents a billion times as strong.

The second point is that the generality of the law—the range over which it is asserted to hold—is far wider than the actual experience it is based on. Ohm discovered his law by making a number of careful measurements, but when he stated the law he did not limit its application to his measurements. He did not write something like, "In all experiments performed by me in January and February, I/E was observed to be constant." The law applies to *all* circuits of the specified sort and all measurements on them, without regard to dates and places. Of course, if it should turn out that the law does not hold in a powerful gravitational field, such as on Jupiter, then it would have to be modified. Either the law would be restated so as to apply only in relatively weak gravitational fields, or, if the effect of the gravitation could be determined, a new factor, G, would be added to the formula.

Thus it is clear that when we accept a law we are accepting more than any particular human being, or any finite number of human beings, can possibly observe. If lightning could have struck wires before men appeared on earth, the current would have behaved according to Ohm's law; and if there are electric circuits when men have disappeared, the same will be true. So if we do know any laws of nature, then we must know them indirectly, though again, of course, our knowledge of them depends somehow upon what we know directly—for example, upon what Ohm saw happening in his laboratory.

There is a third respect in which our knowledge of the workings of nature ventures beyond what we actually observe. If we could watch Ohm in his laboratory and look over his shoulder, we would see him testing a particular metal and length of wire for currents of varying strength and writing down his results. And we would notice that as far as his measurements are concerned, I/E is *not* perfectly constant. Sometimes it is a little more, sometimes a little less, though always the results hover about a certain central value. After a number of tries, if the various recorded figures group themselves pretty densely and seldom deviate more than a few percentage points, Ohm will feel secure in his conclusions that he has found a constant. To be sure, other physicists later on, with more refined instruments, might measure it more precisely, but Ohm will believe himself justified in asserting that in fact the conductor is behaving in exactly the same way each time, and that the small variations in the measurements are due to unavoidable human error in reading the instruments (the volt-meter and ammeter), or to minor variations in the working of the instruments themselves. If there are large variations in the measurements, it may be that the ratio I/E is not constant. But when nature teases him, the physicist doesn't give up easily. He protects his law, within narrow limits, by allowing for a margin of error.

Thus not only does the law, as stated, go beyond the observations, but it may actually deviate from most of them. Evidently Ohm was doing something more than noting approximate regularities in nature: he was in fact inventing a new scientific concept, that of conductance, i.e., an ideally exact and constant relationship between I and E. He chose this particular relationship out of all the mathematically possible ones (such as the product of I and E) because he found it useful for understanding the observations he had made. But the concept itself goes beyond experience.

§ 2. • *The Method of Generalization*

Between what we know directly, by inward and outward observation, and what we know indirectly, there seems to yawn a kind of logical gap—that is, a separation that has to be bridged by inference. How, then, we must ask, can this be done? Granted that we are justified in believing what we observe—how can these observations justify us in believing empirical propositions whose truth we cannot directly confirm?

This question calls, first, for an examination of the actual processes of reasoning by which we do in fact (whether justifiable or not) come to believe indirect empirical propositions. Much can be said (and has been said) about this way of reasoning, but we shall have to be content to single out a few highly significant features. At bottom there are two main processes, distinct though closely related—two methods by which we ordinarily claim to make discoveries about what lies beyond the range of our immediate experience. Familiar as they both are to all of us, for philosophical purposes we must try to look at them with fresh eyes, as if we had just heard of them and were willing to take nothing for granted.

The first method is to *generalize* from what we observe. Let us imagine a man of moderate intelligence whose distant relative sends him a barometer for Christmas. As sometimes happens, the instructions are lost, and the inscriptions have been knocked off in transit. He has no knowledge or curiosity about the instrument, but it looks impressive, so he hangs it on the wall. Admiring it from time to time, on different days, he notices that the column of liquid rises and falls. Eventually he may come to realize that when it falls quite low, a storm of some kind generally occurs within twenty-four hours. Is this a coincidence or is there a connection? Our observer takes the step from "generally has been" to "generally is (including past, present, and future)"—that is, his thinking moves from a proposition about certain cases that he has observed to a broader proposition whose scope includes an indefinite number of cases that he has not observed. This broader proposition might be a universal generalization: "All instances of the barometer's falling are followed by stormy weather." If he is more intelligent, he will of course take into account that the observed correlation between barometer and weather seems to occur independently of the season, the time of day, the state of his health, and so forth. And his generalization will be made more secure by these considerations—it will be more highly confirmed, or, as would often be said, it will have a greater probability of being true. Our observer has made a discovery. And his belief in the generalization involves the claim that it will survive the impact of future experience—will remain tenable despite what is observed tomorrow and the next day, and as long as there are barometers and storms.

The process of generalizing, then, begins with something known about a certain class, or set, of cases, and draws a conclusion about a larger class that includes both the original known cases and others as yet unknown. The larger class may be called a "population" (not necessarily of people), in the statistician's sense; the smaller class is a "sample" of that population. The problem of the generalizer is to insure that his sample is chosen in such a way (with such care, taking such precautions) that it will be a representative sample, that is, give him a true picture of the whole class. Now, the techniques of sampling are complex and cannot be worked out in detail without some elaborate mathematics. But one aspect of the process is of special philosophical interest: it is that the size of the sample has some bearing upon the amount of trust we place in the generalization based upon it.

This is easy enough to see in the barometer case. If our observer noticed once that the barometer went down and that it rained heavily within twenty-four hours, he could dismiss this as a mere coincidence. For if the barometer is going up and down with the tide, or if its changes depend on whether the television set is on or off, then the chances are that sometimes it will go down before it storms. But then if he continues to watch it each day, he will sooner or later find that its changes have nothing to do with the TV—that it sometimes goes up or down whether the TV set is on or off. So suppose our assiduous observer sees the barometer's fall followed by a storm once, and then again, and a third time, and a fourth, . . . he will also begin to feel that that is something *more* than a coincidence. Indeed, his confidence in the correlation will rise with every fall of the barometer. He will become bold enough to foretell the weather to his friends and risk their ire if he is wrong. In time he may become so confident that he loses interest and ceases to keep track of any further cases. But up to this point, we can say that each time a new observation is added to the sample in his possession, the generalization "Falling barometer is always followed by storm," becomes at least a little more dependable.

On the other hand, of course, if he observes a few cases where the barometer goes down and no storm follows, his confidence will be greatly weakened. Then either of two things may happen—but these are best illustrated by a different sort of example. Suppose a dermatologist is testing a new vaccine against skin disorder. He vaccinates some of his patients and waits to note the results. Some of those who are vaccinated will not be helped at all; they are the recalcitrant cases. Some of those who are not vaccinated will clear up anyway. If the proportion of those who improve is no higher among the vaccinated subjects than among the unvaccinated ones, he will have to conclude that the vaccine does them no good. At least, he clearly has no good reason to *believe* that his vaccine is useful. Now suppose, on the other hand, that only 10 per cent of the unvaccinated subjects improve within the month, but 80 per cent of the vaccinated improve; and suppose further that approximately this ratio continues over a period of several months. Here the generalization that the doctor may accept is a statistical one—that 80 per cent will be helped. It does not enable him to predict with certainty what will happen in particular cases, but he has apparently found a regularity of a kind; and again each month that goes by will, up to a point anyway, make him believe more strongly in his law.

Both the doctor and the barometer-observer are thinking in an effective and orderly way and getting results. And their thinking seems to be guided by a certain rule, which we shall call the *rule of repetition:*

> When two things (events, characteristics) are observed to be repeatedly associated with each other (simultaneously or in succession) in a regular way (that is, the percentage of cases in which they are associated is constant), *count on the association to continue, with a degree of confidence that increases with each case observed.*

There are several points to notice about this rule of repetition. First, the association may be of events (falling barometer, bad weather) or of characteristics (atomic weight of 107.88 and melting point of 961° centigrade). Second, the association may be successive (as in the barometer case, where one event follows the other) or simultaneous (as with the properties of silver). Third, the association, or correlation, may be 100 per cent or some smaller percentage. Fourth, when the number of observed cases becomes great, each new case will increase our confidence less and less, but still it will be further supporting evidence.

In singling out this rule for special notice, we do not by any means wish to imply that it is the only consideration that is relevant to the dependability of a generalization. To avoid a long and technical discussion and yet call attention to a fundamental philosophical problem (which you yourself can follow up as fully as you wish, once you understand it), we take this rule as an example. There is, however, the matter of whether the cases in the sample are selected randomly to avoid a biased sample, and there are various methods of insuring that the sample is randomly selected. But suppose we have two samples selected by the same random method; then the rule of repetition tells us that, other things being equal, the larger sample is to be taken as the better evidence for the generalization.

One implication of the rule must be kept in mind throughout our discussion. If the dependability of a generalization can in principle be increased without limit, then there is no final or absolutely conclusive degree of dependability that it can attain. It cannot, by any number of observations, be placed for all time beyond the reach of further experience; it cannot be rendered immune to the very possibility of refutation or rebuttal. And this for two reasons. First, remember that the generalization is based upon a sample. Some samples of any population are representative of the whole, some are not. Imagine a population consisting of one hundred people, of whom fifty are Republicans and fifty Democrats. Suppose we put their names in a hat and draw out some samples of four, reshuffling each time; the samples might come out this way:

Samples	Democrats	Republicans
A	4	0
B	3	1
C	2	2
D	1	3
E	0	4

These are the possible permutations. And of them only one, Sample C, gives an accurate picture of the whole population, for in that sample the party affiliations are divided in the same proportions as they are in the whole. If we were to generalize from Samples B or D, we would be badly thrown off, and if we were to generalize from A or E, our conclusion would be hopelessly mistaken. Of course, if we already know what the whole population is like, we can easily see what is a good sample and what isn't. (If we, in fact, draw ten samples, more of them will probably be like Sample C than like the others.) But when we do not know what the whole population is like—when it is just the point of the investigation to discover what it is like—then we can never arrange matters ahead of time to guarantee that our sample will be representative.

The second reason why the generalization must remain, to some degree, provisional—subject to correction by later experience—is just that it applies to the unknown as well as the known. When we generalize, our belief outreaches the evidence and runs a risk—a risk that may sometimes be, for all practical purposes, negligible, to be sure. If we generalize about a relatively small class of objects, such as all the 14 children in a certain family, of whom we have met three, then it is true that the time may come when we have met all 14, and since there are no more left, our generalization cannot be overturned by any future experience—assuming that no more can be born. But at that point what started out as a generalization ceases to be one and becomes something different, namely a summary of the 14 observations. It is essential to a generalization, by definition, that its scope stretches beyond the evidence for it.

Though a generalization cannot be made safe against all conceivable observations that might upset it, one generalization, it seems clear, can be made safer than another—more likely to withstand the results of future discoveries. And, if our analysis thus far is correct, it also seems that every generalization is reached by a process of inference that is regulated by the rule of repetition. In this sense, the rule is fundamental to all generalizing, including, of course, the generalizing that has given us the known laws of nature. But if that is so, we can now raise a philosophical question about the rule itself: what justifies us in following this rule? In other words, what good reason have we for assuming that the beliefs about nature which we form with the help of the rule are in fact true beliefs? To this question we shall later return.

§ 3. • *The Method of Hypothesis*

There is a second method by which we make empirical discoveries. For a first uncomplicated example of this method we may imagine a man coming out of the store to his parked car and finding a dent in the middle of the side that faces the street. From the size, depth, shape, and position of the dent he infers that another car has backed into his and driven away. If his evidence is solid enough, he knows about the other car and its activities indirectly. But here he is not generalizing from a sample. It is a different process of thinking that leads to his conclusion: he begins by wondering what *made* the dent, and he ends by accepting the conclusion that seems to be the most satisfactory way of accounting for its presence. This procedure—of noting a fact to be explained, proposing a tentative explanation, and then testing it by further observations—is the *method of hypothesis*.

The hypothesis in this case (H_1: "A car backed into mine") is indirectly confirmed, and regarded as fit for belief and action, if it is a good explanation of the facts that are to count as evidence for it. It would not be an explanation at all if there were not some true generalization that connects the explaining event with the event to be explained. The man already knows, from past experience, that when car A backs into car B with a certain force, it will, when withdrawn, leave a grievous dent of a certain conformation in the body of car B. Nor did he have to perform a great many experiments to establish this, for, knowing the great uniformity in bodily weakness that is a consequence of modern methods of car manufacture, he could be pretty sure of his generalization after this sort of accident happened a few times. Because of this general fact about the effect of any backer-up on a parked car, the hypothesis that in this case there was a backer-up *explains* the observed dent on the car. This is the heart of empirical explanation. Whether there are any other sorts of explanation is here left an open question; but when the ordinary person says to himself, "Ah yes, that explains why the boss has been irritable lately," or, "That explains why my car uses so much oil," this is what he means. And when the empirical scientist confirms a theory, he does the same thing: he shows that, in the last analysis, it is the most satisfactory way of accounting for the observed facts.

When we have devised a hypothesis to explain some observed fact or group of facts, our next endeavor is to see what further evidence, if any, can be obtained to support it. And to do that we try to make predictions from that hypothesis. That is, assuming for the moment that the hypothesis is true, and taking into account various relevant laws that we have already discovered, what else would we expect to observe if we were in a position to? *If* someone has backed into our car, and *if* the man standing behind the store-window staring out into the street has been there all the time, and *if* he was wide awake, then (considering what we know of human beings), *if* we go and ask him whether he saw another car back into ours, *then* he may be expected to say yes. A good many assumptions have to be made to get this prediction (some of them are not stated), but ordinarily if someone who claims to have seen the accident tells us about it, this will be further confirmation of our hypothesis. And *if* there was an accident, and *if* the driver is honest, *then* he has left a note—so we look to see whether there is one. If there isn't, this may be taken to count against the hypothesis, or it may be taken to refute one of our auxiliary assumptions (that the driver is honest).

Now, as we increase the amount of evidence for the hypothesis without finding any evidence that destroys it, we follow a rule very much like the rule of repetition. But this is not the point to be stressed here. For whatever evidence we finally accumulate, we may be left with a choice among hypotheses. Consider Hypothesis H_2: a car body repairman, desperate for business, put the dent in with a hammer. True, it looks like a bumper-dent. But no one is in a better position than he to imitate one. True, the man in the store says he saw a car back into ours. But then he must have been bribed to throw us off the scent. True, there is an apologetic note on the windshield. Forged. And so on. With ingenuity, we can generally invent an alternative hypothesis. At some point, we are faced with the necessity of making a choice. And one of the important rules that seems to guide us in this choice is a *rule of simplicity*.

> When two incompatible alternative hypotheses explain the same facts, and neither can be eliminated by available evidence, then, other things being equal, *choose the simpler of the two hypotheses.*

This does not mean, of course, that we must choose the simplest hypothesis we can think of—it must be complex enough to fit the facts, and no one can set any arbitrary limits on the degree of complexity to be tolerated in our empirical theories.

To apply the notion of simplicity throughout the whole range of science, we would have to make it much clearer than it has yet been made. Other things being equal, the physical theory that gets along with the fewest kinds of basic particle or process is the simplest one. We also want to speak of one mathematical formulation as simpler than another (that is part of what is meant by "elegance"), and of one process as being simpler than another (say, alternative hypotheses about the origin of the solar system). Judgments of simplicity are bound to be least exact in such ordinary situations as the dented car. But even there we see that one hypothesis (H_1) involves only an accidental motion of the car a few feet too far, whereas the other hypothesis (H_2) involves a special motive, deliberate damage, a far from normal and healthy psychological condition, and, perhaps, bribery and forgery as well. All this is just too much to swallow, when the first hypothesis takes care of the same facts with greater intellectual economy.

The status of the rule of simplicity is not beyond doubt. It does not seem to be the only principle that is followed in deciding between two alternative hypotheses that are equally successful as explanations. For example, if we had no other basis of choice, we would prefer to explain the dent by a backed-up car rather than a wrench thrown from a helicopter (and carried off by a passer-by), merely on the ground that the former kind of event happens more frequently than the other. Some philosophers of science have argued that the rule of simplicity can be reduced to this principle of frequency, or to some other principle. But it has a strong claim to be considered as at least one of the guiding principles in terms of which we can say that one explanation is better than another.

Again, we must bear in mind that hypotheses, when confirmed in the way we have sketched, are, like generalizations, inherently provisional. There are two reasons for this. First, no matter how many alternative hypotheses we have rejected because they either do not explain all the facts, or run afoul of some of them, or manage to explain them only at the price of being highly complicated, we can never guarantee that no further, better hypotheses can be thought of. And second, no matter how much evidence has been amassed to support any hypothesis, it is always conceivable that on some future day we shall be able to derive further predictions from it, and that these predictions may turn out to be false—that is, to conflict with what we observed. But of course some of our hypotheses are so well supported by so much evidence and have maintained themselves so long against their rivals that we can be fairly certain that they are true, or at least that they are an important part of the truth.

Like the rule of repetition, the rule of simplicity (which is also called the "principle of parsimony") confronts us with a philosophical problem. For again the question arises: what justifies us in following this rule? In other words, what good reason is there for thinking that hypotheses adopted in accordance with this rule are more likely to be true, and to hold up under further investigation, than those that are not? To this question we shall also return.

§ 4. • *What Is Science?*

We can now give a more precise and enlightening definition of "empirical knowledge" than was offered at the start of this chapter: our empirical knowledge consists of what we know either by direct observation or by the methods of generalization and hypothesis. Conceivably there are other methods, quite distinct from these, that should be classified with them as yielding empirical knowledge. If so, they can be added to the definition. But other methods that have been used, or tried, for obtaining knowledge seem either to be of a very different order or to reduce to the methods of generalization and hypothesis. For example, the appeal to authority is a method of obtaining empirical knowledge, as we do from the psychiatrist or economist or garage mechanic, but this is not a fundamental method, for these experts can only tell us what they, or their colleagues, have discovered by observation or by inference to generalizations or hypotheses.

We are unquestionably all interested in obtaining empirical knowledge, and cannot get around in the world without it, but most of us are interested in it only fitfully, partially, and piecemeal—only when we need it for a practical purpose (or are convinced that such a purpose will later turn up). And we make out with comparatively low standards of acceptability. But some of us are, so to speak, specialists in this field, whose concern with empirical knowledge is far more intense, constant, wideranging, and disinterested, and whose standards of admissibility are considerably more stringent. These are the empirical scientists. And because of their activities, a certain segment of our total empirical knowledge is classified as belonging to and, in one sense, constituting various sciences. Thus Newton's first law of motion and Ohm's law belong to the science of physics, the Freudian theory of the unconscious to the science of psychology. But your knowledge of the name of your aunt or the number of rooms in your house doesn't belong to any science, presumably.

Science as a product (though one that is constantly undergoing revision) is the collection of all the particular sciences. But it is not easy to say what a particular science is. For instance, we usually call physics a science but not philately, psychology but not literary criticism. Yet philately (like numismatics) might be regarded as a minor branch of history or archaeology, and some would claim that literary criticism is at least capable of being developed into a science. Certainly a science is not just a collection of empirical knowledge about some distinguishable group of objects or events (postage stamps or landscape paintings); it is a systematic body of knowledge, in that laws and theories are connected, one building upon, one logically more fundamental than, another.

Science is not only a systematic set of propositions; in another sense, it is an activity, or enterprise, and what makes an activity scientific is, basically, the method or methods that it uses. Scientific knowledge, in this sense, is knowledge reached by a scientific method. But if scientific knowledge is empirical knowledge, then the methods by which it is reached are just those we have discussed: observing, generalizing, and hypothesizing. When they are used by the scientist, they are often used differently, in some ways, from the way the man in the street uses them: the observations may be more careful and more numerous; they may involve technical apparatus such as microscopes or voltmeters; they may be made under controlled experimental conditions; the generalizations and hypotheses may be formulated quantitatively, in terms of measurable characteristics; the connections between laws and theories may be exhibited with mathematical rigor. And finally, new concepts are invented for greater explanatory power. Except for this last point, all these are quite clearly refinements of the basic methods; the difference is a difference of degree. Of course, the consequence of these developments is a great increase in reliability and this is an important matter: at its most successful, science provides grounds for a much higher degree of confidence than ordinary life usually affords for our common-sense generalizations and hypotheses—such as that barking dogs don't bite or that an apple a day keeps the doctor away.

The last feature mentioned above does make a significant difference. According to one view, we do not have *a* science until we invent new concepts that do not appear in common-sense inquiry at all. Some of them seem superficially quite close to ordinary ones—mass (in physics), utility (in economics), status (in sociology), intelligence (in psychology)—but they are really different. Some are very far from any ordinary concepts: probability-wave, gravitational field, id, chromosome, valence. This is one of the creative aspects of science, perhaps its most remarkable feature. But again the use of such concepts in hypotheses does not imply an abandonment, only a further development, of the basic methods.

It seems appropriate to speak of the methods of observation, generalization, and hypothesis as *scientific methods*. This title may be thought to dignify them unnecessarily, and perhaps some would rather say that science is only glorified common sense than that the man in the street uses scientific method. But "common sense" covers a great many other things and is often mingled with other methods that are by no means scientific. Empirical knowledge in general, then, is knowledge obtained by scientific method. When some of this knowledge is comparatively well confirmed and systematically related, and when it creates new concepts, it is a science, or at least on the verge of becoming one.

Empirical knowledge, whether in its fully scientific form or as the unsystematized conclusions of ordinary experience, evidently makes up a significant part of our stock. It has many merits, too, for it is not only accessible in some degree to all men, insofar as they have senses and a modicum of sense, but it has lately been growing fast. It is evidently of immense practical utility, since our possession of well-tested natural laws and of sound theories makes possible all sorts of productions and constructions that are found desirable by human beings. Moreover, the excitement of the chase for empirical knowledge and the satisfaction of finally resolving old gnawing puzzles and mysteries of the world about us are both intrinsic enjoyments that empirical knowledge provides.

It is perhaps then not too hard to understand how it comes about that some philosophers have dared to raise a bold and searching question: the question whether in fact *all* our knowledge is really empirical—whether this is not the only kind of knowledge that we need or can obtain. To show that this is so would, of course, not be an easy task if we had to run through samples of every branch of knowledge and prove, by careful analysis, that we learned them by scientific method. It is plausible to place the burden of proof upon anyone who claims that there are kinds of knowledge *other* than empirical; the first move is up to him. For, in the first place, as we have said, no one is likely to deny that *some* of our knowledge is empirical, but some philosophers have denied that there is any other sort. And in the second place, it would certainly be simpler and therefore (all other things being equal) more satisfactory to say that all our knowledge is ultimately of one type, rather than to suppose that there are two or more irreducible types.

But there are two very strong lines of argument that can be leveled against the proposal to regard all knowledge as empirical knowledge. First, there are various limitations that have been placed upon scientific method, various areas of apparent knowledge into which, it has been held, this method cannot go. This set of objections we shall consider next. Second, there is an even more disconcerting claim that the very use of scientific method rests upon certain true propositions about the world, which must be presupposed if the method is to be justified, and which consequently cannot themselves be established by the method. This claim is to be examined below.

ON THE LIMITATIONS OF SCIENCE

A method of doing something is a set of rules and procedures that can be deliberately followed; and its value as a method is presumably to be tested by its results. From this point of view, scientific method has certainly been a notable success. Huge volumes of *Chemical Abstracts,* textbooks, scientific journals, and monographs testify to that. No doubt there are areas in which our knowledge so far is somewhat less impressive—especially some aspects of our own behavior. The question is why. Is it because these problems about why people act as they do are too complicated to yield to us without a more intensive study? Or is it because we are using the wrong method?

The general issue which we are now approaching has been discussed ever since the beginnings, in the Renaissance, of what we know as modern science; but it is more sharply and vigorously debated today than ever before. We would like to know whether or not scientific method is in principle extensible to all areas of human experience and concern. Wherever and whenever we are interested in obtaining reliable knowledge, is this the only method we can count on? Or are there strict boundaries beyond which it cannot be successfully, or even intelligibly, applied?

At any given stage in the course of human history, there will, of course, be frontiers of knowledge—horizons beyond which we as yet can only surmise or speculate, if indeed we can form any ideas at all. And since the life of mankind is presumably finite, no matter how much it may be prolonged there will remain, when man is gone from the cosmic theater, secrets that he never penetrated, facts he never unearthed, laws he was never able to track down.

But these limitations upon the scientific enterprise are inherent in its nature, its very tendency to expand indefinitely. For the answer to any question always makes another question askable; that is why we cannot in practice answer all questions. There is, however, another charge against the very enterprise itself: that certain kinds of question are completely inaccessible to it. According to some philosophers, we already know enough of certain areas of experience to be sure that scientific method is inherently incapable of telling us all that we want to know, and can know, about them. Hence there must be another way of knowing. It is this claim that we must now weigh.

§ 5. • *The Abstractness of Science*

A familiar criticism of science focuses upon its *abstractness* and its interest in *quantitative relationships*. What does it mean to say that science is abstract? If you are looking for constants in nature, you are looking for relationships (statable if possible in mathematical terms, as proportions, sums, fractions) between certain features of the world. Thus, you might say that Boyle's law ignores many properties of gas—its smell, for example —and mentions only the relation among pressure, volume, and temperature. Newton's first law of motion abstracts the inertia of physical particles and leaves out of account their shape, color, and taste. And it is with examples such as these in mind, no doubt, that the critic of science attacks.

Even if we admit, he says, that science gives us partial truths, its scope is severely restricted: it gives us relationships between things, not the things themselves; it describes the structure of the world, but has nothing to say about its immediate qualities; it studies the general and leaves the particular out of account; it seeks for quantitative laws and therefore must ignore those things such as beauty that cannot be measured. With regard to the individual and the qualitative, science is incompetent and helpless.

When this argument is put succinctly, it is not hard to see some, at least, of the misunderstandings upon which it is reared. Surely, for one thing, though he talks about "science," the critic is thinking only of physical science in part of his argument. Of course, the physicist makes a very considerable abstraction from the world, as when he says that the human arm is an example of a lever. What he leaves out is enormous. But his is only one of the sciences. He may ignore color and smell, but these are not ignored by the chemist who is interested in knowing what combinations of substances produce certain sorts of smell, or by the psychologist who is interested in knowing how the perception of one colored area is affected by surrounding it with other colors. There is nothing in the nature of science that forbids it to try to explain qualities of any sort. And if there is no widely agreed-upon science that deals with beauty, perhaps that is because of certain unsettled questions about what beauty is. If, for example, it is, as some hold, a perceived quality, then its explanation is a task for the science, or subscience, of psychological aesthetics, which is a branch of psychology. There doesn't seem to be any reason in the nature of the case why we could not hope to understand the causes and effects of beauty.

A more judicious appraisal of the first criticism of science becomes possible if we turn from talking about sciences to talking about scientific method. The critic, thinking of science on the model of physics and of scientific laws on the model of Boyle's or Planck's constant, assumes that science is inherently and intrinsically quantitative. But we have seen that the two scientific methods of generalization and hypothesis do not necessarily require measurement at all. To be sure, the quantitatively stated law is a goal, an ideal, for the scientist—it is what he would like to have, for many reasons. But you can be scientific about—in the sense of using scientific method on—things that cannot, as yet, be measured: manic-depressive psychoses, indigestion, the consequences of the farm-subsidy price-support program. Admittedly, it may not be possible in some of these cases to attain such highly probable knowledge as the physical sciences provide, but we may hope to make it dependable enough for reasonable action. At any rate, this does not seem to be ruled out at the start.

There is also the charge that science is concerned with generalities, with structural and functional relationships, but not with the individual thing. Insofar as it seeks for laws, of course, a science is general: it does not want to know how *this* or *that* falling body behaves, but what the general principle is. But insofar as a science uses the method of hypothesis, it may be interested in particulars. The astronomer is interested in the moon and the earth and how they came into being; the geologist is interested in the White Mountains or the Grand Canyon. These are particular things. Still, it might be said, the scientist's interest in the particular is somewhat abstract; it is always for him an example of something general, a mere instance. He does not enjoy it and cherish it in all its full concreteness, as an individual, unique and unrepeatable. It is not this mountain, with all its own qualities, but only its mountainness, or its graniteness, or its exemplification of some geologic process that he sees in it, or cares to see in it—speaking as a geologist, of course, not as a human being.

We can reply that every science selects, but that there is no feature of the mountain that couldn't be studied by some science, or at least couldn't be investigated by scientific method. Yet this may not satisfy the critic. He may say that when the mountain has been divided up among a number of disciplines, each interested in his own selected features, the mountain as a whole, as an entity in itself, will be left out. This is a puzzling claim. Suppose we have completely explained the parts of the mountain, and all its aspects, and the relationships among those parts and aspects: what remains to be explained? Is there anything else to be puzzled about?

The argument we are analyzing is that scientific method is necessarily restricted in its application because of its abstractness. Whether or not the case can be made out convincingly in relation to mountains, there is another realm in which it carries more weight. This is the realm of human nature. For human beings, of all the things under the sun, are special and unique. And if scientific method can only cope with what is not unique, but in principle repeatable, then here is a very large limitation.

It is worth nothing, first, that this argument is in danger of proving that scientific method cannot be used at all—a conclusion that would reduce the argument to absurdity. Each time Galileo rolled the brass ball down his polished groove, the situation was a little different, of course— dust was settling, the assistants were walking about, carts were rumbling by in the street. At every moment the state of the world is unique. And every particular thing is unique in some respect—the only one of its kind. Some things are more individualized than others: they have more properties that nothing else happens to have; they are the only one of more kinds. Some people, for example, are highly individual; others are more like what you commonly encounter, rather dull and uninteresting. The point is this: if the argument is that people are unique, then this holds for all entities, including amoebas and molecules; if the argument is that people are more different from each other than amoebas and molecules are, then this individualization is a matter of degree.

The next question to ask, then, is why the dust and rumbling carts didn't make Galileo's experiments impossible. When something happens, the scientist may want to explain it, to know what caused it. Presumably its occurrence depended on certain events and conditions that preceded it.

The cause may be a relatively small and simple set of conditions, or it may be very complex; the scientist speaks of the number of "variables" involved. One of the remarkable things about Galileo's discovery is that the motion of the ball, its rate of acceleration, turned out to be a function of so few variables. And in this respect, of course, it is at the opposite extreme to most human behavior. For when a man chooses a career as a high school teacher, or gets married, or becomes a Buddhist monk, his action probably depends upon a large number of variables. Perhaps not; perhaps his drive to teach high school was so strong from an early age that nothing short of death could have deterred him. But on the other hand, it may have required a very special conjunction of circumstances—his arrival at a certain stage of development, the influence of family and friends, the inspiration of an admired teacher, a sudden opening of opportunity, and so on —to bring it about.

In any case, it is clear that, generally speaking, the greater the number of variables upon which an event depends, the more difficult it will be to explain it fully. And human nature is no doubt extremely complex. But this is, so to speak, a technical difficulty; it does not show that the enterprise is hopeless. Something more must be advanced to make that point. That is the purpose of the word "repeatable" in the argument. But the suffix of this word is ambiguous. The explainability of an event does not require that it should be repeatable in practice, or that it should be repeated. There might have been only enough fissionable material on earth to make one atomic bomb. Nevertheless, that one explosion could be explained. Of course, the explosion would be repeatable in principle—but so would anything else, including the birth of the sun and the voyage of the Mayflower.

§ 6. • *Science and Human Nature*

The discussion of this last point brings us to the consideration of some parallel arguments for the limitation of science—arguments that also bear upon the special character of human nature. Can scientific method be applied to the understanding of human beings? And if it can, is it the only, and sufficient, method? These questions are profound and searching ones. They are not to be dismissed by the retort that we can't tell until we try, that scientific method is already being applied here, and that some success has been achieved. The critic does not, of course, deny that psychologists and others have employed the methods of generalization and hypothesis in the study of human behavior, and have offered explanations of some human behavior and also some alleged laws. But he claims to know, independently of scientific method, some things about ourselves as individuals that reveal human nature to be inherently beyond the capacity of science to understand. And he supports this, moreover, by sharp attacks upon the supposed achievements of human sciences. The much-prized "explana-tions" of significant human behavior, such as those given by the depth-psychologist, are often speculative and questionable; the so-called "laws" that have been "discovered" about human behavior are either false or else vague and loose, and far from being laws in the sense of the natural sciences.

These are very significant claims, and you can see that they have far-reaching implications, which we shall not be able to do justice to here. But let us see how far we can go. What do we know about ourselves, ac-cording to the critic, that shows the inapplicability of scientific method to human nature? The first claim, uniqueness, we have just discussed. Three others are frequently advanced: (1) Our feelings and thoughts are essen-tially private, known only to ourselves, whereas scientific method can only deal with what is publicly observable. (2) Our feelings and emotions are subtle and constantly changing, and therefore not describable in words, whereas scientific method can deal only with what can be described. (3) Our actions are free and subject to no laws, and therefore both the method of generalization, which looks for laws, and the method of hypothesis, which presupposes laws, are inevitably frustrated when applied to human behavior.

The privacy of our inner life is a fact that bears upon a hard problem that we shall have to meet on its own terms in the following chapter. But as far as our present problem is concerned, enough may perhaps be said to show that the first argument is dubious. It is true that the public charac-ter of scientific knowledge has often been stressed—its accessibility to any-one with the relevant evidence. But the publicity of the laws and theories of science is not at all incompatible with the privacy of some of the data on which they may rest. Consider the hypothesis that you have an inflamed appendix. There is no question that this can be known by a great many people—if they are interested. One of the important items of evidence may be the pain you feel in your side. Now, this pain is private in one sense: it can only be felt by you; only you can have that bit of evidence. If that were the only evidence at all relevant and you could conceal your pain, then no one else could know about your appendicitis. But the proposition that you are feeling a pain can itself be a hypothesis for someone else who hears you speak of it or sees you wince. And so his evidence that you have a pain becomes, indirectly, evidence that you have appendicitis. If P is evidence for Q, and Q is evidence for R, then P is indirect evidence for R. In some cases, it may not be as good evidence for R as Q is when Q is directly observable, but in other cases it may be just as good. The doctor can know you have appendicitis at least as well as you do—though of course he also depends upon other evidence besides your report of the pain.

Thus insofar as there can be externally observable evidence for in-ternal states, the privacy of thoughts and feelings by no means prevents us from verifying hypotheses about them or using them as data for the verification of other hypotheses. Suppose, however, there were subjective states that *cannot* be externally manifested; let us call them "ultimately private." They would have to be states that do not produce, or correlate with, any behavior, and do not correspond to any observable physiological conditions, such as an increase of adrenalin in the blood, a rise in the pulse-rate, flushed cheeks, tensed muscles, etc. If a person were in such an ultimately private state of mind, he himself would know it, and would know it empirically, in the sense we have given to this term. But could it be known by anyone else? Two points of view are possible here. (1) We might concede that in this case another person, B, could never empirically know A's state of mind. But this is not a limitation upon scientific method. For B could not know A's state of mind in *any* way. (2) We might hold that when A is in such an ultimately private state of mind, B cannot know this by scientific method, but he *can* know it by another method. This position would require an alternative theory of knowledge, which we shall not discuss here. Meanwhile, of course, we must bear in mind that many philosophers doubt that there is such a thing as ultimate privacy.

The argument just considered branches off into another argument that may nevertheless be developed somewhat independently. When one person endeavors to provide others with evidence of his own inward states, in many cases he must do this by means of language. If he is very much excited, he will show it, no doubt; but to let his friend know that he is thinking of staying home in the evening rather than going to the movies, he will need more than gross and obvious behavior. His thoughts are communicable in words. But it can be argued that this is not so true of his emotional and feeling states. How can you be precise about love? How can you describe it exactly, or formulate exact hypotheses about it? Doesn't the very attempt to describe it alter it beyond recognition—so that it is bound to slip through the web of language?

That there are difficulties here cannot be denied; and it must even be acknowledged that they quite often do impose limits upon the range of our empirical knowledge of human nature. The difficulties can be exaggerated; after all you have said *something* about your emotional state when you describe it as "love." And though this blanket classification leaves out much that is important, you can, by further words, make us understand more clearly and distinctly just which sort of love it is. No one seems to have proved that there is a necessary and definite limit to this refinement of description. But to make out the proposed case against scientific method, one would have to justify two claims, as in the preceding argument: first, that no matter how hard we try, certain qualities of our psychological states must in principle remain unknown to others insofar as their knowledge of our states is obtained by scientific method; and second, that nevertheless these qualities *are* known to others, in some other way.

The next argument is based upon the theory that human beings have free will. If our choices are free in the sense that they do not occur in accordance with any law, then it does seem that, as far as these events are concerned, scientific method is balked in its aim. We shall inquire into that in the following chapter.

Our main purpose here is to confront the two positions, to make it clear that the issues are fundamental, and then to leave further reflection to the reader. If there is no inherent bar to a scientific understanding of human behavior, then there is no reason not to hope and work for genuine social sciences. If there is such a bar, the best we can expect in the way of "social studies" will be collections of observations, some loose generalizations, and more or less common-sense theories.

These conflicts over the limitations of science have led to a great deal of thinking, in recent years, about the methods of the social sciences—and they have also aroused much discussion about the nature of historical study. History, we assume, is not itself a social science, but it certainly deals with human behavior, or, better, human actions. And it purports to give explanations of particular actions: Caesar's decision to cross the Rubicon in defiance of the Roman Senate, or the United States Government's decision to drop the atomic bomb on Hiroshima. A number of philosophers in recent years have defended the special character of historical explanations, or at least their radical difference from explanations given in physics, in astronomy, or in meteorology. Some of the arguments we have been discussing have been urged with some force in this area: that historical events are unique and unrepeatable; that they depend on an indefinite number of variables; that we cannot state, in any complete and precise way, a single general law of history; that when we explain a historical event, we therefore cannot hope to base our explanation on a law, as we do when, for example, we explain a thunder storm with the help of a tested generalization about certain meteorological conditions.

All these, and other, arguments deserve careful consideration, and they have been the center of attention in recent philosophy of history. Much can be said on the other side. But in any case, even if historical explanations do turn out to be rather special in certain ways, and even if there are severe restrictions on what we can expect from history in the way of laws, it does not seem as though we have here a limitation on science. Certainly the historian's explanations are empirical, in their content and in their support: President Truman's character and motives in 1945, and the assumptions of his advisers, are open to their direct experience and to our indirect inferences. That they feared a great loss of life if Japan had to be invaded is a theory that helps to explain why the bomb was dropped (whether it *justifies* that decision is, of course, another matter). And it is hard to see how such an explanation could be given at all unless *some* kind of true generalization connects the motive with the action: that under the circumstances, a President of that character may be expected to put the saving of American lives highest on his scale of preferences.

When historical explanation is regarded in this light, it seems to be a special case of empirical explanation.

§ 7. • *Science and Ethics*

There are two other extremely general and important limitations that have been alleged against scientific method, one of which we shall barely mention, the other of which we shall say somewhat more about.

The first criticism of scientific method is that though science may be equipped to inform us about significant features of the world of nature and perhaps even human nature, it cannot reach beyond nature and tell us about the supernatural, if it exists—or even whether there is a supernatural world or not. This criticism opens up a number of problems in the philosophy of religion that we cannot take up here. The question "Does God exist?" ostensibly admits of only two answers. But those who ask that question divide very fundamentally with respect to the way they require an acceptable answer to be supported. Those who base their belief in God on faith, or on some form of nonrational apprehension, must, of course, go beyond science: they lay claim to a kind of knowledge that cannot in principle be afforded by scientific methods. But there are many others who do not try to answer the question in that way. They may, for example, base their belief in God on the various sorts of order or purposiveness or design that can be discovered in the world; and anyone who argues this way is, in effect, regarding the existence of God as an empirical hypothesis to be tested by evidence drawn from observation. But in that case, it is pertinent to ask whether the theistic hypothesis is clear and consistent, and whether it is the simplest hypothesis available to explain what it does explain.

The second criticism is that even if science can cope with all factual questions about nature and supernature, it is still handicapped in another sphere: normative questions—questions of value—are quite beyond its competence.

This limitation is so often alleged, even in the popular press and mass media, that it is confidently accepted and echoed even by the man in the street who would claim to know little else about science. One thing he is sure of: that science cannot tell us what the world *ought* to be like, but only what it *is* like; that science has nothing to say about what is right and good; that it is silent about the ends we should pursue, though it provides us with valuable instructions about the means. Deciding how the bridge is to be built is supposed to be a scientific question, and the engineer is the one to whom this task is to be entrusted. But deciding whether there is to be a bridge at all is a radically different sort of question; how can the engineer, as engineer, answer that?

We take note of this important idea here chiefly to get it on the record, but an adequate discussion of it will have to be postponed. In Chapter 4, we shall consider ethical judgments; this will cast some light on the relation between science and ethics. If our beliefs about what is right and wrong, about what is good and bad, are in the final analysis empirical beliefs, like our belief in the strength of bridges and the political consequences of raising taxes, then presumably they can be warranted by scientific method. Perhaps ethical propositions are a special kind of empirical proposition. On the other hand, if ethical propositions are fundamentally different, then it may be that they constitute another kind of knowledge. To them scientific method would be irrelevant; for them it would be inadequate. And this fact would indeed impose a significant limitation upon the range of scientific method. Clearly the issues here, as we untangle them, will have a number of threads, and this is all we propose to say of the matter for the present.

But once we have asked about the relation of science to ethics, we may take advantage of this opportunity for a short digression into a related question that is widely and often heatedly discussed. This is itself an ethical question, or can be posed as one: suppose that scientific method *can* be applied, at least within some limits, to human beings and their behavior; nevertheless, *should* it be so applied? A deep mistrust of science, and anxiety about the consequences of its very success, are reflected in this question. There are two aspects of the matter: fear of what the scientific method may do to those to whom it is applied, and fear of what it may do to those who apply it.

To mention the word "experiment" in connection with human beings is to summon up, in the minds of many of us, grisly reflections that we would happily forget, if we dared: the Nazi surgeons experimenting on the Polish women with freezing temperatures and deliberate infections, the more humane but also somewhat hair-raising behavioristic conditioners of Aldous Huxley's *Brave New World,* and the would-be manipulators of massive public opinion and taste who are paid large sums by political parties and advertising agencies as "behavioral engineers." Some of the distaste for the idea of a science of human nature comes from a deep feeling that even if we could consider human beings scientifically, we had better not: isn't that to treat people as means, rather than ends; to dehumanize them into mere things?

But that nightmare is the result of old connotations attached to science by its detractors. If "science" sounds too cruel and inhumane, too vivisectionist and hospital-like, think again of scientific method. To apply scientific method to human beings is, after all, only to make a deliberate and systematic attempt to find out, as far as we can, why we behave as we do. Of course, if we are able to discover some reliable psychological laws, there looms the possibility of guided change. It is the same in every field of science. In the early days of work on the atomic bomb, according to James B. Conant, some physicists hoped that the constants of nature would turn out to be such that peaceful controlled use of atomic energy would be possible, but not explosions. If the world had been designed with human welfare in mind, we might have been spared one of our most tremendous problems. But it turned out we could not have one without the other. So, if we discover, in detail, how schizophrenia comes about, we will not only perhaps know how to cure it, but also how to induce it if we wish. But clearly the wish to do so is not produced by the discovery nor is it encouraged by the discovery. The discovery of viruses has not, in general, increased medical appetite to spread them about—though there are always people around (some in positions of great power) whose first thought, on learning of viruses, is to wonder how they can be used as a weapon.

In any case, as was pointed out in the preceding section, the method of experiment is not one of the defining features of scientific method. Hypotheses and laws rest upon observations, and the best-confirmed ones generally rest upon deliberately controlled observation, that is, experiment. To obtain the most complete knowledge of human beings, of how they are made insecure, or creative, or rational, or loving, we may have to experiment, in a broad sense. For example, when we think of some new methods of combating juvenile delinquency, or improving the teaching of mathematics in elementary schools, or aiding underdeveloped countries, how do we begin? With what is called a "pilot project"—a small-scale controlled, carefully planned program. After it has run for a suitable time, we try to measure its success or failure and understand it in terms of the conditions it faced, so that we can decide whether or not to institute it on a larger scale. Such a pilot project is an experiment on human beings, in the broad sense. It is a use of scientific method. But it need not be demeaning or degrading—indeed, those who have been guinea pigs in such projects often feel the thrill of discovery and the satisfaction of making a contribution to knowledge, and for many of them it is a most memorable experience.

For the most part, of course, the evidential data on which our knowledge of human beings will rest must come from careful and sustained observation of activities that go on in any case—schoolrooms, political conventions, juryrooms, sales conferences, gang fights. Of course there will be conflicts of value: to get some of the information we need in order to understand these things well, we will come up against other important aspects of life, such as the right to due process in a trial (when we try to make motion picture records of juries coming to a decision) and the right to privacy (when we barge in on people to ask for details of their sex life). In these and other cases, we cannot fanatically say that knowledge is the only, or the most, important thing at all times. We know it is one of the most important things, and we have to decide in particular cases whether the sort of knowledge we are after is important enough to override other considerations.

Besides the supposed dangers of regarding man in a spirit of scientific inquiry, there is another source of alarm. Does not scientific method produce in those who use it an attitude that is coldly intellectual and detached? When a philosopher proposes that all knowledge is empirical —when he recommends that we base our beliefs on empirical evidence alone—isn't he asking us to be calm and rational all the time, never to trust our feelings and give way to emotions? As if anyone could decide to get married by analyzing the prospective bride or bridegroom and setting up hypotheses about the probable consequences of the union. Might as well let a digital computer select your spouse. Love is something else.

A reply to such appealing protestations is likely to seem too hard-boiled, but the fears are groundless, the interpretation mistaken. There are certainly situations in which one does well to give way to his emotions. Sometimes you want to get married, sometimes you want knowledge—if it is the latter you want, then you have to use the method that will secure it. Of course, if you want to get married *with* knowledge, then at some point in the proceedings some thinking will have to be done; there is no escape from that. Fortunately some of the evidence required is fairly readily accessible, either through introspection or by a ready inference from the other person's behavior. But when the couple try to find out whether they have enough to live on, whether they can agree on the bride's taking a job, whether their political and religious beliefs are sufficiently compatible, etc., they are using scientific method, even if it sounds cold to say so. It is not certain that once they raise these questions they are doomed either to part or to enter a bloodless partnership. The only coldness in the scientific method is that it obliges us to accept a proposition when the evidence is adequate, whether we like it or not; the warmth it rejects is the comfort of self-deception.

And this suggests one further reflection to conclude on. The attitudes required for the most effective and successful use of scientific method are in themselves ideals of high ethical value: the courage to think independently, the humility to transcend personal wishes, the resolution not to deceive oneself or others. A discussion of science and ethics, however brief, that failed to note the ethical quality of the principles guiding the use of scientific method would remain sadly incomplete.

ON THE PRESUPPOSITIONS OF SCIENCE

When you open your eyes in the morning and look out the window, what you see is mainly dependent on what there is to be seen rather than on what you hope or expect to see. We say "mainly" because experiments in the psychology of perception have shown that in certain subtle though important ways what we actually see may be influenced by our expectations. But if the sun is shining, you will certainly observe it, whether you had hoped for sunshine or for rain. And it does not seem that in making this observation you need to rely on any prior assumptions about yourself or about the world. A very different sort of case may be made out, however, when it comes to matters of fact that we know by inference: say, the age of the sun or the generalization "Rain before seven; clear before eleven." For here it can be argued that when you use the methods appropriate to the verification of these propositions, you presuppose certain other propositions about the nature of the world—you take for granted, that is, certain assumptions without which these methods would not be used.

The sort of presupposition presumably involved here needs to be made quite clear. We use a method because we hope for success, and we find it reasonable to use the method if we have some justification for believing that this hope will be fulfilled, or at least is more likely to be fulfilled than not. Otherwise, why not consult the gypsy's tea leaves or gaze into a crystal ball? But if we must have a good reason for using scientific method before we use it, then this reason, obviously, cannot be provided by scientific method itself; it must be obtained in some other fashion, from some other source. From this it would follow that we could have no empirical knowledge at all (beyond direct observation) unless we also had some knowledge that is *not* empirical. In that case, it could not be true that *all* our knowledge is empirical: indeed, this doctrine would be self-refuting.

Such, in a general form, is the argument we are now confronted with. It aims to disprove the view that all knowledge is empirical—not, as with the arguments previously considered, by marking necessary boundaries of scientific method, but by exposing its indispensable presuppositions. If science, or indeed any use of scientific method at all, cannot really be knowledge except on the prior guarantee that the world is a certain kind of world, then science rests upon metaphysical foundations. For such a general presupposition about reality would presumably be a metaphysical proposition.

Many candidates have been put forward for this position as presupposition of scientific method. Some of them perhaps need not cause concern. For example, it is sometimes said that we could not use scientific method for knowing the world unless the world were *knowable*. To such a claim one would surely be justified in replying that, of course, the world cannot be known unless it can be known (that is what "knowable" means), but that does not mean we must know that the world is knowable before we try to know it, for, indeed, how else can we discover whether (or to what extent, or in what respects) it is knowable, except by trying to know it? You tell whether something is bounceable by trying to bounce it. If there really is no other access to the world than scientific method, then we are justified in using it without any assurance at all, beforehand, that success is a sure thing—just as a man desperate for a bounceable substance will try anything he can lay his hands on.

A second proposal raises harder questions. It is that scientific method presupposes the trustworthiness of memory. You cannot accumulate evidence for a theory unless you bear in mind the evidence already obtained; you cannot generalize from a number of instances if you forget each instance as soon as you have it, or if you remember incorrectly what you have found. Now, we must all admit that sometimes, at least, our recollections are mistaken; we remember what did not happen and forget what did. Can we be reasonably sure that on the whole, or by and large, let us say, our recollections are reliable, and are justifiably taken as data on which to build our scientific laws and theories? Of course, if the dependability of memory could itself be shown empirically, there would be no problem. But it looks as if this will not work. If you say, "In the past, more often than not, my recollections have proved reliable, therefore my future ones probably will," it is apparent that you are assuming the reliability of your memory of the proved reliability of your memories, and so taking for granted what you thought you were proving. But this is a complex problem, and there are others equally fundamental that are somewhat more approachable.

§ 8. • *The Simplicity Criterion*

To bring out the sort of problem involved in the argument for presuppositions, we shall confine our chief discussion to two proposals that grow directly out of discussions earlier in this chapter. You remember that in our somewhat schematic account of the two scientific methods, at a certain point in the use of each method, we invoked a special maxim. Take the method of hypothesis first. At a certain stage in the development of an explanation of some phenomena, as over and over again in the history of science, the investigator is confronted with the choice of two hypotheses, each of which has a great deal to recommend it, and neither of which, at that time, can be decisively ruled out by experiment. According to the rule we stated, he is to choose the simpler hypothesis (everything else being equal). This rule we put in the form of an imperative sentence: "Do so-and-so." But suppose the scientist does not just spinelessly obey our command; suppose he asks for a reason why he should obey it. In effect he is asking why he should use this particular scientific method, since the rule is built into the method itself. So the question is serious.

What would serve to justify this imperative? No one, of course, can assure him that if he chooses the simpler of two available hypotheses he will always be right, for sometimes the simpler one turns out later to be false. Yet, we believe, it is still reasonable for him to choose the simpler. The question is, why? Can we assure him that, in the long run, if he always chooses the simpler hypothesis he will be right more often than he is wrong? Or, better, that if the whole history of his science, or his branch of science, is guided steadily by this rule, then it will probably converge more and more, as it develops, upon the nature of reality?

One solution to our problem consists in trying to show that the criterion of simplicity does not stand in need of any defense. This argument has not been very well worked out, and we shall not pursue it far.

What is it to explain something, anyway? We distinguish an explanation of certain phenomena from a mere description of the phenomena because the explanation connects up a number of facts, relates them in some way, establishes an order, and gives us in this sense a scientific understanding of them. Thus *comparative* simplicity is involved in the very concept of explanation. An explanation must be simpler than what it explains, or it will not count as an explanation at all. So it might be argued that a fuller grasp of what we are after in explaining will, in a way, make it clear that the simpler explanation does better, more adequately, exactly what all explanations are supposed to do.

And, indeed, simplicity does seem to be almost a defining characteristic of *rationality*. Certainly one of the key symptoms of the psychosis called "paranoia" is a persistent tendency to choose and act upon one of the less simple of available hypotheses. The paranoiac, when he leaves his house and sees someone dressed like a mailman coming down the street, does not simply infer that it *is* the mailman. He is convinced that it is his wife's lover in disguise, or that it is a foreign spy who is following him and probably has been hiding in his garage all night, hunched over a short-wave radio, while assembling a brace of plastic bombs. The paranoiac's delusions must, in general, also include the belief that he is threatened (which is why he himself is dangerous), but the credit he places in his fantasies is not deterred by their elaborate complexity, far in excess of what would be required to explain his observations. We do not mean to turn this into an *ad hominem* argument. If one asks, "Why should I not choose the more complex and colorful hypothesis?" we don't simply say to him, "You're crazy." Yet maybe his question amounts to this, "Why should I not be irrational?" There is something strange about this question. But let us set it aside for a time.

If the simplicity criterion does require a defense, then there are two main ways of providing one. The first we may call a metaphysical defense: the rule of simplicity is to be followed because, the natural world being what it is, it is the rule most likely to be successful. Following the seventeenth-century philosopher Leibniz,[1] let us conceive of the natural world as created by a benevolent and omnipotent God whose goodness and power are such that they must inevitably express themselves in the most economical, and even elegant, way. The world will then be one in which

[1] See his *Discourse on Metaphysics*, §§ 1–6.

the great possible variety and immensity of things are combined with the simplest, most coherent, order. From this proposition we cannot, of course, infer how simple that order is, in the last analysis; but we can infer that, as our grasp of its complexities increases, there will tend to be compensating visions of larger patterns of relationship, and whenever we are so fortunate as suddenly to come upon a simple principle that seems to have vast applications—such as the notion of a conservative system or the inverse-square relationship—we are justified in feeling a certain amount of awe, for we have opened up a new aspect of the glory of God.

There is no doubt that many scientists felt something like this in the seventeenth century, and some do today. However, it is not the understandable emotion aroused by this view, but the argument behind it, that must affect us now. *If* the postulate of God is accepted, and the suggested restrictions made, then it does seem that we might have a metaphysical justification of the rule of simplicity. For if we know antecedently to our empirical inquiry that the world is as simple as it can be, considering its richness, then it is reasonable to expect that the simpler of two adequately explanatory hypotheses is probably nearer the truth. So, for example, the mystically minded Kepler was sustained through many drudging years of computation by the burning conviction that God was essentially a mathematical designer and that the laws of planetary motion could not help but turn out to be neat and tidy and beautifully harmonious with each other. And Newton expressed his metaphysical faith that "Nature does nothing in vain."

This way of justifying the simplicity criterion for selecting hypotheses may work, granted its basic postulate, but it does not itself seem to conform to that criterion, considering the host of further problems it brings in its wake. We must know not only that God exists but that he is wise and good and economical and perhaps even an admirer of beauty. And that is a good deal to establish—independently of any empirical evidence. The appeal to empirical evidence to establish the existence and nature of God would, of course, raise the possibility of a serious dilemma. For that appeal, as in the argument from design, makes the proposition that God exists itself an empirical hypothesis. In deciding to accept that proposition as a postulate, must we then employ the criterion of simplicity? On the one hand, it seems we must, to be consistent: we do, for example, when we choose to explain the design in nature by the hypothesis of a single deity, rather than three or four—for polytheism (a well-run committee of gods, let us say) would explain the order of nature just as well as monotheism, but superfluously. On the other hand, we must not apply the simplicity criterion to the postulate on which the criterion itself is to rest, for then we shall be arguing in a circle. And, in any case, it is a question whether any empirical argument for God can really use that criterion, for it can be argued that if God is infinite in every way, the proposition "God exists" is the most complex hypothesis conceivable, because so much is packed into it. In that case, perhaps any alternative hypothesis that explains the facts would be simpler than this.

The second way of justifying the simplicity criterion is a straight-forwardly inductive one. There are two main senses of "inductive," a broad and a narrow one. In the *broad* sense, all arguments are divided into two forms: deductive and inductive. And the inductive arguments are those that claim to secure for their conclusions some degree of probability, or acceptability, that falls short of certainty. In this sense, both of the basic scientific methods are inductive: supporting a hypothesis by giving evidence for it, or supporting a generalization by citing instances of it. In the *narrow* sense, induction is the same as using the method of generalization: it consists in establishing a general proposition by a set of particular facts.

Now we can try to base our recommendation of the simplicity criterion on a suitable generalization about hypotheses. We might say, for example, that it is best to choose the simpler of two hypotheses because more often than not, in the past, this choice has proved successful in some way. If the simpler hypothesis works more often than not, this is a reasonable defense. To make it convincing, however, we have to give a clear meaning to the term "work" when applied to a hypothesis, and there are many different ways of doing this. Let us consider one possibility.

Suppose at a certain time we have a set of facts and two hypotheses to explain them: H_1 and H_2. Suppose H_1 is simpler, and we choose it. Choosing means accepting it: applying it in practice, in the laboratory, clinic, or production line. It means trying it out, probably in combination with other hypotheses and generalizations, basing further experiments or observations upon it. The hypothesis is, to speak, held in readiness for confrontation with new relevant facts as they turn up. A relevant fact is either one that fits in with the hypothesis, is explained by it and therefore supports it, or one that conflicts with the hypothesis and therefore counts against it. Now suppose the very next relevant fact that swims into our ken is one that either tells in favor of H_1 or counts against H_2. Let us call this fact a "trial" (thinking an analogy with preliminary contests in a complicated tournament). We can say that Hypothesis H_1 has survived that trial, and in that sense has "worked" so far.

Now, of course, the metaphysical defender of simplicity will hold that, in the long run anyway, the simpler hypothesis will work longer (that is, through more trials), simply because it is nearer to the truth—for a true hypothesis will never conflict with any new fact and so will always continue to work. (The situation is more complicated in actuality, no doubt, because, for example, some of the apparent facts that we discover will not be facts at all; so it is possible to "refute" a true hypothesis by inaccurate observations.) But without a metaphysical justification, we can only argue in some such way as this: if more often than not, when we have a pair of rival hypotheses, the simpler one works on the next trial, then it is reasonable to choose the simpler of any two rival hypotheses we are confronted with.

The evidence on this question is not all in. Philosophers would argue in different ways. Some would say, for example, that the simpler hypothesis, just because it makes fewer assumptions, runs a lesser risk of conflicting with observations and so is in principle safer. Others would say that even if the simpler hypothesis did not turn out to be true more often, it would always be the convenient one to test because if it turns out to be wrong, we can put our finger on the error more readily. But such arguments as these open up questions that lie beyond our present scope. The main point at the moment is simply this: to try to justify the simplicity criterion inductively is to shift the burden of the issue in a radical way; for now the defense of the simplicity criterion rests upon a prior generalization about the working of hypotheses. And so the logically more fundamental question is this: how can the method of generalization be justified? This is the problem we must now face up to.

§ 9. • *The Problem of Induction*

When we examine the other scientific maxim turned up earlier—the rule of repetition—we encounter a somewhat parallel set of problems, but even more fundamental ones, since explanation presupposes generalization, but not vice versa. All of these problems, by the way, belong to the branch of philosophy that is called the philosophy of science, and they are in the forefront of contemporary discussion and debate. Much disagreement still persists, despite important clarifications and discoveries that have been achieved in recent decades, and our treatment here, as with the problems about simplicity, will be quite elementary.

The rule of repetition, which is what we seem to follow when we draw conclusions about whole classes from observations of subclasses of those classes, authorizes us to feel more confident about any such conclusions as the size of the subclass increases. The rule is, of course, loosely stated, and would have to be qualified in various ways if we had opportunity here to deal in detail with the auxiliary methods of sampling: for example, the methods of randomizing the samples, so the observed instances of the generalization will not be misleading, and the methods of stratifying the samples, where it is already known that certain factors may interfere with the randomness. But even if the rule is loosely put, it says enough to bring out the problem. For the question is whether that rule can be given a rational justification. This is the *problem of induction*.

It may be well, before considering some of the proposed solutions of this problem, to remind ourselves what the philosophical stance of the inquirer must be here. Imagine, then, two friends, Neutron and Positron, who sit beside a pond and watch a fisherman. They know nothing of the pond, and little of fish, but they observe that the first fish he catches is a yellow perch. And so is the second, and the third. (He is lucky.) After this has happened seven times, there is a period when the fish don't bite, and Positron turns to his friend and says, "I bet you that the next fish he catches, if any, will be a yellow perch, too." Now, from a practical point of view, of course, it would be strange if Neutron took that bet—unless Positron gave him very good odds, or the wager was small. Such behavior would almost be a test of irrationality, like accepting the more complex of two hypotheses. Just in the same way, if half of the first six fish were yellow perch and half sunfish, it would be irrational to believe with confidence that the next would be a perch—one might *hope* for perch (since they are tastier), but such hope is in advance of justified belief. So, too, if a psychologist wishing to test the truth of astrology—as Jung did once—gathered one hundred cases of people born under "favorable" zodiacal influences, and one hundred cases of people born under "unfavorable" influences, and found that there were no more successful, happy people in one group than in the other, then it would be irrational for him to accept the astrologer's claim that the stars affect our destinies.

But lay aside the common-sense view for the moment, for Neutron is not a betting man, but a philosopher. And his rejoinder is this: "Granted that the first seven fish have been perch; still, we do not know that there are no other kinds of fish in the pond, and that only perch can be caught here. Nor do we know that only perch will respond to the bait he is using, or succumb to that size of hook. Therefore, I see no good reason to believe any more strongly that the next fish caught will be a perch than I did before he started fishing; and I see no good reason to expect a perch next time any more than any other kind of fish. I know what he *has* caught; I have no reasoned views at all about what he *will* catch. On this point I remain, like my name, neutral. And I am curious to know why you are so sure what the next one will be."

Positron, we may suppose, is a philosopher, too, but a thrifty one, who does not propose to waste arguments where they are not needed. Therefore, he begins by trying an easy answer. "I follow what I call an *inductive policy,* basing my expectations and predictions about the uncaught fish upon my observations of the caught ones. You might, of course, propose a counter-inductive policy, and say that the more perch he catches, the *less* likely is the next one to be a perch, since there can only be a finite number, and they would ultimately become exhausted. But this argument does not apply. For what I am predicting is not that he will catch more fish but that *if* he catches more, they will be perch. I do not claim, of course, to be certain of this, but since the caught fish are pond-fish, like the uncaught fish, they have something in common, and it is therefore more reasonable, if I have to choose between these two policies, to argue from what I know rather than from what I don't know."

Neutron, however, will not be swayed. "I propose," he says, "neither your inductive policy nor your counterinductive policy, but rather no policy at all. It is true that all the fish we are talking about have something in common—they are pond-fish. But they also are different in an important way, for some have been caught and some have not. I don't pretend to know anything about the uncaught fish, so long as they remain uncaught; about them, my mind is completely open. And I don't believe that you can know anything about them, either. You can't argue that what is true of frogs must be true of oysters, or that what is true of sunfish must be true of perch, or that what is true of caught fish must be true of uncaught fish; all these are illegitimate inferences, which a careful thinker will avoid. Experience, to put it in a nutshell, tells us about the things we have experienced, but it tells and can tell us nothing about what we have *not* experienced."

This view of Neutron's—which he learned from certain of David Hume's writings—we shall call the skeptical view of induction, or *inductive skepticism*. It is the view that no good reason can be given for believing any generalization. And it carries many consequences in its wake. For every empirical belief about objects and events beyond what we are observing at a given time owes its credit to some generalization taken as reliable. How do you know, for example, that City Hall did not burn down yesterday—except that *if* it had, *then* you would have heard about it through newspapers or radio or television or by word of mouth? And this "if . . . then . . ." rests upon generalizations about human behavior and about the mass media communication. Therefore, if we have no good reason to believe in any generalization, then we have no good reason to believe in past events (history becomes no better than fable), or in future events (predictions are lucky guesses), or in distant places and people (out of sight, out of existence). Or so it would seem. Neutron, of course, will not deny that we *do* believe all these things, and cannot help believing all these things, just as the victim of hysteria cannot help believing that his arm is broken, though it isn't. But philosophy is not concerned merely to record, or even to explain psychologically, what people do believe; it is concerned to discover what they *ought* to believe, or have a rational basis for believing. And the inductive skeptic concludes that for a very large group of our empirical beliefs there is no rational basis at all.

§ 10. • *The Postulates of Induction*

Evidently Positron, our defender of induction, will have to produce something more fundamental and more searching in answer to Neutron's sweeping denial. And let us now begin by considering what is perhaps the most ambitious and wide-ranging sort of justification that he might give. Is Positron's inductive policy the kind of policy we would be justified in following, no matter what reality happens to be like? If not, what would reality have to be like if we are to be justified? To put it another way, suppose we could find some postulate about reality—a metaphysical postulate —of such a nature that if it were true then induction (generalizing) would be a reasonable procedure. Then if that postulate in turn can be justified, so will induction be.

In seeking out such a metaphysical presupposition of induction, we may have difficulty in finding one that is strong enough to serve its purpose but not so strong as to be utterly indefensible. "Strength" here means roughly how much the proposition commits us to. Thus, for example, suppose Positron were to lay down the following

> *Postulate P_1*: Whenever two things X and Y have been observed to be associated in more than one case, but never X without Y, then whenever in the future X occurs, Y will occur in the same relation to it.

That would be a fine postulate indeed, and very convenient. With its help it will be easy to say,

> The only seven fish caught by the fisherman so far have been perch.
> Therefore, all future fish caught by the fisherman will be perch.

The trouble is that Postulate P_1 is evidently not true. It says too much. We can easily think of many examples where X and Y have been observed to be associated many times, and then have gone their separate ways.

Similar difficulties attend the formulation of another principle that is commonly invoked in this context: the principle of the *uniformity of nature*. A "uniformity" we may consider to be a universal regularity—for instance, Archimedes' discovery that when a body floats partly immersed in a liquid, the product of its volume and density equals the product of the volume and density of the liquid displaced, or that the volume of the body and the displaced liquid are inversely proportional to their densities:

$$\frac{V_B}{V_L} = \frac{D_L}{D_B}$$

We might formulate the principle of uniformity in this way:

> *Postulate P_2*: There are uniformities (constants) in nature.

But this would, of course, be far too weak to help us in the example of the fish—nor would it have been of service to Archimedes. Knowing nothing more than this, we would have no assurance that the fisherman's behavior will happen to constitute one of these uniformities. There might be constants, but no fish-constants. Now let us try the universal form:

> *Postulate P_3*: Nature is uniform throughout.

We shall have to be careful not to make this too strong and demanding. For example, when we generalize from the caught fish to the uncaught fish, it may be said that we assume that the fish population of the pond is the same throughout. But how far does this assumption go? It must not preclude fish swimming in schools, or having favorite eating places. And we certainly do not suppose that *all* ponds all over the world have the same kinds of fish in them. When we generalize about any class of things, of course, we are *affirming* a certain uniformity, but what is the uniformity we assume in advance of generalizing?

It might be said that our assumption is more complex. We can't take it for granted, of course, that all the fish in the pond are of the same kind. But consider Archimedes' problem. Suppose we float a log in the bathtub and discover that his formula correctly describes the situation. Suppose we float the log in salt water, in milk, in crankcase oil, in asparagus soup, and find that his formula correctly describes the relations between volumes and densities in all these cases. Our problem is how far we are justified in extending the formula to all solids and liquids. In other words, have we hit upon a genuine (universal) uniformity, or only a short-range, temporary association? Notice that a formula is universal if it is held to apply to *all* things of a certain kind. Archimedes' formula holds for all solids and all liquids (except, of course, when the solids have a higher specific gravity than the liquids, and so won't float in them). If it held for wood and water but not for rubber and oil, it would still be universal, for it would hold for *all* water and wood, not just for some. But of course it would then not be so broad or general a formula as it is now. If there are physical formulas that hold for absolutely everything, these are the most general of all, but most formulas apply only to smaller—though still very large—classes, such as sound waves, conductors of heat, or magnetic fields.

If we found that the formula applied to wood and water, but not to rubber and oil, we would not simply accept this conclusion; we would make a further inference: namely, that there must be some difference between the two cases that accounts for the fact that the formula holds for one but not for the other. Now this inference can be put in a very trivial form. "Whatever holds in one case must hold in similar cases unless there is some difference"—yes, but since there is always *some* difference (as between water and oil) this could mean only, "Whatever holds in one case must hold in similar cases, unless it doesn't." But perhaps there is a little more to it than this. Suppose we tried the wood and water experiment on Monday, and confirmed Archimedes' principle, and suppose we tried it again on Tuesday, in as exactly similar a fashion as possible, and it didn't work. What would happen then? We could say, well, the difference between Monday water and Tuesday water is just like the difference between fresh water and salt water; the experiments show that the law is less general than was thought, it only holds on alternate days of the week. But this is something we would never say. And the interesting question is, why not?

Let us look carefully at the different ways of talking about these regularities. We might say (never mind whether this is true or false, but only whether it makes good sense): "Archimedes' formula holds for beef broth but not for tomato soup." We cannot say: "Archimedes' law holds for Monday soup but not for Tuesday soup"; that is the same as saying the formula holds on Monday but not on Tuesday. Now there are differences between beef broth and tomato soup; if it held for one but not the other, we could search among these differences for an explanation of the different behavior. Why doesn't it hold for tomato soup? Because it is too thick, too viscous, or some other reason. But the distinction between Monday and Tuesday is merely a distinction in time. Why didn't the formula hold on Tuesday? Because it was too Tuesdayish? That's nonsense.

It seems that the sort of thing we are looking for in a formula like Archimedes' (or Ohm's or Boyle's) is one to which the date would be irrelevant. So whenever there is a difference in behavior on distinct dates, we automatically take it for granted that there must be some other, as yet hidden, difference in what is existing or going on at those two dates, to account for the difference in result. We seem to be taking it for granted that it is quite impossible for exactly the same conditions to be repeated, and yet for the consequences to vary. Roughly: same conditions, same result.

Out of the notion of the uniformity of nature, then, we have apparently elicited a somewhat more definite underlying principle that makes explicit its significant meaning. At this point let us reintroduce the term "natural law" (or "law" for short) with a somewhat more careful definition. Consider a certain sort of event, E, which is preceded by certain circumstances, C, including previous events and conditions. A law then is a true statement of the form "If C, then E," or "Whenever C, then E." For example: when a body emitting sound at a constant pitch approaches a receiver (a human ear, for example), the received pitch will rise, and when it recedes from the receiver, the received pitch will fall. This is the effect discovered and explained by Christian Doppler and known as the "Doppler effect"—it is illustrated by the train whistle that sounds higher as the train approaches you and lower when it passes and goes away.

The principle of uniformity, restated in terms of laws, then becomes

Postulate P_4: Nature is completely lawful; that is, every event occurs in accordance with some law.

As we saw in the case of Archimedes' principle, a law is basically conditional in form and controls a limited number of variables: the rise in pitch in the Doppler effect depends not on whether it is a train whistle or an oboe, but on the nature of the medium, the relative velocities, and whether the sound-source or the receiver or both are in motion. Moreover, a law, in the strict sense, makes no mention of particular times (Monday and Tuesday) or places (Greenwich or M.I.T.) or individual things (the moon or Adam). Many useful generalizations, for example about the population of the United States in the year 2000, are, for this reason, not laws in the scientific sense, though they may lead to the discovery of laws or they may be based on laws. Statements about the moon, for example, even if general in form, are not laws, but may exemplify laws that hold for all satellites; similarly, statements about particular people may exemplify genetic laws that do not mention anyone in particular.

Postulate P_4 says that whenever anything, E, happens, there must be among its total set of antecedent circumstances some limited set of conditions, C, responsible for its occurrence, in the sense that whenever in the future C turns up again, E is bound to occur as well. C is said to be a sufficient condition of E, for its occurrence is enough to bring about E. E is lawful because there is a law according to which it will happen. And we may also say, if we wish, that in this case C *causes* E; so that Postulate P_4 becomes equivalent to P_5:

Postulate P_5: Every event has a cause.

This proposition, the *principle of causality,* is one that we shall have another occasion to discuss, and we do not propose to analyze the notion of causality right now. One qualification would be insisted upon by some philosophers: that the cause of an event is not just its sufficient conditions, but its *necessary* and sufficient conditions. If we include that in the definition of "cause," then of course Postulate P_5 becomes stronger than P_4. That will not affect our present problem, however; if P_5 is true, then P_4 must be true, at least.

One further qualification probably should be inserted here. It is customary to speak of two sorts of "law," the universal sort that we have been speaking of (let us call them causal laws) and "statistical laws," which fall short of that universality, but deal with percentages. What if one were to doubt whether every event is causally lawful, but assert that there is for every event some statistical law true of it? When a light is turned on, for example, he may say, there is no law holding for what individual photons will do, but there is a law that holds very constant about what certain proportions of photons will do. This view raises some difficult problems. It does not seem consistent with Postulates P_4 and P_5, in any case, for it limits the types of events that may be said to be causally lawful. The event consisting of the path of one photon is not, in this view, lawful; the event consisting of the aggregate behavior of the large group of photons is lawful. It is convenient to use the word "lawful" in the causal, or nonstatistical, sense for the present discussion, and this we shall do.

§ 11. • *The Metaphysical Justification*

This may have seemed a long way around to the argument we were about to put into the mouth of Positron in answer to the inductive skepticism of his friend Neutron. But so subtle and far-reaching are these problems about induction and scientific method that we cannot hope to get an insight into them without taking some precautions with terminology, and some of these terms, such as "uniformity," "law," "cause," are so very fundamental in our scientific work and common-sense thinking that they deserve a good deal of scrutiny. At last, we have maneuvered ourselves into a position in which we can consider the metaphysical justification of induction directly.

Suppose, then, we already know that all events are lawful: that there is some limited set of factors, for example, that decides which kinds of fish will be caught under certain conditions, or how far the bobber will sink in the water when we cast the line. Then, according to the argument now before us, we begin our inductive inquiries into nature with a formidable advantage. If we had to start cold, not knowing whether there are laws or not, we could sustain the doubts urged upon us by the skeptic—intellectually, if not in practice. But if we know in advance that every kind of event has its hidden law waiting to be discovered, then any regular associations that we observe can be taken as cues to those laws, and as therefore having a claim upon our assent. We know that there *are* sufficient conditions for every case of the cork's floating; so whatever conditions we have always found present are automatically the best candidates to be the sufficient conditions. And this candidacy is reasonably strengthened each time it is found, for on each of those occasions when we test it, we are eliminating rival claimants and leaving a smaller number of possibilities. If it works in warm water as well as cool, then it doesn't depend on the temperature; if in salt water as well as fresh, then it is not the salt; if in wet weather as well as dry, then it isn't the humidity, etc., etc.

Think of this analogy. Suppose we are shooting dice with someone who uses his own dice and is phenomenally lucky. As he scores one success after another, we begin to suspect that his dice are loaded. He assures us we are mistaken, it is only chance. At one point, let us say, he throws twelve sevens in a row. We are ready to quit. But, he argues reasonably, although this run is highly improbable, it *could* be just chance. In fact, considering all the throws of dice since their invention, it could not amaze us to hear that a run of twelve sevens has occurred; why, then, should we be amazed that it should happen once before our eyes? Maybe these reasonable reflections will not quiet our suspicions, but it is evident that the surprising run does not, by itself, prove that the dice are loaded. However, suppose we know from some independent source that at least one pair of dice out of several being used are loaded; then when we observe this long run we can take it as quite strong evidence that this is the pair. Similarly, the principle of lawfulness assures us that the dice of nature are loaded; our only problem is to find out what numbers are most likely to come up.

If induction becomes reasonable—that is, if its conclusions become worthy of belief—only through the principle of lawfulness or the principle of causality, then these principles, of course, cannot themselves be inductively established. It would not do to argue in the following way, for example: Archimedes discovered a law for floating bodies, Ohm for electric currents, Doppler for sound waves, Boyle for gases, etc.; therefore, since all these types of events are lawful, let us generalize to the conclusion that probably all types of events are lawful. For, first, this generalization would seem to presuppose itself, and beg the question. And, second, even the individual laws could not have been discovered (that is, we could not have reason to accept them) without assuming the universal lawfulness of nature. The postulates must be established in some way quite independent of all our empirical knowledge.

But how is this to be done? If we can prove the existence of a God whose intentions and capacities assure us that the world he makes will be law-abiding throughout, that would be one way—but of course we would have to prove God's existence without the help of the cosmological argument, which itself presupposes the lawfulness of nature, and without the help of the argument from design, which uses the method of hypothesis, and thus depends on our knowing some laws (for example, about the connection of order with intelligence). The alternative would perhaps be to show that the postulates are self-evident in some way, or deducible from self-evident truths. We shall soon explore this line of thought. But first we must consider some suggestions that are less drastic.

§ 12. • *Pragmatic Proposals*

Let us now look at the process of induction in another way. Suppose we do not know, before we begin to inquire, what nature is really like. If we are interested in constants, as a scientist is, then the rational thing to do is to act in such a way that if there are constants in nature, they will appear. There are two possibilities:

1. Nature is lawful.
2. Nature is not lawful.

And there are two ways (let us say, to simplify matters) of approaching this situation:

A. We base our expectations upon the inductive policy.
B. We form no expectations at all.

Now, suppose possibility 2 is true. Then, since there are no laws, we shall not discover any laws. Method B will yield none and Method A will be frustrated. Therefore it does not matter which method we choose. But suppose possibility 1 is true, and there are laws. Method B will not yield them; Method A may or may not yield them, but it is the *only* policy that has any chance of yielding them. We cannot, in other words, guarantee its success, but we may be able to show that it will be successful if *any* policy will. In an analogous way, we might justify fishing in a pond, not on the ground that we know already that it is well stocked (that would be fine if it were possible), but on the ground that if there are any fish there, fishing is the best way to catch them, if they can be caught.

This justification would be modest but adequate: it is that the inductive policy will give us the truth if any policy will. Think of the inducer's problem as one of making reliable predictions on the basis of what he observes. Perhaps we can imagine a world in which no predictions would be possible. For example, suppose nature were governed by a malicious demon who knew everything. In such a world, no sealed predictions would be possible, and whenever we made a prediction, he would arrange for it to turn out false. But can we imagine a world in which the inductive policy would fail us, but some other method would succeed? It would seem that no such world is possible. For if *any* method of making reliable predictions can be used in such a world, we can find out what that method is by using the inductive method (that is, we could note its repeated success). Therefore, no method can be better than the inductive method.

Actually, to show that following the rule of repetition (and, more particularly, the techniques, such as random sampling and stratification, that fall under it) will disclose natural laws if anything will is a complex task that is beyond our power here. But if it can be carried out, it places scientific method once more upon its own feet. For in that case the scientist does not require to rest his work on metaphysical commitments, and he can claim that the propositions he discovers are as well grounded as human beliefs can be. Whether they rate high or low on some absolute scale of assurance, he cannot say, for he knows (as empirical scientist) no such absolute scale. But, in any case, the view that all knowledge is empirical can be consistently maintained.

If there is a standard, taken outside of our empirical knowledge as a whole, against which we can measure the success of empirical knowledge at its best, then perhaps the pragmatic argument even in its sophisticated form cannot be expected to satisfy the skeptic or the metaphysician who builds his case upon the skeptic's doubts. For consider once more the choices and possibilities outlined just above. Suppose nature is not lawful, but we work with Method A; is it really the case that we shall simply be frustrated? How can we be sure we may not be actively *mis*led? We are all familiar with coincidences that we mistake for genuine uniformities, at least for a time; when they break down, we learn that we were mistaken. But suppose all the uniformities we seem to have hit upon, in the small space of time in which man has seriously and systematically studied his environment, are, in the wide expanse of cosmic time, only momentary coincidences. (Quite recently, evidence has suggested that even the force of gravity may be weakening.) Would not science then be, not simply without justification—a mere habit of expecting things to continue to do whatever they are doing—but a complete deception?

In some such way as this, the skeptic may return once more to insist that if absolutely nothing is known pre-empirically (before our scientific method gets under way) about nature, then no policy can be proved ante-cedently any more reasonable than any other, for if the policy permits any beliefs about the unobserved, it may as well permit false beliefs as true ones. The pond analogy cuts both ways, after all, for what is it that assures us that sticking a baited hook in the water is the best way to catch fish, if there are any? To ask the reason for any empirical belief whatsoever is always reasonable and sensible; but to ask for a reason for induction is a very different sort of question. And it is a question to which the skeptic can find only a negative, and the metaphysician only a nonempirical, answer.

There are other philosophers who would answer the skeptic by trying to waive the question itself. Is the question somehow illegitimate, in asking for something that the question itself excludes? If someone asks what hap-pened before time began, we can see what's wrong with that question: there is no "before" time began, for that would be a time when there is no time. The question is self-contradictory. So, too, if someone asks for a good reason why he should regard any reason as good, it is equally impossible to comply with his request. If he is not prepared to accept a good reason when it is offered to him, he will certainly not accept a good reason for accepting good reasons. Nor does it seem that there is anything really profound in his squeamishness about accepting good reasons until he has a good reason for accepting them. It is not as if he just had very high standards of reasoning, and would not accept reasons unless they passed very stringent tests. For the test he has devised is one that no reason can pass. And it is not as if he were merely disappointed in some reasons he had received because they were less decisive than he had hoped. For ex-ample, suppose you are talking with a teacher or critic of the fine arts, and he gives you his reasons for thinking that Picasso is a great painter. After he had done his best, you might still go away grumbling that the reasons he gave did not measure up to those that can be given for mathe-matical principles, or for Archimedes' law, or even for the guilt of Lee Harvey Oswald. Perhaps your complaint is unfair—perhaps the reasons for such aesthetic judgments are to be measured against other standards than those for mathematics, physics, or the law. But at least you have some idea what it is that you are missing in the critic's argument. The skeptic, how-ever, who deplored the absence of good reasons for believing in good reasons, would be in no such position; he could not even have a clear idea what he lacked.

Now let us turn this line of thought against the inductive skeptic. When he asks for a justification of induction and laments its impossibility (as he claims), is his request illegitimate, like that of the skeptic we have just heard? He is not a complete skeptic, for he does agree that when we directly observe something, then we are justified in believing that it exists and has the shapes and colors we observe in it. He is just disappointed that inductive conclusions fall short of the results of observation. But perhaps he is in the position of the one who accepts art criticism to be provided with reasons like the proofs in mathematics or the experiments in physics; perhaps he is demanding of inductive arguments a kind of warrant that they cannot be expected to provide.

It would be fine if we could show, as some philosophers contend, that the problem of induction is unreal in this way—that it only arises because of an illegitimate and self-refuting demand for a kind of justification that is in the nature of the case unprovidable. But it does not seem obvious that the one who seeks a reason for following the rules of repetition and simplicity is wholly out of order, or that his quest is either misguided or futile.

NECESSARY TRUTH

Consider the familiar proposition that nobody can be in two different places at the same time. Why do we believe it? It has the form of a generalization, since it is really about everyone: "All persons are such that if they are in one place at time t, then they cannot be at a different place at time t." Is it then an induction from experience? You have never observed any of your friends, even those you know most intimately, in two places at the same time, so you conclude that probably you never will. But this account will not do at all. In the first place, your trust in this proposition— the extreme assurance that you have of its truth—is far greater than would be justified if you had reached it by generalization from past observations. After all, the fact that you have never *seen* your friends in two places at the same time can't count very heavily, for to see them you would yourself have had to be in two places at the same time—assuming that the two places are spatially separated, like New York and Chicago. If you aren't in two places at the same time yourself, you are in no position to dogmatize about what others may be doing. One might say: you've never really looked. Moreover, to get one really clear-cut case where you can be quite sure that a person is *not* in two places at once, you would have to catch a single momentary view of all parts of space, for as long as there were some part of space you could not observe, you couldn't rule out the possibility that he might also be there, as well as where you observe him.

Yet, in the second place, reflecting on the really inadequate evidence you would have for this proposition, taken as a generalization, you do not find your confidence in it being weakened by these reflections. Here is a curious fact. For ordinarily, if you are open-minded, the strength of your belief in a generalization will decrease when you become convinced that the evidence for it is less than you thought. Are you then just being stub-born when you say, "I don't care how little evidence for this proposition I have, it is still certain that nobody can be in two places at once"? Or is this a perfectly justifiable reply?

Perhaps. But only, it would seem, if there is a way of justifying be-liefs that does not have recourse to evidence at all.

§ 13. • *Self-evidence*

Suppose someone demanded a good reason for believing that nobody can be in two different places at the same time. What sort of reason could be given? We might say something like this: "To be in two places at once, a person would have to be two people, instead of one, but it is impossible for one person to be two people." Does this help? It might well be rejected as begging the question. A carping critic could reply, "I don't agree that in order to be in two places at once, a person would have to be two people; you are only saying that because you take it for granted that one person cannot be in two places at the same time, and this was what I asked you not to assume, but to prove." And our argument does seem somewhat circular. Yet when it is rejected, our belief in the proposition will hardly be shaken. At some point we are likely to say, "But don't you *see* it? It's as clear as can be to me; how can I make it clear to you?"

It might help to point out a second feature of this proposition: that nobody has to worry about its ever being refuted, for it seems completely immune to all opposing evidence. Suppose you left a friend peacefully chatting away at the coffee shop and drove as fast as possible for several blocks to a barber shop, where you found him getting a haircut—having been there, according to the barber, for some time. You would still not admit that he was in two places at once. The more you became convinced that it *was* the same friend, the more you would be sure that somehow he managed to get there ahead of you, and that the barber is teasing you. Or, on the other hand, the more you are convinced by further testimony that "he" had been in the barber shop while you were seeing "him" in the coffee shop, the more certain you would be that "he" is two different people, probably identical twins. Without more evidence, it might be hard to choose between these two hypotheses—as is commonly the case when the magician is at work producing apparently impossible events—but you wouldn't for a moment take the third choice and abandon the proposition. After all, if a thing *could* be in different places at the same time, there would be less magic in the magician: some of his most striking effects could readily be accounted for by *this* hypothesis.

But what if you saw the same person at two different places in the same room, with your own eyes? Again, you would have several choices, even if you did not suppose that what you apparently saw was true. If both figures looked and acted alike, it would apparently be a case of double-imagery, as when you press your eyeball with your finger or when your eyes fail to focus properly. If they acted differently, one sitting and the other standing, why they may be two people made up to look alike—or one of them may be a hallucination. These are all reasonable possibilities; what is not a reasonable possibility is that the same person is in both places.

This is why our proposition is hard to doubt: it offers no intelligible alternative. We can conceive of alternatives to the most probable of empirical hypotheses, but can we really conceive of a person being in two places at the same time? Conceivability here, it is to be noted, is not the same as imaginability; many things that are impossible to form a clear (visual or auditory) image of may yet be precisely conceivable—for example, a tree with 3,781 leaves or a chorus of 9,999 voices. Even so, the criterion of inconceivability may prove troublesome, and we shall return to it later. For the time being, however, let us use it. Whether or not it is adequately clear, we shall say that the proposition we are considering is one whose denial (that is, contradictory) is inconceivable.

The special characteristics we have found in the proposition "Nobody can be in two different places at the same time" are somewhat overlapping and certainly in need of more analysis, but let us bring them together here to define a much-used and much-abused term. We shall say that a proposition is *self-evident* when it is (a) true, (b) known to be true without needing to be inferred (deductively or inductively) from any other propositions, when (c) no possible experience could force us to retract it, and (d) its denial is inconceivable. Whether a given proposition is or is not self-evident by this definition can of course always be disputed: but perhaps we have made out at least a fair case for saying that the proposition "Nobody can be in two different places at the same time" is self-evident.

Many philosophers are unhappy about the idea of self-evidence, because of the mischief that it has undoubtedly caused in the history of human thought. They point out that once you admit that some propositions might be self-evident, there is no holding back the credulous and the dogmatic: anything that they believe strongly and stubbornly they will claim to be "self-evident" and refuse to give up in the face of adverse evidence. That the claim to self-evidence can be abused is no doubt true. But we can stick to our distinctions even if others won't. For example, it is sometimes asserted that in the Middle Ages it was self-evident to people that the earth is flat; that it was self-evident to the Greeks that heavenly bodies must move in perfect circles; that it is self-evident to many people today that divorce is immoral, and so on. But none of these could be self-evident by our definition. It was *evident* to the medieval man that the world was flat, and perhaps he even found the alternative impossible to imagine; but it was possible to conceive an alternative, even if only to reject it with horror because people would slip off; and he certainly thought he had evidence in favor of the flatness-hypothesis. A *self*-evident proposition would be its own witness, carrying its warranty about with it, standing in no need of external support.

Propositions have *seemed* self-evident that were really not. But that does not show that none are, or that self-evidence is merely a mask for prejudice and superstition. At least for the time being, let us hold our minds open on this point and see what can be done with the concept of self-evidence. When combined with another basic concept, it provides a definition of a highly important philosophic term, "necessary proposition." To *deduce* a proposition, Q, from another proposition, P, is to show that Q follows logically from P, or, in other words, that P can't be true without Q's being true. Now let us say that a necessary proposition is one that is either self-evident or is logically deducible from self-evident propositions.

To show, for example, that the proposition "Every triangle can be inscribed in one and only one circle" is necessarily true, we give a geometrical proof. We draw the perpendicular bisectors of the sides of the triangle, find the point where they intersect, and show by a series of congruence-proofs that this point is equidistant from all the vertices of the triangle. Therefore a circle centered on this point and drawn through one vertex will pass through all three vertices. In carrying out this proof we are of course relying upon previously proved theorems, and their proofs can be traced back to the basic axioms and postulates of the system. At bottom will be found such propositions as "Things equal to the same things are equal to each other." This *seems* to be self-evident. In fact, some of the basic propositions needed for the rigorous working out of Euclid's geometry were so evident to him that he did not even mention them, and it was not until 1901 that Hilbert reformulated Euclidean geometry in such a way that everything used in the proofs is stated explicitly. For example, Euclid assumed that when a line connects a point inside a circle with a point outside the circle, that line must intersect the circle. What could be more obvious than that? Yet it is neither stated by him as an axiom nor proved as a theorem. He does not even provide a way of distinguishing clearly the inside from the outside of a plane figure, and that is one of the reasons why it is possible to prove in his system some paradoxical theorems —as that every triangle is an equilateral triangle.

Notice that, by our definition, a self-evident proposition may also be provable, though it does not *need* to be proved. It might turn out, for example, that the proposition "Nobody can be in two different places at the same time" can be deduced from still simpler or more basic propositions, but it would still be self-evident if its truth can be grasped without depending on that deduction. Other propositions, like many of Euclid's, do not show their necessity so plainly, so to speak, and that is why they stand in need of proof.

§ 14. • *Logical Truth*

A proposition that is not necessary is said to be "contingent." And it is clear that empirical propositions are all contingent. What you observe before your very eyes you may feel certain of, and with justice; but you can perfectly well conceive it as different. The sky is blue, but it can be conceived not to be blue. And so with indirect knowledge. The earth revolves around the sun, but we can conceive of the sun revolving around the earth instead—as Ptolemy did.

A very important consequence follows. If no empirical propositions can be necessarily true, then if there are necessarily true propositions they cannot be empirical ones. So if we can be said to *know* some necessary propositions, then not all our knowledge is empirical knowledge.

One step of this brief but powerful argument must now be carefully examined. In what sense are necessary propositions *known?* Consider first this peculiar proposition: "If the institution of marriage were abolished, then there would be no more divorces." If someone who was alarmed about the divorce rate proposed this as a method of lowering that rate to zero, we should wonder what to think of him. It is a drastic, not to say defeatist, measure. We would not say, "Why didn't I think of that myself?" for it is the kind of thing that anyone might have thought of, but no sensible person would say. There is something queer about it as a solution to the problem.

The proposition "Where there is no marriage, there is no divorce" is a necessary proposition, no doubt. Yet it is curiously weak. It doesn't really say anything—or anything very important—after all. What it gains in necessity it seems to pay for in significance. Suppose we tried to give a deductive proof of this proposition, the way geometrical propositions are proved. The first thing we would do is examine the meanings of some of its key words. What does "divorce" mean? Let us define it as "legal termination of marriage." Now suppose we substitute this new term for "divorce" in the proposition we are concerned with, and get:

Where there are no marriages, there are no legal terminations of marriage.

This proposition is logically equivalent to the following one (in other words, they imply each other):

Wherever there are legal terminations of marriage, there are marriages.

To make the meaning of this proposition a little more explicit, let us write it this way:

Wherever there are (a) marriages plus (b) marriage-terminating legal processes, there are (a) marriages.

Now, if we take out the particular words here and substitute the letters, we get the following formula:

Wherever there are *a* and *b,* there are *a*

or, in a slightly different form,

Anything that is both *a* and *b* is *a*.

We must pause at this point to consider exactly what we have been doing in this series of steps. It may seem like a bit of legerdemain, but in fact it is by no means arbitrary. Every step was orderly. By some steps we moved from one proposition to another that is logically equivalent to the first; by other steps we moved from one proposition to another that says the same thing in slightly different words. By another step, we removed certain words from the proposition, and substituted letters for them. And the point of this was to bring out the *logical form* of the original proposition. To give a full account of this notion of logical form would take us a good way into the study of logic, but it will serve us quite well at this time if we agree upon a distinction that can be made by the logician quite exactly. In any given proposition, some of the elements are counted as its form and some as its content. The logical form of "All horses are quadrupeds," for example, is

All *a* are *b*.

But the logical form of "All horses are horses" is

All *a* are *a*.

The letters are *variables,* standing for any term, but no term in particular.

By our series of steps we came out at the end with a proposition of a special sort, "Anything that is both *a* and *b* is *a*"—let us refer to this as Proposition L, for the sake of brevity. What is special about this proposition is that it is a truth of logic, or a *logical truth*. Thus our series of steps consists in reducing the original proposition, "Where there is no marriage, there is no divorce," to a logical truth. This cannot be done for all propositions, of course. If we had started with, say, "Where there is no marriage, there is no happiness," we would have wound up with the final formula "Anything that is *a* is *b*," and this is not at all a logical truth. What, then, is a logical truth?

This question, again, is by no means susceptible of a brief answer that is wholly adequate. But an important part of the answer might be produced this way. Given Proposition L, we can construct an indefinite number of propositions by substituting words for the letters *a* and *b*, but we must substitute the same word for *a* and the same word for *b* throughout. In this way we get:

All red fire engines are red.
All blue skies are blue.

All green grass is green.
All purple cows are purple.
Etc.

Inevitably all these *have* the same logical form. They are also all very true. If anyone wishes to insure that he will never be at a loss for words yet will take no risk of being caught in error, when he is talking about matters he knows nothing about, here is a method for manufacturing conversation. Well, you can hardly call it conversation, for it is pretty monotonous. Nor will it convey any information about the world. We ask him whether the local fire engines are red or (as in some cities) white, and instead of answering our question (for he might make a mistake), he replies, "All the red ones are red, and all the white ones are white." Which leaves us no better informed than we were before. It wasn't worthwhile asking him, for with a little practice we could make up just as good answers ourselves, and without bothering to look at any fire engines at all.

Let us say that these propositions are true just by virtue of their logical form. When we consider any one of them, we see that its logical form is of such a sort that whatever other words had been put in instead would have made no difference to its truth. Now it is a peculiar proposition that would remain true no matter what words you put in. "All horses are horses" is like that. But "All horses are quadrupeds" is not. For its logical form, as we saw, is "All *a* are *b*," and it is easy enough to make false propositions out of this logical form—by substituting "birds" for *a* or "carnivores" for *b*, or by substituting "quadrupeds" for *a* and "horses" for *b*. Thus, let us define a logical truth, for the time being, as a proposition containing variables, such as *a, b, c,* which yields a true proposition no matter what words are substituted for the variables, provided they are substituted consistently throughout (same letter, same word). The propositions we get from logical truths by such substitutions are themselves logically true—that is, true by virtue of their logical form.

There are many important logical truths, some of which may be noted now. The proposition "All *a* are *a*" is called the principle of identity. There is the principle of contradiction, "No proposition is both true and false," and its companion principle, the principle of excluded middle, "Every proposition is either true or false." There are truths like "If *a* is included in *b,* and *b* in *c,* then *a* is included in *c,*" which is one principle of the syllogism, where the letters stand for classes of things. Propositions like "All red fire engines are red" or "Tomorrow either it will rain or it won't," which can be constructed merely by putting some appropriate words in appropriate places in logical truths, we shall call *basic analytic propositions.* And they are self-evident. Now if you feel uneasy about self-evidence, and find it hard to see what sort of process it is by which we are supposed to recognize the self-evidence of a proposition, a definite answer can be given, at least as far as these simple analytic ones are concerned.

To recognize *their* self-evidence is simply to recognize their logical form and understand that they are made true by their logical form alone. That is what their necessity consists in. Of course it is another question, still awaiting us, whether there are self-evident propositions whose necessity does not depend solely on their logical form.

§ 15. • *Analytic Propositions*

Now, consider once more the proposition "Whatever is *a* and *b* is *a*." If our neurotic conversationalist wanted to make his remarks slightly more interesting, or at least partially disguise their triviality, he might introduce one variation. Suppose that instead of "red fire engine" he introduces a new term "rengine" and, instead of "white fire engine," the term "whengine." Now he can say something that at first glance seems new: "All rengines are red, but whengines are always white."

But of course these are not frightfully interesting to us, because we know how he arrived at them. Step 1 consists in choosing a logical truth:

Whatever is *a* and *b* is *a*.

Step 2 consists in substituting words for the letters:

Whatever is both red and a fire engine is red.

Step 3 consists in substituting for certain words another word that is defined as synonymous with them. The definition is: "Rengine" means the same as "red fire engine." Substituting according to this definition, and changing words around for naturalness, gives us:

All rengines are red.

Since this proposition is derived from a basic analytic proposition, let us call it a *derived analytic proposition*. And because its derivation involves only the substitution of synonymous terms, it has the same meaning as the basic analytic proposition from which it is derived, so it must be equally necessary—though perhaps not equally self-evident.

Any proposition that is either a basic analytic proposition or a derived analytic one we shall call simply *analytic*—meaning that it can be arrived at by starting from a logical truth and using only the following procedures: (a) substituting words for variables, (b) substituting some words for others according to accepted definitions, (c) substituting equivalent propositions for one another, and (d) rearranging the grammar without changing the meaning.

Notice that the series of steps by which we arrived at "All rengines are red" exactly reverses the order of steps by which the earlier proposition about divorces was reduced to a logical truth. Here we begin with the logical truth and wind up with the proposition. But since each step can go both ways, the two proofs are equivalent, and we could have built up the divorce proposition in the same way. Let us call this second series of steps a "proof of analyticity." To prove a proposition in this way is to show that its truth is a necessary consequence of its logical form and the meaning of its words. The proposition (for example, "Abolishing marriages will eliminate divorce") is proved to be true by definition—which may or may not have been obvious before the proof was given.

The denial of an analytic proposition is *analytically false,* or logically impossible. The proof that a proposition is analytically false follows a course that reverses the proof of positive analyticity. We assume, say, that there are countries that have divorces but no marriages and, with the help of suitable definitions and logical truths, deduce a contradiction: that in those countries there are marriages and also no marriages. This shows that the proposition "In some countries there are divorces but no marriages" is analytically false. "Cows lay eggs" is false, but not analytically false, for it does not imply a contradiction.

A proposition (true or false) that is neither analytic nor analytically false (that is, self-contradictory), is called a *synthetic* proposition. This means that its truth or falsity is not determined merely by its logical form plus definitions, and therefore it is not empty in the way that an analytic proposition is.

Sometimes it is not wholly clear whether a proposition is analytic or synthetic because the definitions of its terms are not immediately apparent, and in these cases it may be helpful to go at the problem in a more round-about way by asking how we assign meanings to the various terms. An interesting example appeared in our earlier discussion. Ohm's law, which was mentioned there, is sometimes expressed as the equation

$$I = \frac{E}{R}$$

Is this equation analytic or synthetic? Now, all three letters stand for magnitudes, and the question is how we go about determining what numbers to substitute for them in actual cases—what operations we perform. I stands for the amount of the current, which is given in amperes, and to measure that we connect an ammeter into the circuit and read off the result. E stands for the electromotive force, or difference in potential over the circuit, and to measure that we connect a voltmeter in parallel with the circuit and read off the results in volts. R stands for the resistance, which is given in ohms, and how do we measure that? We don't measure it directly; we decide what the resistance is by measuring the current and the electromotive force and dividing the second by the first, using an equivalent transformation of the equation:

$$R = \frac{E}{I}$$

When we reflect upon the actual way in which these equations are used, then, we see that they are not themselves tested in the physics laboratory but are used as a means for calculating R when E and I are known. In short, they are definitions of "resistance." Or, more accurately, they become true by definition once we agree to define "ohm" in terms of "volt" and "ampere"; so they are analytic propositions, not synthetic laws. Does this mean, then, that Ohm didn't make any discovery after all—that he did no more than introduce some new definitions? Not at all: what Ohm discovered is the synthetic proposition that in a homogeneous metal conductor at a given temperature the current is proportional to the electromotive force; and he discovered that the constant of proportionality depends upon such variables as the kind of metal, the length, the cross-section area. These are his synthetic statements. Because they are true, the definition of R becomes possible and useful, and the equation important. But the equation itself is not the same as the law, for one is analytic, the other synthetic.

Whether a proposition is analytic or synthetic, as we have seen, depends upon the definitions of its key terms, and this circumstance can make for a troublesome problem sometimes. For when two people who are engaged in a discussion use different definitions of some term without acknowledging it and realizing it, the same sentence may be synthetic for one but analytic for the other; or when a key term shifts its meaning in the course of a discussion the sentence may shift from being synthetic to being analytic, or vice versa. For example, consider the sort of dispute that can arise over the frequent assertion that everyone acts at all times to benefit himself: that all persons seek to maximize their own good, whether or not this is at the expense of others. Let us call an action "egoistic" if it is motivated by the desire to maximize one's own good; *psychological egoism,* then, is the thesis that *all actions are egoistic.*

Suppose the psychological egoist (or egoist, for short) broaches his theory: that whenever anyone acts, his motive is always to maximize his own good. Propositions about motivation are clearly empirical and synthetic, and anyone who objected to the egoist's view as a slander upon human nature would naturally try to think of examples to refute it. "What about the civil rights worker, the freedom rider—and never mind whether you agree or disagree with him. When he takes the risk of being jailed or fined or shot or beaten by the police for doing what he believes, surely his motive is not to maximize his own good, but to help others." The egoist's reply is that even if we think the freedom rider is altruistic—even if he thinks so himself—there is a hidden self-regard in his action. After all, he wouldn't do what he is doing unless he wanted to, would he? "Well, but I have a friend," the anti-egoist may reply, "who hated the thought of going on freedom rides, and feared it, and wished he could escape it—but still he believed he ought to help others in this way, and so he did it." Again the egoist will answer: if someone does his duty rather than following his inclinations, that only means that he wants to do his duty more than he wants not to—and so he is really doing what he wants to do, after all.

There are a hundred subtleties that can come into this kind of dispute, and we cannot trace them all here, even though there is much of philosophical interest and importance to notice. One can imagine this conversation moving on for some time, while the anti-egoist offers various examples and tries to overcome the egoist's theory. But from the small sample we have before us, the main features of the dispute emerge. For the egoist has hit upon a formula that is unbeatable—whatever action, however noble, his opponent cites, he will always reply that if the person acted that way, it can be presumed that he was doing what he desired to do, and hence was motivated by the desire to maximize his own good by fulfilling his own greatest desire. Since the egoist has a universally effective reply, the anti-egoist must recognize, when he catches on, that his arguments are hopeless —he has no chance to win. But does that mean simply that the egoist has better evidence to support his theory?

This is not really the case, of course. For not only can every action that has actually occurred be explained egoistically by the egoist; any *possible* action that we could even conceive of can be equally well explained in the same way. If the freedom rider had stayed home by his comfortable fireside, that would still have been an egoistic action. But a theory that no conceivable evidence could refute is a highly suspect theory. We are bound to wonder whether, like the promises of an evasive politician, it owes its safety to its caution—whether it may perhaps be saying nothing at all.

And the dispute between the egoist and his critic does seem to have led to this outcome. For in effect the egoist was determined to say that whatever a person does is what he wants to do. The fact that he does it is decisive. The egoist doesn't make a special study of a person's motives in each case; he simply waits until the action is taken, then says that is what the person wanted to do. But obviously in this way the statement "Everyone always does what he wants to do" becomes analytic—it means nothing more than "Everyone does what he does." The next step is tacitly to redefine "egoism" so that it takes on a new, broad meaning. Thus "desiring to maximize one's own good" is used in such a way that it means only "wanting to do something." Since "wanting to do something" means no more than "doing something," it is no wonder that the theory of psychological egoism becomes impregnable to attack—for it becomes practically equivalent to the uninformative tautology "All actions are somebody's actions." It certainly is impossible to refute that.

To show how this works out in detail would require more analysis, but we shall have to leave that to you. We do not say that psychological egoism has been a totally worthless theory, for the attempt to debunk superficially altruistic behavior can on occasion expose motives that are genuinely self-regarding. Nor do we say that the fallacious defense for the theory discussed here is the only defense that could be offered. We do say that psychological egoism often is defended in this way, and that as a result it becomes necessary but analytic, so that no synthetic consequences can follow from it (for example, that it is futile to try to bring children up to be generous). And we add that unless the anti-egoist in such a discussion sees how the senses of the words are shifting, so that a statement that started out as synthetic becomes analytic through redefinition, he will be at least frustrated, and quite possibly misled.

The importance of distinguishing between analytic and synthetic propositions should, then, be apparent. The synthetic proposition is meaty, has a content, commits the believer to something, and calls for substantial support. The analytic proposition, on the other hand, is empty of reference to the world and follows directly from the general principles of formal logic plus chosen definitions of certain terms. Though certain types of analytic statement are of the greatest importance for some purposes, there is a sense in which, even when true and accepted, they do not amount to knowledge. This is a crucial point, if it can be made out. It doesn't seem that anyone can increase the total quantity of his knowledge by committing to memory a new set of statements that he never thought of before, when they are all of the form "Cows are cows," "Coulombs are coulombs," "Endocrines are endocrines," and so on. Indeed, he can accept these, in the sense of disdaining to question them, without even knowing what coulombs or endocrines are. So they certainly add nothing to his knowledge of zoology, physics, or organic chemistry. And the same may be said of more complex analytic statements, like "Brown cows are cows" or "You will never find horns on an animal that is neither brown nor horned."

There is no trouble about saying, if we wish, that analytic propositions are true, and of course if they are true they are necessarily true. Their contradictories are inconceivable, for the very good reason that they are *self*-contradictory: we cannot conceive how cows should fail to be cows, or circles round, or how people could be divorced when they were never married in the first place. But these inconceivabilities are not a consequence of the way the world is, so to speak, but of the initial principles of logic and the definitions we choose to give for the key words. So we might choose to say that analytic knowledge is not really knowledge at all.

Nevertheless, though we *could* use the term "knowledge" in this restricted sense, we do not need to. Nor shall we do so here. We shall speak of knowing analytic truths—but we shall call this "analytic knowledge," to mark its special character.

We have found one important connection between the two sets of distinctions we have been making. We first said that propositions may be either necessary or contingent, and later that they may be either analytic or synthetic. Now we can draw this conclusion, at least: that all analytic propositions are necessary. The same conclusion may be put in other words: all contingent ones are synthetic. Our two pairs of terms give us

four theoretical compartments in which we might classify all true propositions: (1) necessary and analytic, (2) necessary and synthetic, (3) contingent and analytic, (4) contingent and synthetic. But we now see that
the third compartment is bound to remain empty: there cannot be any
propositions that are both contingent and analytic. On the other hand, the
first and fourth compartments quite obviously have many propositions in
them: all the examples of analytic propositions we have just been discussing are necessary, and therefore belong in the first compartment; and all
the examples of contingent empirical propositions we discussed earlier are
synthetic, and therefore belong in the fourth compartment. The question
that remains is this: what about compartment No. 2?

Are there, in other words, any propositions that are both necessary
and synthetic? This question poses one of the most fundamental of all the
problems of knowledge.

We have been inquiring whether all knowledge could be empirical.
That all knowledge is empirical is a theory of knowledge, and one whose
truth would be important to discover: it is called *empiricism*. But it seems
clear, from what we have just been discussing, that this thesis cannot be
true as it stands. For we know some necessary truths, and these cannot
be empirical. If they are self-evident, they are not based on observations in
any way; and if they are deduced from self-evident propositions, they are
neither empirical generalizations nor empirical hypotheses. Some knowledge seems obviously to be nonempirical.

On the other hand, at least some of this necessary knowledge can be
explained as analytic, and analytic knowledge, as we have seen, is empty
of any reference to the world. This kind of knowledge does not pose any
special problems to the empiricist, and so he can restate his view in such
a way as to take account of it. Let us define empiricism, then, as the theory
that all *synthetic* knowledge is empirical—or, in other words, that all
knowledge is either empirical or analytic knowledge.

Now we see the importance of the question about synthetic necessary
truth. The empiricist can explain how synthetic contingent truths are built
up from observation as generalizations or hypotheses and he can explain
how analytic necessary truths are built up from logical truths and definitions. But he cannot explain how there can be any truths that are both
synthetic and necessary. So if such truths exist, empiricism is false.

Let us use the term *a priori* for knowledge that does not depend on
experience for its support. Generally this term is used as synonymous with
"necessary," just as the term "factual" is often used as synonymous with
"synthetic," so that some philosophers speak of "synthetic a priori propositions" or "factual a priori propositions." It will be somewhat more
convenient here, however, if we apply the term "a priori" to knowledge
rather than to propositions. When we speak of a priori knowledge, then,
we shall mean knowledge—in some way independent of experience—of
necessary propositions.

The theory that there is such a thing as synthetic a priori knowledge is called *rationalism*. This definition makes rationalism contradictory to empiricism. Both cannot be true; either there is a synthetic a priori knowledge or there is not. Rationalism and empiricism are often contrasted in less striking ways, but it seems best to state the issue sharply. If rationalism is defined as the view which "emphasizes the role of reason in human knowledge," and empiricism as the view which "emphasizes the role of experience," why then is it a simple matter to reconcile them by pointing out that when the physicist verifies a hypothesis he is both reasoning and appealing to experience. This is all very well, but it loses sight of the epistemological problem. For the important question is whether we, as human beings, have or have not two fundamentally distinct ways of knowing.

§ 16. • *The Principle of Lawfulness*

To see what is at stake in the dispute between rationalists and empiricists, we must take a close look at an example of alleged synthetic a priori knowledge. Many sorts of propositions have figured in this dispute—religious, ethical, mathematical, logical, etc. But the most convenient example for us—and an illuminating one—lies close at hand in the discussion we have just concluded. For if, as some philosophers hold, the scientific enterprise rests upon some antecedent assurance that nature is lawful throughout, or that every event is in principle explainable in terms of a cause, then here, surely, is a fine specimen of synthetic a priori knowledge —the principle of lawfulness, or, as it is often called, determinism. Thus Kant, for example, made an elaborate and brilliant attempt to prove that this principle, which he took to be clearly synthetic, is a necessary truth that we cannot dispense with. It is, he argued, a principle that guides us in ordinary life, where it is never questioned on the common-sense level. And it provides both a guiding principle and an ideal goal to the empirical scientist. The proposition that every event is lawful is certainly not susceptible to refutation by experience: you can't prove that any particular event *has* no law. And Kant also argued that this principle plays a fundamental role in our very concept of reality. How, for example, do we distinguish dreams from waking experiences, or illusions from correct perceptions? We take it for granted that what is real hangs together in a lawful system, and when chairs in dreams behave in ways that cannot be fitted into a coherent system of mechanics, or when pink elephants defy the laws of physiology, we call them "unreal" or nonexistent.

It is important to see that Kant and others have made out a strong case for the view that we do take the principle of lawfulness for granted, without questioning it. There is one very important ground (to be considered in the following chapter) on which many philosophers do question it, at least verbally. But though it is easy to *say* that some natural event—the falling of a tree—might have had no cause, is it really easy to *think* it? It would mean that that event just happened spontaneously; there were no antecedent conditions, such as lightning striking or rot eating away its innards, that would explain the falling and would have enabled us to predict its falling had they been known beforehand. It would be, from a human point of view, like a miraculous event, save that the miraculous event is supposed to have a supernatural cause. Can we really suppose that a tree might fall with absolutely no cause? And if just one such event has occurred, why not more? Why does any event require a cause if some do not? Could we justify our belief that *some* events are lawful, if we cannot prove that *all* are?

Nevertheless, the principle of lawfulness, for all its pull on our assent, has been denied, and with especial force in recent years. The principle of uncertainty, proposed a few decades ago by Werner Heisenberg, still plays a central role in quantum physics, and while no one can guarantee that it will never be superseded, it is the best we know now, and must be taken account of. Unfortunately, its philosophical significance is still much debated, for what it actually implies is variously interpreted. It states that it is physically impossible to determine precisely at one time both the position and the velocity of a microphysical particle; the more exact one of these measurements is, the less exact must be the other—the degree of indeterminacy being stated by the principle. But what is the reason for this physical impossibility?

According to one interpretation, it is due to the fact that our instruments inevitably interfere with the particles we are trying to measure. But that makes it sound like saying that you can't be sure the refrigerator light goes off when you shut the door, because you can't look in when the door is shut. That would be consistent with a perfectly lawful behavior on the part of those little particles.

According to another interpretation, the fact is that the particle simply doesn't *have* both exact position and exact velocity at the same time—as traditional Newtonian particles used to do. Therefore its future behavior cannot be predicted exactly, for if we want to know where a particle is going we must know where it's heading, with what speed, and where it is now. Thus within limits we may predict, or we may predict what the average particle of a large group will do, but there will be, let us say, two different photons that take slightly different paths with no difference in the preceding conditions in terms of which one could discover a law accounting for the difference in path. Now, it is difficult to see how the physicist could show that there *cannot* be any such distinguishing conditions. Clearly, as he says, he can't make his prediction using only the concepts that served in Newtonian mechanics, but how can he rule out the possibility that there are other features of the situation—unknown characteristics internal to the photon, or undiscovered characteristics of the field in which they move—

that do cause the difference in path? It doesn't seem that he can refute the principle of lawfulness.

But perhaps that is not, at least from Kant's point of view, the important thing; the question is not whether the principle is true, but whether it is necessarily true. What is unsettling is that quantum physicists—at least some of them—say that they can get along without the principle of lawfulness, that they don't need it and don't miss it. That events have causes is undoubtedly a deep-rooted conviction in the human mind, but perhaps it is no less a prejudice for all that. There are, indeed, a number of strange features of quantum theory, anomalous and paradoxical notions, that run counter to cherished assumptions about the physical world. For example, we take it for granted that an object that moves from one place to another must traverse a continuous path in between; but some of these little particles move by jumps, simply disappear at one place and turn up at another, without crossing the intervening space. Again, we think that if two separate streams of particles are moving through two small holes, and we cover up one hole, it can't make any difference to the other particles, who aren't looking around to see what their companions are doing; but yet it does. Perhaps the time will come when we may have to admit that a person —or at least a photon—can be in two places at the same time. It will be a wrench, but let us not be dogmatic.

This is certainly a powerful argument, and it shows how difficult it is for us to separate in our minds propositions that are logically necessary from propositions that are merely very familiar and obvious or long taken for granted. This is precisely why the empiricist is uneasy about the rationalist's criterion of necessity—the inconceivability of the opposite. Is this really an objective test? Not long ago mathematicians thought it inconceivable that there could be the same number of things in a whole class as in part of the class (e.g., the same number of whole numbers as there are even numbers), yet now find this perfectly conceivable. The only really objective test, says the empiricist, is whether the contradictory is self-contradictory. If you can show that, then you have shown the proposition is necessary. But this is the test of analyticity, and if it is made the test of necessity, then analyticity and necessity must go together. Which is precisely what the empiricist holds: all analytic propositions are necessary, and all necessary propositions are analytic.

Now the rationalist, if he is to save the necessity of the principle of lawfulness, has two choices. The first choice is to show that, for all his blithe talk, the quantum physicist does not really abandon his belief in lawfulness. Here the discussion gets very technical, for there is no way to carry it on except to go into the actual working of the uncertainty principle in quantum physics. As far as we can see, this question has not been settled among physicists or among philosophers of science, and we are not qualified to deal with it. (However, you may wish to follow it up.) The second choice is to cling to a distinction between the microphysical level of photons, electrons, etc., and the macrophysical level of ordinary physical objects, mattresses, bullets, footballs, sputniks. Never mind the first level for the time being, until we know more: it may be that microphysical events are not lawful, in the sense in which we have been using this term, and that only statistical laws can be hoped for in that realm. But events on the macrophysical level are, the rationalist may insist, just as lawful as ever, and nothing can shake our confidence in that. Nor is this just a stubborn unreasoned feeling.

The question is, how can such a distinction be maintained? There is one rather drastic method to use. These microphysical entities are, after all, a rather queer lot anyway: it is an odd story that the physicist makes up when we ask him, for example, what is going on in the center of the sun, and he tells us about hydrogen atoms fusing into helium atoms, and larger ones being built up by neutron capture. We do not question the interest and the usefulness of his story: after all, can he not predict that when, some 5 or 6 billion years from now, 12 per cent of the hydrogen has been converted into helium, it is the beginning of the end for the solar system? But none of these processes can be directly observed; are they then *real* in the same sense in which chairs and tables are real?

This line of thought develops into a certain view of the unobservable entities of physics: that they are "constructs," or made-up notions convenient in predicting what we do observe but not to be taken as a picture of reality. The rationalist might preserve the principle of lawfulness for the macrophysical world by identifying that world with the "real" world and using the principle of lawfulness as one of the criteria of reality. This is part of what Kant was in fact doing—though of course he did not face the problem posed by Heisenberg's principle. He said that we do and must distinguish, as was noted above, between what is real and what is unreal (illusory), and he argued that we cannot make this distinction without the help of the principle of lawfulness. The general structure of his definition might be sketched (incompletely) as follows:

> "E is a real event" means "E conforms to the following conditions:
> a. it is in space and time;
> b. it is a change in a property of a substance (principle of substance);
> c. it is lawful (principle of causality); . . ."

and so on. When you define a word in this fashion, by listing the conditions under which one is permitted to say that the word applies to something, such a definition is called an "implicit definition," or a "postulational definition."

Thus, by way of analogy, suppose someone picked up a copy of Hoyle's book on games, and read certain propositions under the heading "Contract Bridge." For example: the game is played with a deck of 52 cards in four suits; one card is dealt at a time; ace is high; four players play as two teams. . . . Now he might be puzzled to know what sort of propositions these are. They don't seem to be analytic propositions, for cards are not dealt one at a time by definition, and indeed in some other games are dealt several at a time—no self-contradiction there. On the other hand, they don't seem to be merely contingent propositions. A newspaper may report of the latest International Bridge Tournament that North bid six no trumps or that East opened with his ace of hearts. These are contingent propositions, reports of what actually went on. But a proposition like "Ace is high" has a certain necessity about it; it *must* be high, in bridge. Are these rules, then, really synthetic necessary truths?

In this case the answer is clear: they are necessary, but not synthetic. For they constitute collectively an implicit definition of "contract bridge." Contract bridge is the game played according to these rules. If you don't follow the rules, you aren't playing the game, by definition. The analytic character of the rules is hard to see when we consider them one at a time, but when we see how together they actually define the game, their analytic nature is revealed. So, too, with the postulational way of making the principle of lawfulness necessary: the principle becomes necessary, but analytic, since now, in effect, it says that all *real* events have causes, but this is true by the stipulated definition of "real."

The issue between the rationalist and the empiricist over the principle of lawfulness is evidently a complex one, which must be left unresolved here. Yet one further alternative must be mentioned, to make the record reasonably complete. For since the issue is so tangled, some philosophers have been strongly tempted to see whether the whole issue could somehow be avoided. They are not convinced that the principle of lawfulness can be shown either to be necessary or contingent, either synthetic or analytic. But since these classifications of propositions are exhaustive, there is only one conclusion to be drawn: it is not a proposition at all. Suppose that "Nature is lawful" is really an imperative, a command, in disguise: that its substance is, "Seek laws!" or "Let us seek laws!" Then what makes it seem synthetic is that this resolution or advice really enjoins an action, tells us something to do—maybe even adds some encouragement like "Keep it up, old boy; don't be discouraged!" though it cannot promise success. And what makes it seem necessary is that it points out a duty, perhaps in this form: "If you want to be a scientist, seek laws!" We don't have to obey, of course, but we see that if we don't obey, then we really aren't acting as scientists at all.

The view, so briefly sketched here, that the principle of lawfulness is really an imperative, wipes out, of course, a good deal of the discussion in §§ 10–12 of this chapter. We saw that certain maxims, in an imperative form, are involved in scientific method—that to use this method is to resolve to obey these imperatives. The problem of induction was whether or not the imperatives rest upon the presupposition that nature is lawful. According to the present view, that presupposition is itself an imperative, of a more general sort. It may still be backed up, as an imperative, by some such argument as this: "If you don't seek laws, you won't find them; but if there are any laws, then you may find them when you look." And that may be the most that can be hoped for.

Yet to make plausible this solution, or dissolution, of the problem of induction, we must grant one assumption that is not easy to grant. How could we have been fooled? Here we thought the principle of lawfulness was a proposition, because it was formulated in a declarative sentence, but all along it was an imperative sentence in disguise. Now, it might be pointed out that some declarative sentences have a kind of imperative function. "It's getting late" under certain circumstances may be taken to mean, "Go home." But this does not show that "It's getting late" ceases to be a proposition, either true or false. In fact, it loses its imperative force if it is not taken as expressing the speaker's belief. Similarly, we may wonder if the full force of the principle of lawfulness can be preserved if it is not a proposition at all.

CHAPTER THREE

❧

HUMAN NATURE

When we ask what is distinctive of human beings in the world of living things, a number of important concepts come to mind. By way of opening things up for the present chapter, then, let us consider these concepts briefly. Some of them will be given a more extended and searching treatment later.

Consider *consciousness,* for example. The term "conscious" is by no means easy to define, save by the somewhat evasive method of listing near-synonyms: aware, awake, sensible (as opposed to insensible). Certainly to be conscious is to be in a state of having feelings, thoughts, sensations, or other experiences. Consciousness, of course, we do not think of as restricted to human beings; the higher vertebrates possess it, and perhaps even the lowly crustaceans. We may doubt whether the earthworm or oyster is conscious; but if the one can feel pain (however dull) from the fishhook and the other the irritation of the pearl, then they have a dim consciousness, at least. We may be confident that the amoeba and the white birch tree are not conscious, even though from time to time they exhibit behavior that mimics awareness. Consciousness varies in degree—in scope and intensity, articulation of thought, subtlety of sensation, depth of feeling. And human beings, we assume, have it in a higher degree than all the other beings we know of.

It is sometimes said that man alone possesses a special kind of consciousness, capable of reflecting upon itself. Self-consciousness consists not only in thinking, but in thinking about thinking, in knowing that you know. And indeed it does seem doubtful that even the most advanced nonhuman organism has this capacity.

Consider *mind.* Under what conditions should we say that a living being has a mind? Human beings have; flowers and trees do not. A dog or a cat, a porpoise or a chimpanzee, has a mind, though not as good as those of most humans. Our test here may be certain capacities for behavior: an organism has a mind if it can overcome obstacles to its aims, solve problems, work out flexible and alternative strategies. In this sense, mind is what the experimental psychologist measures as *intelligence*. Though intelligence can be less or greater, the human level of organic evolution is marked by the highest degree so far known to us.

Can this difference in degree be made a difference in kind? One of the oldest attempts to define human nature was Aristotle's: man is the rational animal. Though some philosophers still cling to it, modern psychology makes it difficult to preserve. A rational animal is presumably a reasoning animal, and certainly reasoning is what the chimpanzee is doing when he learns to use poker chips in a slot machine to get bananas, or the rat when he figures his way through the maze. But is human reasoning on a plane radically different from anything that lower animals are capable of? The twentieth-century philosopher Ernst Cassirer and others in his wake have suggested that the difference lies in the ability to use *symbols*—that is, not merely to learn to react appropriately to stimuli, but to manipulate language, to develop abstractions, to intend, with the help of signs, something far distant in time or space. Man is the symbol-using animal, according to this view. Indeed, it may be symbolic processes that constitute self-consciousness, since it is by formulating our thoughts in words and other symbols that we become able to examine them.

There is one other very important term that we are wont to apply to ourselves, but seldom if ever (and then only perhaps facetiously) to other animals. A human being is, or can be, a *person*. No doubt a dog or a cat can have a *personality* (so some owners would claim)—that is, a recognizable individual manner of behaving—but it is not, in the full sense, a person. The concept of what it is to be a person is extremely difficult to explicate. It involves, at the least, the consciousness of being the same self over a period of time, of having goals and purposes, and of having a role or status in relation to other persons—if that is not too circular a way of putting it. Being a person, in the full sense, seems to be at least in part a social property—or at least the capacity to act socially. And this was another definition that Aristotle once suggested: man is the social (or civic) animal. Again, human beings are not the only creatures that have societies and organized cooperation; but in man these interindividual relations are lifted to a different plane through language and culture and become interpersonal.

These sketchy and preliminary remarks may be enough to suggest some questions that can hover in the background as we proceed. But let us now select one of the most fundamental and philosophically important of the terms we have mentioned, "mind," and consider more directly the problems it raises.

THE MIND-BODY PROBLEM

§ 1. • *Mental States and the Self*

Imagine yourself writing a letter to a distant friend describing what you have been up to during the past week. A good part of the letter may turn out to consist of sentences beginning with the letter "I" or ending with "me": "I walked . . . I wondered . . . I got pretty tired . . . I swam . . . I thought of you . . . The air felt fresh and cool to me . . ." All these sentences are about the same person, the person writing the letter—namely, you. And what they describe are various activities that you engaged in.

These activities are evidently of very different sorts. And for some practical purposes it would be useful to classify them in certain ways. One important method of classification might be according to the parts of you that are required for a given activity. If you sprained your wrist, for example, you might not be able to swim, but you could still walk. We can ask, what do you walk *with?* And one might answer, "With my legs, of course" —mentioning the limbs that play the most prominent and obvious part in the action. But it would be a mistake to overlook the cooperation that is also required from the heart, lungs, eyes, and the inner ear that helps to keep you in balance—not to mention the brain. It is, in the last analysis, the whole body that does the walking or swimming.

What about wondering and thinking? No doubt you couldn't do these things either without the cooperation of certain bodily activities—in the brain, in the nervous system. Still, they are not actions performed primarily by any particular organs or limbs—you don't think *with* your head or your hands. These activities we tend to place, when we reflect upon the matter, in a different category from walking and swimming. They are *mental* activities, rather than physical ones.

As for getting tired—well, this is perhaps ambiguous. In one sense, tiredness means carbon dioxide piling up in the blood, muscles not responding so quickly to stimuli, a general slowing down of actions—and in this sense, it is physical. But it can also mean certain feelings—weariness, aching muscles, and the increasing effort of movement. And in this sense tiredness is said to be mental. So getting tired might be called both physical and mental, or neither one more than the other. And indeed, most of the specific actions we would single out for mention have both physical and mental aspects. Even swimming, for example, is not the same as floating; it involves thought, intention, effort, voluntary decision.

We want to know whether this common-sense distinction between the mental and the physical is philosophically defensible. But first we must see how it is usually made. The distinction between two sorts of activity may itself hinge upon a distinction between two sorts of events, or states, involved in our activities. (An event can be regarded as a series of states, or a state as an event with minimal change.) To think about somebody far off, to have a sensation of coolness, to feel tired, is to experience a mental state; mental activity seems to be activity that involves only, or predominantly, mental states.

Can a clear and satisfactory distinction be made between mental states and physical states? What we need are some criteria or properties by which we can tell whether or not a given state is mental. Three such criteria have been widely employed by philosophers.

The first criterion of the mental is *lack of spatial location*. A bodily movement always occurs at some point in space; it has a place. But it seems ridiculous, at first glance anyway, to ask where a thought is, or how distant one emotion may be from another. And so, some philosophers hold, by applying this criterion we can always distinguish the mental from the physical. But what about a pain, which is obviously mental? We can certainly ask where a pain is, and the answer—"In my big toe"—seems to locate it in just the same way as it would locate a physical object if given in reply to the question "Where is the splinter?" Can't a feeling of tiredness be spread throughout the body?

There is an ingenious way of answering the objection to the first criterion. It is well known that a person can have a pain in the toe even if he does not have a toe—if it has been amputated. But he certainly can't have a splinter in the toe, if he has no toe. This strongly suggests that the expression "in the toe," when we are speaking of a pain, means something quite different from what it means when we are speaking of a splinter. Perhaps "pain felt in the toe" is really a description of the pain itself—it is a toe-type pain, and might better be hyphenated "pain-felt-in-the-toe," to show that the spatial reference involved is not strictly a location of the pain but part of the feeling itself. If you dream of a horse in your room, it doesn't follow that the dream is in your room, or the dream-horse is in your room, but only that you have had a horse-in-your-room-type dream.

On the other hand, it might be argued that even if a pain-felt-in-the-toe has no precise location in the toe, it is certainly located somewhere—namely, in your body. Some things acknowledged to be physical, like clouds and magnetic fields, have no definite boundaries and are hard to pinpoint. An idea, granted, is not in your head, any more than it is in your foot; but if someone asks, "Whose idea was that?" we can point to the one who had it, and what we point to, is, after all, a physical body. Perhaps mental states, then, *can* have physical locations.

So the first criterion of the mental is subject to some dispute. The second one is *privacy*. A physical object, event, or condition (let us stick to the macroscopic level in this context) is said by some philosophers to be, at least in principle, publicly observable. It may in fact be observed by no one, or by one person—say, the first to climb to the summit of the mountain or to descend so far into the ocean depths. But if it makes sense to speak of more than one person observing it, then it is physical. If it makes no sense to speak of two people observing it, then it is essentially private, and therefore mental.

This criterion is applied in the following way. Consider physical tiredness, as exemplified, say, in sluggish movements and slow reactions. You can observe these conditions in your own body, and anyone else who happens to be looking can do the same. So they are public. But as for mental tiredness, the feeling of tiredness, how would this be observed? One can only observe it (experience it) by *having* it, and therefore *your* feeling of tiredness is private to you. For if someone else were to observe it, he would have to have it; then what *he* had wouldn't be yours any more, but his—there would be two distinct (though similar) mental states, your feeling and his, and each would still be private. Even if he were hooked up to you so that whenever you felt tired he would always have the same feeling, that would still not make your feeling public, for his feeling would not be yours, and he would not be observing yours, but only his own.

That is one line of argument. Perhaps what it suggests is that when it comes to feeling (and other mental states), it is confusing, or even mistaken, to speak of "observing" them. The doctor can observe your swollen glands without having them. But when something cannot be observed without being had (a pain or an emotion), then perhaps we should not call this observation at all. Then the privacy criterion would be stated this way: mental states are states that cannot be observed (strictly speaking), but only had; physical states are states that are in principle observable. Because of the fact that so many of the words we use in describing people cut across the distinction, the criterion may at first seem implausible: can't the mother *see* that her child is tired? But the criterion can always be applied by making the proper distinctions. There is mental tiredness, which can't be seen by anyone, but only felt by the child. And there are the effects, the symptoms, the behavioral manifestations of this feeling, which the attentive mother notes.

The alleged privacy of mental states can perhaps be clarified by reference to another useful philosophical concept. A mental state, it might be said, is a state such that first-person propositions about it are *incorrigible*. Other people may be mistaken in their belief that you have a headache, even though you give all the signs of it; but you cannot help knowing whether or not you have it. "I have a headache" seems to be known with certainty and conclusiveness by the person who truly utters it. Note that we are talking about conscious mental states here; if there are unconscious mental states, this criterion would not apply. But philosophers have sometimes questioned whether the concept of unconscious mental states is self-contradictory or unintelligible. As far as conscious states are concerned, if there really is such a thing as incorrigibility—the impossibility of being mistaken about some proposition—then it provides a possible criterion of the mental.

The third criterion is the most difficult of all: *intentionality*. Mental states are forms of consciousness, and consciousness is said to have an essentially referential character: we cannot be conscious without being conscious *of* something; a thought is *about* something; an emotion is directed toward an object, and so forth. The object does not have to exist; we can wish for a Utopia that will never come. "Intentional" is used here in a very special sense that has little to do with its ordinary senses; the intentional character of hatred, for example, is its implicit reference to someone or something that is hated. A chair or a tree does not have this intentional character, but an emotion does.

If this notion of intentionality can be made reasonably clear, we must ask whether it is either a sufficient or a necessary condition of being mental. A good case can surely be made out for saying that it is sufficient. A signpost pointing to the turnpike might seem to have an intentional character; it constitutes a reference to something else. And a signpost is not mental. But it is only people who can intend the turnpike (that is, think of it, yearn to arrive at it); the sign is merely an aid. Is intentionality a necessary condition of being mental? It has been argued that some mental states are not intentional. What about a generalized state of vague anxiety, for example—where, as we say, the patient doesn't feel anxious about anything in particular? But it seems that something must be troubling him; perhaps he is anxious about everything—the most familiar object fills him with nameless dread. Or what about pains? A headache just is a headache; it may be caused by overwork, eyestrain, or late hours, but it can't be said to be *about* (or of, or toward, or in reference to) any of these things. We might say that the headache is an ache referring to the head, just as a pain-felt-in-the-toe is a pain referring to the toe. This is evident in the case of the person who has no toe—he can only be said to be feeling painfully about (or in reference to) a nonexistent toe. Perhaps the apparent location of a pain is its intentional character.

Suppose that, with the help of these three criteria or others, we can make a distinction between two kinds of state, mental and physical. This would seem to be a very fundamental distinction, with important consequences for various fields of thought—psychology, ethics, religion. And of course it immediately raises philosophical questions. The primary one is this: what is the relationship between the mental and the physical? This is the *mind-body problem*.

We shall tackle this problem shortly, but there is one preliminary point that may require some explanation. In speaking of the mind-body problem, instead of the mental-physical problem, we jump from adjectives to nouns, and our haste may land us in some dubious inferences unless we are cautious. The word "mind" is a very handy one for many purposes and clearly in some contexts it is legitimate: you have something on your mind, you are afraid you are going out of your mind, your mind is on what you are doing. All these things could be expressed in other ways, without using the word: you are thinking of something, you are distraught, you are intent on what you are doing. But when we want to refer loosely, unspecifically, and collectively to such mental activities, we use the word "mind."

But does this word mean something more? When we are tempted to use it in a way parallel to the word "body," it develops a new philosophical sense. There is the body and there are its physical (bodily) states: it is the body that has those states, or is in them, and it seems that the states could not be there without a body to support them. So, again, there are mental states—but states of what? States of mind, we say: it is the mind that is in those states, or has them. Now the mind is thought of as a kind of thing, a substantial entity of some sort underlying our mental states. This is one very old and very important theory about the mind—let us call it the *mental-substance theory.*

Much in our experience lends support to the theory. First, our ordinary language suggests that you cannot have mental states unless they are states *of* something, and something that is not itself a state but an object in its own right. If "I" and "me" are to have a referent, must they not refer to a particular thing? Second, there is the appeal to individual introspection: some philosophers have claimed that each of us is conscious of being a self, a core or center of awareness, distinct from, but somehow underlying, our constantly shifting experiences. Third, there is the presumption of self-identity. You are the same person you were long ago, though altered irrevocably by the passing of the years. In what does this sameness consist? You don't have the same body you had in your childhood days—every one of the old cells is gone. But something about you must be the same (the argument runs): that is your mind. And since the thoughts and feelings and sensations you have now are different from what they were, your mind must be something distinct from all these mental states.

Other philosophers have rejected these arguments for a substantial self. First, the logic of our ordinary language is not decisive for a philosopher. Granted that the word "I" refers to something; it does not follow that I am a single unitary thing. And granted that there are states of mind; it does not follow that the mind is something distinct from all its states. Some philosophers (especially those who have followed Hume) claim that their introspection reveals no such single mental substance within: when I look in upon myself, said Hume, I find only this and that thought, or feeling, or desire, or wish, or color, or sound, etc., etc. And third, perhaps the identity of the self through time and change can be accounted for without presuming an underlying changeless substance. It might consist, for example, in certain continuities of experience. Sense-experiences reappear in memory, binding the earlier to the later time; anticipations are fulfilled;

every change of hope or of ambition occurs against a background of certain temporary constancies of experience—when you are deciding not to be a fireman after all, you are continuing to enjoy baseball; and when you are losing your taste for baseball, you continue to maintain your interest in ancient Egypt. If you lost all your memories at once, and changed all your thoughts and feelings, you really would be a different self.

There are many difficulties in this project of explaining self-identity without the mental-substance theory—and some of these difficulties are not yet overcome. But enough progress has been made to lead some philosophers to suppose that a simpler theory will ultimately be shown to be acceptable. According to the *collective theory,* the mind is simply a collection of mental states, bound together more or less tightly by their mutual intentions. If the states must still be states of something, then they are states of a person—a person being something that has both mental and physical states, that can add two and two and also digest a dinner.

However the mind itself be analyzed, the further question of its relationship to the body also remains. In calling this the mind-body problem (its conventional name) we do not wish to beg any question about the nature of mind. As will be seen presently, this problem concerns the connection between mental and bodily states (or events), and it arises for any philosopher who makes the original distinction between these two kinds of state.

§ 2. • *Dualistic Theories*

One very familiar sequence of events might be summarized in this way: your stomach muscles contract after some hours of not eating (W), you feel hungry (X), you decide to eat something (Y), you reach out for the apple on the table (Z). These events would ordinarily be said to constitute a *causal* series, each event providing an explanation of what follows. Why did you reach out for the apple? Because you felt hungry. Why did you feel hungry? Because you hadn't eaten for some time, so your stomach muscles contracted. The role of event Y in this series may be a bit more puzzling—at least some philosophers would find it so. But if deciding to eat can be regarded as a particular action—like saying to oneself, "I know I should watch the calories, but this time I'll forget them"—then this action could perhaps quite properly be said to have been caused by the antecedent feeling of hunger and to have been causally efficacious in producing the consequent movement of the arm.

Now what is remarkable, and philosophically interesting, about this little story, in terms of the distinction we have just been considering, is the way it passes back and forth between the two types of event, mental and physical. If, for the sake of perspicuity, we use primes for the mental events, and plain letters for the physical ones, and let arrows stand for causal connections, the sequence might be diagrammed as follows:

Mental events

X' ⟶ Y'

Physical events   W   Z

This diagram represents one answer to the question about the relationship between the mind and the body: mental events and physical events enter into sequences in which either can cause the other. This is the *interactionist theory.*

The philosopher who first tried to work out a sharp and definite distinction between the mind and the body, Descartes, also adopted this common-sense solution to the problem that his distinction raised. Yet he and several others who followed him were much troubled by the interactionist thesis. The difficulty (if it is one) lies in the extreme dissimilarity of the two types of event. If physical events are spatially located, while mental ones are not, and if mental events involve consciousness, while matter is wholly insentient, then how can events of such radically different sorts be causes or effects of one another? It's easy to understand how one moving body can transfer motion to another, but the notion that a movement in the body somehow provokes a thought has been regarded by some philosophers as transparently absurd.

Still, what is so absurd about it? Must we assume a priori that A and B cannot be causally connected unless they are of the same type? Experience does not bear this out. The heat produced by the dynamite is enormous, but that heat is not in the dynamite before it explodes, or in the electric current that explodes it. Of course if we think of minds and bodies as substances, their interaction may be more difficult to conceive. But if we are just dealing with two kinds of events, then why is it impossible that laws of some sort should connect them? Certainly there is much mystery about the connection—we do not know how tranquilizing drugs transform a tense or brooding person into a calm and cheerful one, nor how a gentle electric current through the cortex can bring to vivid consciousness long-buried memories. We do not know how an unhappy home can lead to chemical changes in the body that help to produce symptoms of psychosis. But if there is anything that we do know it is that you can change people's mental states by drugs, and that we can make our limbs move by deciding and then trying to move them.

This first supposed difficulty with interactionism may be left at this stage, while we turn to consider a more fundamental question. Suppose we work backward from the final event of the sequence, the reaching out of the hand, and press our request for an explanation more closely and more scientifically. We do not propose to go into the physiological details, but only to remind ourselves that they exist. It is worth bearing in mind that what we have called the level of physical events really consists of two levels, which for some purposes it is important to distinguish. We can speak of *overt behavior* (the reaching of the hand, for example), that is, gross bodily movements open to ordinary observation. And we can speak of *internal processes* going on inside the organism, which we know about through scientific study—the stomach contractions, the events occurring in brain and nerve cells, etc. Now, if we ask the physiologist to explain to us what caused the hand to move, he will begin by showing how certain muscles contracted. Why? Because of certain electrical discharges in the neurons. What triggered these discharges? Impulses sent out by the brain along the efferent nerve cells in the spinal column. And what caused these impulses to be sent? Certain electrical and chemical activities in the motor part of the cortex and in the cerebellum. And what was the cause of these? Certain impulses sent up to the brain, along the afferent nerves, by the muscles contracting in the stomach from lack of food to digest.

Now, the physiologist's story has certain very interesting features. First, note that it takes us from event Z back to event W—it bridges the gap between the original physical event we considered and the final one in our sequence. Second, it bridges this gap in a convincing way (despite certain segments of the process that are still not fully understood), and in detail, showing us step by step how one event led, or could have led, to the next. But third, it is a story told completely in physical language; it concerns only physical events and states and objects, with no mention of feelings of hunger or acts of will.

A rather startling consequence follows. Suppose we think of this whole process as taking one minute and let our main events occur at 15-second intervals, beginning at 12:00 noon. Then if Z occurs at 12:01 we will say that Y′ occurs at 12:00:45. Let us assume that our subject is under observation by a psychologist, who asks him questions about what he is feeling, thinking, etc., and notes the answers down along with the time as recorded by his stop watch. At 12:00:45, the subject reports that he is deciding to succumb to his temptation to eat the apple. Now suppose the subject is also under observation by a physiologist, and to make the situation simple and colorful we may suppose that the subject's cranium is painlessly probed by all sorts of electrodes, recording events within. If we ask the physiologist, then, what is going on at 12:00:45, he will report to us that there is an unusual burst of electrical activity of a certain sort in a certain sector of the cortex. Now if the physiologist is right when he says that this cortical activity (which is of course wholly physical) is the cause of the arm movement, then the psychologist would have to be wrong if he told us that the decision to eat was the cause of the arm movement. For if the cortical activity is a sufficient condition of the arm movement, then no other condition is required for it to occur; the mental decision adds nothing, is of no avail; everything can be accounted for without it.

When we draw out the implications of this line of thought, we get a different picture of the relation of mind to body:

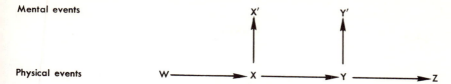

This theory is usually called *epiphenomenalism,* because it makes mental events an "epiphenomenon," or by-product, of physical events. What this means can be seen in the diagram. The sequence of physical events forms a complete and self-sufficient causal process, in which every physical event can be explained in terms of those physical events and conditions that preceded it. Corresponding to some of the physical events are certain mental events that depend upon them. Physical events cause mental events, but not vice versa. There are subtly different versions of this theory. For example, in the diagram just above, when a mental event is simultaneous with a physical one (a feeling of hunger with certain activities in the brain and nervous system), the mental event is said to be caused by the physical one. Those who prefer to confine the term "cause" to a temporal sequence (ruling out simultaneous causation) would rearrange the diagram as follows:

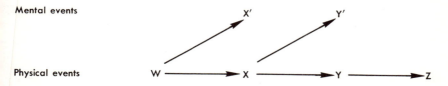

In this version, X' corresponds to X, and Y' to Y, but we would say, for example, that the stomach-muscle contraction (W) has two effects: a physical one (the message sent to the brain) and a mental one (the feeling of hunger).

Either version of epiphenomenalism can lead to another step in the argument. Many philosophers have been bothered by the asymmetry of epiphenomenalism. If you feel a headache as a result of being hit on the head, this is quite in accord with epiphenomenalism; but if it seems to you as though the constant pain of your headache was what made you take the aspirin, the epiphenomenalist says you are quite mistaken about that—what really happened is that certain neural and muscular processes were set in motion by the very physiological conditions that produced the headache, and these caused you in turn to take the aspirin. It seems odd that causal relations should go in one direction but not the other. And if there is any objection to interactionism on the ground of dissimilarity, it would hold against one-way interactions as well as two-way ones.

Other philosophers have made much of another point about our familiar experience. Sometimes we can tell a kind of story different from the physiologist's, one that (at least for some time) mentions only mental events and yet is quite coherent and internally complete. Wondering whether he could afford a new car (we might say), So-and-so thought how nice a car would be, and how beat-up his old one was, and then he added up in his mind the raise in pay that he was expecting, considered other possible drains on the budget, and finally concluded that he could afford the car and should go down the next day and order it. This is a story about what was going on in his mind, and it, too, can be treated as a causal story. It was the thought of the old car's condition that intensified his desire for a new one; and it was the sequence of arithmetical computations that led to his conclusion that he could afford to buy.

By such reflections as these, some philosophers have concluded that in fact we have two separate series of events. If we want the explanation of a physical event, the answer should be in physical terms; if we want the explanation of a mental event, the answer should be in mental terms. And each of these systems is complete in itself and independent of the other. This theory is called *parallelism:*

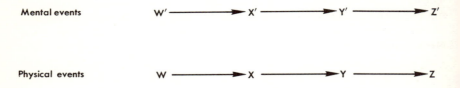

Certain doubtful, or at least artificial, presumptions are required for such a scheme. The parallelist, for one thing, will have to introduce unconscious mental events. When the stomach muscles contract, for example (W), the feeling of hunger (X') occurs shortly thereafter, but the subject doesn't directly feel the muscles moving, as he does when he moves his arm. To make the parallelist system completely deterministic, however, the series of mental events, like the series of physical events, must have no gaps in it.

Now there are several curious features of this theory, and it is not generally regarded as very plausible. That reality, in the last analysis, consists of two entirely independent streams of events—which, however, match each other at all points—is a conclusion that one would be reluctant to accept, on account of its complexity, if there is any satisfactory alternative. What would drive us to that acceptance? Only an unshakable conviction that the mental and the physical somehow can never interact. If we make no such commitment at the start, there is no need for parallelism. And perhaps there is even no clear sense to it. For what does it mean to say that W' causes X'? If that means no more than that W' always occurs as a sufficient condition of X', the same may be said of W—for given the parallelist scheme, W cannot occur without being followed by X', just as W' cannot occur without being followed by X'. It seems then that W is just as much the cause of X' as W' is. Moreover, W' is just as much the cause of X as W is.

Interactionism, epiphenomenalism, and parallelism can be classified together as dualistic solutions to the mind-body problem, because they do not question the distinction between mental and physical events, but accept it as ultimate. Those philosophers who are dissatisfied, on various grounds, with all of the theories we have been discussing have explored the logical alternative of dissolving the distinction itself. If it seems so difficult to put the two kinds of event into an intelligible relationship, once they have been torn asunder, the reason may be that they should not have been separated in the first place. We must now look into this possibility.

§ 3. • *The Reductive Theory*

Metaphysicians who aim to make their account of ultimate reality as clean and tidy as possible often claim to be able to show that one kind of thing, A, which at first seems quite different from B, is really B after all. We are all, of course, familiar with this kind of discovery. Perhaps you thought that that fine detergent, Deterjo, was much superior to its chief rival, Desmirch, but *Consumers Union* found out that it was the same stuff under another name. On one level of analysis, a circle and an ellipse are sharply distinct, yet with the help of the notion of a mathematical limit, we can say that a circle is just an ellipse in which the two foci collapse into one. Of course, in these cases the reduction of one category to another has limitations. In the first case, it was only the name that was different, and names are not very fundamental properties. In the second case, the basic difference between circles and ellipses is not really canceled out; it's just that we see them as more closely related. But an apparently new disease that turns out to be a slightly variant form of an old one, or an apparently new microphysical particle that turns out to be a familiar one in special circumstances, will perhaps serve as an apt parallel to the metaphysician's kind of reduction—except that the latter is operating with so much larger and more general categories.

The mind-body problem can be swept away, or at least rendered fairly innocuous, if the duality on which it rests can be reduced to a unity—if, in other words, we can show that one of the two kinds of state, or event, is really a special case of the other. And of course there are two ways in which we might proceed—at least in theory.

When the philosopher Berkeley argued that material objects, including not only things outside our bodies like stones and roots, but brains and stomachs, too, are really collections of sense data (or, in his word, "ideas"), this theory, if it could be proved, would seem to dispose of the mind-body problem. We don't mean that the mind-body problem cannot be stated in Berkeley's system—for even he could make a distinction between mental ideas, so to speak (tickles and sorrows), and physical ideas (shape and weight), and one could still ask about their relationship. Nor would he have to be skeptical about interactions between them, seeing that the things interacting would be fundamentally of the same sort. Berkeley did not himself wish to speak of ideas as having causal connections with each other—because causation for him was a form of action, and ideas (he said) are passive. But suppose we moved from Berkeley's idealism to a Humean form of neutral monism—that is, the view that the elements of reality (sense data, feeling data, thoughts, etc.) are neither mental nor physical. Then the very same pink color patch, when combined with certain feelings and thoughts, would be part of a mind, and when combined with a certain shape and weight would be part of a body—so there would be nothing to arouse philosophic worries in the statement that this mind and this body can interact. No one would be tempted to become a parallelist or an epiphenomenalist.

This seems a suitable occasion to say a little more about idealism. In Berkeley we find the two kinds of idealism, epistemological and metaphysical, and the former is used as an argument for the latter. Metaphysical idealism is the proposition that reality is mental or spiritual in nature. And one (but only one) of the ways of arriving at this conclusion is Berkeley's argument that objects such as chairs and tables cannot exist independently of minds, but are really collections of mental states. Another is the argument that physical properties are essentially relations to minds.

Pluralistic idealists, like Leibniz and Berkeley, hold that reality consists of a number of finite spirits or selves. Monistic idealists, like Hegel and Bradley, hold that reality is one single absolute spirit, or ultimate self. Not many philosophers today are idealists, but anyone who intends to think very seriously about philosophical problems should know something of what idealists have believed, where they have gone wrong (if they have gone wrong), and what they have taught us (which is much).

We can also turn in the opposite direction and inquire whether the mind-body problem can be solved by regarding mental events as physical events. Of course, such a view appears shocking and absurd at first glance; but that is not necessarily a fatal flaw—though it means that to make the view convincing would require a certain amount of careful and powerful argument.

When we say that "A is the same as B," we can mean two very different things. We say, "A crime is the same as a violation of the law." And we say, "The War between the States is the same as the Civil War." Now, in the first example, what we are stating is really a definition, or equivalence of intension: the term "crime" and the term "violation of the law" mean the same properties. Because of this, the first proposition is a logical necessity; it would be self-contradictory to say that a crime was committed but no law violated. But, in the second example, there is no such logical necessity. The term "War between the States" does not *mean* the same as the term "Civil War." But the two terms, having different meanings, nevertheless apply to the same war—which in one part of the country is described one way, and in another, another. They have the same *extension.* At some future time, if our extant records should be largely lost, a curious historian might gather together the records that remain, and begin to piece together the history of two great American wars. To make the illustration graphic, let us assume (without any general aspersions upon his scholarly profession) that this historian is slow witted but systematic in his investigation. He puts all the documents concerning the War between the States in one pile, and those concerning the Civil War in another pile. He begins by writing up the history of the former. Now he turns to the latter. At first, naturally, he gets a very different picture of what was going on. But gradually, as he compares places and dates, he realizes that the two battles of Manassas were the same battles as the two battles of Bull Run, that the Battle of Antietam was the Battle of Sharpsburg, etc. And he is forced to conclude that there were not two wars, but one. He has discovered an identity; and this is the discovery of an empirical fact, not a logical necessity.

It is important to see clearly the distinction between these two kinds of sameness—of meaning (intension) and of reference (extension)—because it also applies to the proposition that mental events are the same as physical events. In short, there are two ways in which this thesis can be formulated and defended—or, better, there are two different theories, which we shall call the *reductive theory* and the *identity theory.*

According to the reductive theory, to begin with a blunt summary, words that refer to mental states are synonymous with (can be fully analyzed into) words that refer only to physical states—so that when we talk about mental events, what we really *mean* are physical events. This is a materialist theory of the mind. How could it be made plausible? Well, let us begin with the word "anger." We say, "So-and-so is angry," and offer this as a description of his state of mind. What do we mean? To see what we mean, we must ask how we *know* that So-and-so is angry. Let's say he turns red in the face, clenches his fists, tightens his lips, raises his voice, and so forth. Not every angry person shows his anger in the same fashion, but we could draw up a list of items of what might be called anger-behavior —all those publicly observable ways of acting that would provide evidence of being angry. Would it then be plausible to say that the proposition "So-and-so is angry" really means "So-and-so is exhibiting certain items of anger-behavior"? (Then "So-and-so is *very* angry" might mean "So-and-so is exhibiting *extreme* anger-behavior"—his face is very flushed, his voice very loud, etc.)

Obviously this attempt to translate "angry" into a language of physical behavior is too simple so far. In the first place, when we say that someone is angry we are not just reporting his present behavior, we are implying something about his future behavior—the likelihood that he is about to bang the desk or throw a punch. The reductionist can easily add this, but we may still be unsatisfied. For, in the second place, we test a proposition that is alleged to be logically necessary by asking whether its contradictory is self-contradictory. In this case the test is a double one. We ask whether it is (logically) possible for a person to exhibit anger-behavior, even though he is not really angry. And we ask whether it is (logically) possible for a person to be angry even though he exhibits no anger-behavior. If either of these can happen, "angry" cannot mean the same as "anger-behaving."

The first question is really about acting. Can we conceive of an actor so perfect that, to every intent and purpose, he can convince us that he is angry, even though he is not at all? Some actors of the so-called Method school would say that they can't work themselves up into a really convincing performance unless they evoke in themselves some trace of the emotion they wish to express. But that does not imply that a Hamlet can't pretend violent rage at Claudius unless he is actually ready to kill him. The reductionist might try one escape from the difficulty: to describe someone as angry is not merely to report behavior, but to predict it. So when we see someone flushing and stamping and yelling and grimacing, and uttering words of threat and contempt, we may not know at first whether this anger-behavior is a case of anger or not—but we wait to see whether it issues in further anger-behavior. When the actor finishes the scene, and comes out to take a bow, we know that he wasn't really mad. But this doesn't fully answer the objection. For perhaps we can imagine two men going through the same anger-behavior over as long a time as we wish—even until death —the one really angry, the other an unusually gifted actor. Their behavior is the same, but only one is angry. This would show that anger is not the same thing as anger-behavior.

A similar line of thought might be suggested by the second test of the alleged synonymity. This question is about ideal self-control. Can we conceive of a person who is inwardly seething with anger, but who, through rigid self-discipline, is able to conceal that anger completely from others— by exhibiting no anger-behavior at all? Again it seems at least conceivable, however difficult we all find it to be in practice. And if it is conceivable, then the emotion of anger cannot be reduced to movements of muscles.

But this does not discourage the reductionist—it only spurs him on to more complex and ingenious proposals. Granted that there can be a distinction between anger and anger-behavior, it does not follow that anger is something nonphysical. We are overlooking part of what is going on in the organism, the inner processes that are also (he says) a part of being angry. The rapid pulse rate, the increase of adrenalin in the blood and of electrical activity in the brain, for example—these are the inside of anger (physiologically speaking), as overt behavior is its outside. So it is perfectly correct to say that a person can appear angry even when he isn't—this only means that he exhibits overt anger-behavior without internal anger-processes. Your magnificent actor can fool his public when he shouts,

> *Here, thou incestuous, murderous, damned Dane,*
> *Drink off this potion . . .*

But let the physiologist note the state of his blood, heart, and brain, and the physiologist will not be taken in. And again, it is perfectly correct to say that a person can appear calm and collected while inwardly raging—however, "inward" here does not refer to unique mental events, but only to hidden physiological indications of tension and disturbance. Surely if a person *is* in a disturbed state, there must be *some* physical circumstances that would reveal this state, though only to special instruments of measurement.

If we include in the definition of any mental state, then, two sets of physical states, external and internal, we can provide a fairly plausible account. At least, it is not readily refutable. The theory that this can be done in every case—the reductive theory—is also called *behaviorism*. This term is perhaps dangerous to use without some warning—some psychologists call themselves, for example, methodological behaviorists, meaning that they choose to confine the data of their science to what can be obtained from public observation (that is, to internal and external physical states). Others who have called themselves behaviorists take a more radical line, and affirm (as we have said) that in fact the only things we can really talk about, in the last analysis, are physical states. Of course, for ordinary purposes, it is handy to have a word like "angry," as a shorthand expression for a list of physical states that it would be tedious to enumerate. But insofar as we make sense in describing how people feel (or think or experience), it is these states we are talking about.

To sharpen the issue raised by the reductive theory as far as we can in this book, let us take one more step. Suppose someone tells us he has just invented the perfect robot. It looks in every way like a human being, it acts in every way like one, it responds to all physiological tests like one, and so on—but it is a machine; it cannot love or hate, it only goes through the motions. How would you like to have it for a wife or husband? A great many interesting and profound philosophical discussions can be set going by this question.

For example, one might say, suppose you had such a spouse, wouldn't you feel something was missing? Could you really love something that doesn't feel love itself? But, on the other hand, how would you ever know? How do you know that your own spouse—or your best friend—is not a perfect robot? If such things are possible, then perhaps that is what everyone is. But this is ridiculous. Therefore, there must be something wrong even in talking about, or trying to think about, such a robot. The reductionist would say that it is logically impossible: to exhibit love-activity is (by definition) to feel love. The reductionist would no doubt dismiss the robot argument with a forthright dilemma: if the robot exhibits overt behavior without the inner physiological processes, it is not in love by the behaviorist definition; if it undergoes all those inner processes of human beings, as well as exhibiting the overt behavior, then it is not a robot at all but an artificial (man-made) man or woman.

The reductionist's opponent, on the other hand, has two choices open to him. One is the mental-substance theory. If the mind is an entity that may, or may not, be placed in some special relationship to a particular body—so that the body has *that* mind, or that mind *that* body—then the distinction between the robot and the human being is metaphysically definite. A human being is a robot with a mental substance attached, or closely associated. There is a "ghost in the machine," as the Cartesian mind has been characterized by a leading contemporary philosopher, Gilbert Ryle. The second choice may be foreshadowed here, though its full significance will come out later. Suppose that the mental states of an organism depend upon its physical states—the dependence being statable in certain psychophysical laws. On this assumption, it would be psychophysically (not logically) impossible to have two organisms in perfectly similar physical states, one having a particular emotion and the other lack-it. The reductionist's opponent could maintain this and on this basis reject the fanciful notion of the robot-mate.

And he would have one more card up his sleeve, which some philosophers would consider to be a trump. A few paragraphs back, the question was raised whether, if the human being and the robot were empirically indistinguishable, it might not be conceivable that all of us are robots. But there may be a hitch in this. The human would know whether he felt love or not, even if no one else did. *You* know that you are not a robot; and you know this in a way that no one else does. Even if you are no actor and pitifully incapable of concealing your emotions, you are aware (it has been argued) that your feeling of anger is something different from your physical states. And this can be very simply shown. For you do not have to look at your face in the mirror to find out whether you are angry—and you certainly don't have to go to the physiologist and ask him to test your blood pressure and adrenalin level. Hence when you say, "I am angry," you cannot *mean* "I am in such-and-such physical states," because you can know you are angry while knowing nothing of those states. And that, if true, seems sufficient to refute the reductive theory.

§ 4. • *The Identity Theory*

There is one other fundamental theory about the relationship between mind and body. It can be reached by various logical roads, but let us begin by returning to a common-sense distinction that had to be pushed into the background to make any form of behaviorism plausible. An analogy might be helpful. In speaking of any common disease, we usually distinguish between the disease and the symptoms of the disease. We can imagine a naive disease behaviorist who insists that the disease is nothing more than the sum total of all its symptoms; but we would not choose him for a physician, since he might think that he can lower the fever with aspirin, cover up the skin rash, and treat all the other symptoms separately, he has done all that needs to be done for a cure. We would remind him that to have a disease is to be attacked inwardly by some bacteria or virus, and it is this attack that requires his attention. A sophisticated disease behaviorist would be willing to include the bacteria along with the symptoms as part of his definition of "diphtheria" or "measles," or whatever, and that would be an improvement. But we might protest that, too, and say that the bacteria are not on the same level as the symptoms—they are, in fact, the *cause* of the symptoms. Even if all the symptoms could somehow be stopped, so long as the bacteria lurk in the interior, carrying on their aggression against the body cells, you would still have the disease.

And the same would usually be said about states of emotion. A person's overt anger-behavior is, in very much the same way, a symptom of his state of mind, because it is the effect of it. We say, "He threw the golf club at the tree because he was mad." But again, when we consider the matter, we are dogged by the same dualism we met with earlier. For when he threw the club his arm and muscles moved in certain ways, and these events can be explained satisfactorily (to the physiologist) only in terms of events in brains and neurons. It seems that the question "What caused him to throw the golf club?" can be given two answers:

1. his anger
2. his brain states

Now these are different answers—they do not mean the same thing at all (if we reject behaviorism). They are both true answers (it can be argued) because they could be verified. And yet they *cannot* both be true, because if either is the sufficient condition of the effect, the other cannot be playing any causal role.

The identity theory proposes to escape this dilemma by a very simple stroke: the anger and the brain states are the same thing, and since that one thing (event or state) is the sufficient condition of the effect, both answers are true, even though they are not the same answer. To see how this can be, suppose we ask a question framed in terms of our earlier example: "Which war led directly to the ending of legal slavery in the United States?" Answers:

1. the Civil War
2. the War between the States

These are different answers—in the precise sense that they do not have the same meaning (since a civil war need not be a war between states, and a war between states need not be a civil war). Yet they are both true; they do not contradict each other, because they both denote the very same event, which can be described in different ways.

According to the identity theory, the same is true of our brain states. They have certain physical properties, which can be studied by the neurologist. And they have certain mental properties. Anger is just the way certain brain states feel, so to speak, to the organism that is in those states. The mental states are not something added on, but the same thing from a different aspect, or angle, from which appear certain properties that are not open to the physiologist probing the brain from the outside. It is no use trying to refute the identity theory by saying that if emotions were in the brain, the physiologist would *see* them when he opens it up. Emotions aren't seen, they are only *felt*. But wouldn't the physiologist have to detect them, then? Yes, he does—or, in principle, could. He discovers the electrical activity in the brain, and this is precisely the emotion.

One objection to this theory may be put as follows: if X is identical to Y, then every property of X is a property of Y, and vice versa. The Vice President of the United States is the same person as the presiding officer of the Senate (by constitutional requirement)—and therefore, if the Vice President is bald, so is the presiding officer. No getting around that. If anger is identical to a brain state, and a brain state is located in space, the anger is located in space—and it must have all the other properties that a brain state can have, too: voltage, for example. Now, it's true that we might speak of high-voltage anger, but that would be a metaphor. Strictly speaking, the argument runs, anger is neither here nor there, it cannot be four centimeters long, or equal to such-and-such a fraction of a volt. According to some philosophers, these statements would be not just false and silly, but utterly meaningless. And in that case the identity theory cannot be true or even make sense. Whatever it is in the mind that is anger and whatever it is in the brain that is electrical cannot possibly be the same thing.

Questions about what is meaningless and what is meaningful are often not easy to resolve. The identity theorist can make out something of a case by explaining, at least, why the identification of anger and brain states might *seem* silly and perhaps nonsensical, even though it isn't. Imagine, for example, a poorly paid policeman who moonlights as a waiter in a fancy restaurant. Logically, of course, whatever one does the other must do, since they are the same person. When we point out the policeman in the daytime, we can say, "He waits on table at night." But *while* he is working as a policeman, we wouldn't think it appropriate to refer to him as a waiter. Suppose we said, "The policeman was generously tipped, and the waiter directed traffic." These remarks have some absurdity about them. In the first case, people would think the policeman was taking graft, and in the second case they would think the poor waiter had lost his wits. Similarly, when we are talking about certain kinds of things, we refer to what a person does in the brain-state language, and when we are talking about other kinds of things, we use the emotion language. But it is confusing to mix them.

Whether or not you are satisfied with this reply to the first objection against the identity theory, let us turn to the second one, which is the inverse of the first. A brain state is a physical state, a state of the body. If we say that is identical to a mental state, aren't we saying that matter can think? And isn't this the greatest absurdity of all? Some philosophers would regard it as a necessary truth that matter cannot think. If that is so, we must again return to some form of dualistic theory, with its attendant problems. The identity theory is a simpler one, in an important respect. That is, it requires only one set of real entities, rather than two—though it does not do away with the distinction between mental and physical *properties* of those entities. But if the identity theory is too simple to be acceptable, in view of the richness and complexity of our experience, then it must be abandoned without regret.

The question is whether it is indeed too simple. Why can't matter think? Suppose the opponent of the identity theory challenges it this way: "Have you ever run across any pieces of matter that think?" "Why, yes, every day—there's a crowd of people; each one is certainly material, and each thinks (sometimes). A human being is a thinking piece of matter. Why not?"

"But you confuse me," the dualist might reply. "One of us must be begging the question. I say that matter by itself clearly can't think; it needs a mind to do that; and since people think, they cannot be *merely* matter." But who is begging the question? We point out chimpanzees that think, and porpoises, and worms and fish that learn to run a (very simple) maze. Those are physical organisms, and they are examples of matter thinking. But the dualist replies, "Then they must have minds of some sort. Show me some matter that obviously doesn't have a mind, and yet that thinks— say, a heap of bricks, a newspaper press, or a storage battery." But this, of course, is an unfair request. Whenever we show him a piece of matter that thinks, he dismisses it as an unsuitable example, by alleging that it must have a mind, so it is not pure matter. Certainly he has fixed things so he cannot be refuted, but only by assuming what he was supposed to be proving.

What the dualist may be taking for granted here is that if molecules cannot act in a certain way when they are separated, then they cannot act in that way when combined. It is as though one said that a cable is made of thin wires, and thin wires cannot lift a freight car, therefore a cable can't lift a freight car. One atom by itself can't think, of course, and even quite complicated sets of atoms might not be able to. But it doesn't follow that groups of atoms can't think when they form into certain kinds of molecules and are related in certain organic ways. Emergence is not logically impossible. Is there anything in the very definition of matter that *logically* excludes the possibility that matter can think? The identity theorist can see none.

This whole problem, puzzling as it is, has been in some respects clarified (though perhaps in others still further complicated) in recent years by the development of the great computers, the so-called "electronic brains." These are properly called machines. And as everyone knows, they do the kinds of things that thinking organisms do to show that they are thinking, and thinking intelligently. They do just about everything of this sort—some things not so well (for example, composing music), some things better, or at least faster (analyzing masses of data, solving certain kinds of equations). So the question arises quite naturally: do these machines think?

A number of important and profound questions can be provoked by this one, and we shall have to limit ourselves to a few that bear directly upon the identity theory. If mental states are identical with certain kinds of physical states, then wherever there is one, there will be the other. We do not know enough of the processes in the cortex, for example, on which various kinds of sensations and feelings and thoughts depend, to be able to plot the correlation exactly, to say just what state the brain is in when someone is adding two and two and getting four. And of course we are even farther from being able to make a brain, or part of one, in a laboratory. To make a brain would be to produce a group of cells of a certain sort, undergoing the same activities as our brain cells, and we may suppose that if we were to do this, that brain would experience mental events. That would be a reasonable generalization from what we know of human physiology. We could apply the same test, in an emergency, to our neighbors. Ordinarily, of course, we guess how others feel from their behavior, but if we believed they were concealing their real feelings, then appropriate neurological study (if that were legal, as fortunately it is not) would reveal whether or not their brain cells were overstimulated.

But a computer is not, except by analogy, a brain—it is only a model of one or a substitute for one. And no matter how cleverly it imitates a brain, or even surpasses it, we have no reason to believe that it is conscious of what it is doing. There is no problem for the identity theory here. It is an empirical question whether a process involving a certain array of transistors is or is not accompanied by any mental states. It is conceivable that one day, when we have decided to fit out a computer with sensory organs, speech-box, and so on, we shall be in a position to ask whether it experiences thoughts and feelings. If the answer is plausible, we might accept it. It has been argued (by Michael Scriven, for example) that under certain carefully contrived conditions, we might have the same reason to believe a computer if it told us it has thoughts and feelings that we have to believe the people next door.

It seems, then, that it is because the computer is not made up of living cells that we are not inclined to believe that it thinks, strictly speaking—however effectively it solves problems for us. But this does not show that matter can't think; it simply reinforces the position that only matter of certain sorts, in certain combinations, can think. And this position cannot be refuted by pointing out that matter of other sorts, in other combinations—much less unorganized matter—cannot think. But, of course, it is odd to speak of matter thinking—in the same way it is odd to speak of the waiter making an arrest. We don't classify a human being as a piece of matter except for certain purposes, when we are not concerned with his thinking. The teacher could address all his students as "chunks of matter" or "collections of cells," and these would not be false descriptions—they would just be somewhat deprecating. It is not, in the usual way of speaking, bodies that think, but *persons* who think—and who swim, sing, fall in love, and enjoy the protections of the Constitution.

It may be that through this concept of the person as a whole individual being, the oppositions and conflicts expressed in the mind-body problem can be reconciled. Some recent philosophers have thought so. Starting with the notion of a physical organism complicated enough to possess higher-order faculties, to use symbols and relate to others in terms of mutual acknowledgment of rights and needs, and to adopt long-range goals, we build up the concept of a person who has various levels of reality. To this individual, predicates of all sorts can be applied. And distinctions can be made. It may be convenient to distinguish between more or less predominantly mental and more or less predominantly physical activity, depending on how deeply conscious thoughts and feelings and desires are involved. But there need be no dualism here, no call for any ultimate division of the person into two entities. The personal pronoun has the same reference whenever the same person uses it—say, in the examples given above in §1. There will still remain a great deal to be discovered about the causes of these kinds of behavior and their interconnections—perhaps enough to keep scientists occupied for a long time to come. But that is an empirical task, which the philosopher cannot take up. All he can do to help is try to sort out the confusions in our thought, in the categories with which we approach the task, so that they will not hinder the empirical scientist in his work.

FREEDOM AND DETERMINISM

When we speak of human beings as free, we may have in mind many things—certainly, range and variety of activity, flexibility of response, the power to extend one's capacity to cope with his environment through language, tools, machines, and social organization. "Freedom" has many other senses, posing other problems to philosophers. There are political freedoms and economic freedoms—which we spell out with the help of prepositional phrases: freedom *from* want, freedom *of* religion, freedom *to* participate in the political process. It is always clarifying to make explicit the kind of freedom, or the sense of the word "freedom," that is in question—and one way of doing so is to say what we are contrasting freedom with. Thus "free" when applied to a newly emerging country means absence of colonial status or an end of being governed by another country. And "free" as applied to an individual may mean no longer being behind bars, or no longer being excluded from an equal opportunity to share in the good things of one's society, or any one of many other things.

The kind of freedom with which we are chiefly concerned now is a metaphysical freedom, *freedom of the will*. And the problems we shall consider are defined by what is thought to contrast with, or to conflict with, freedom of the will—namely, *determinism*. Our first step will be to make this issue, or supposed issue, as clear and explicit as possible.

§ 5.   • *The Free Will Problem*

The principle of determinism, as we have remarked earlier in this book, is the proposition that every event has a cause, in the sense of sufficient condition—or, perhaps equivalently, that every event is lawful. The word "perhaps" acknowledges the possibility of a distinction that has been maintained by some philosophers. For example, it has been argued that if the steady-state theory of creation is correct, and hydrogen atoms pop into existence at certain intervals and at a constant rate, then this continuous creation is lawful (that is, constant), but not caused. But when we speak of a law in connection with determinism, we shall mean a general proposition of the form "If C, then E," where C is a set of conditions such that whenever they occur, E always follows. And in that case C, or some subset of C that we may single out for special notice (as when we say that the accident was caused by a slippery road), can be said to be the cause of E.

Determinism applies to all events, including human acts of will—if there are such things. The concept of the will is a very puzzling one, and the more we think about it the more puzzled we can get. But if we are careful we can perhaps avoid confusion. Think of two occasions on which you raise your arm. On the first occasion you start to salute the flag. On the second occasion you demonstrate a physiological quirk: you stand in a narrow doorway, with your arms down, then try to raise them sideways; when they encounter the sides of the doorway, you press hard against the doorway for several seconds—and when you step out into the room, your arms move upward of their own accord, without any effort on your part.

In the first case your movement is *voluntary;* in the second it is involuntary. Some of the differences can be described in this way: in the first case, the movement of the arm is connected with a mental event, or a series of mental events: you think of an act to perform (saluting the flag), you want or are inclined to perform it, you exert an effort (slight, no doubt) to begin to perform it, by raising your arm. The process may be more complicated than that: you may feel some disinclination to act, such as tiredness or conscientious scruples, you may pause to deliberate, to consider not acting, to think of pros and cons, and you may have the experience of coming to a decision, making up your mind, and choosing consciously between two alternatives. In this case, let us say your action is *deliberate,* because it is preceded by some deliberation: it is an act of choice. All deliberate actions are voluntary, but not all voluntary actions involve deliberation (the salute to the flag, on ceremonial occasions, may be quite automatic).

Now, according to the determinist, all of these actions—involuntary, voluntary, deliberate—are determined. The manner in which they are determined makes the differences, and they are important differences for many purposes (as we shall see later). But in every case, there is a sequence of events, more or less complex, in which one set of events leads lawfully to the next; in the end, if we knew enough, we could explain every event in terms of its antecedent conditions—and predict each event from those conditions. In making such predictions, as we frequently do with people we know well, we do not, of course, make the mistake of telling the person what we predict—if he is stubborn, that might make him do the opposite just to spite us. One way to get someone to cut down smoking may be to tell him that he is unable to do so—but it depends on the sort of person he is. In any case, predictions have to be made with respect to closed systems—that is, systems in which the prediction does not introduce a new cause that the prediction itself fails to take into account.

A process of deliberation may be crudely pictured as follows:

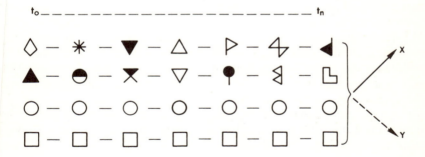

In the successive states of the mind, there are certain comparatively stable factors, represented by circles and squares (previously acquired dispositions, memory traces, inherited traits, etc.), and certain variable factors, represented by other figures (changing impulses, sensations, thoughts, feelings, etc.). The determinist will say that the state of the person at each moment is caused by his state just prior to that moment—plus, of course, the conditions in the environment that may suddenly impinge upon him. Among the thoughts that will turn up and recur during this process of deliberation are thoughts about possible actions. Suppose the situation is such that the person must either reach out to take a bribe that is being offered to him, or turn away—he is a policeman who has stumbled on a numbers game runner at one of his favorite "drops," and he must decide whether to get on the syndicate's payroll and overlook these gambling activities or arrest the runner and take him to the police station. There is a period of uncertainty, conflict of feelings and thoughts, and painful hesitation. At time t_n it comes to a climax and ends in a resolution. The policeman reaches out his hand for the bribe (action X), instead of refusing (action Y).

The determinist's thesis, then, is that the conditions at t_n (Ct_n) are the sufficient conditions for the policeman's choosing X—that given his character and his recent experiences and the peculiar circumstances, he must take the bribe—"must" in the sense that his taking the bribe is an instance of some psychological law which always holds, even though we may not be able to formulate it very precisely. So there is a sense in which, though he could imagine himself doing Y, and even could want to do Y (at least with part of himself), he could not do Y. For him to do Y under conditions Ct_n would be in violation of a psychological law. Perhaps he has always been more concerned about getting money than about abstract principles: he resents the fact that his income is too small to support his wife and seven children; he believes it is perfectly safe to take the payoff; and he knows that some of his fellow policemen do the same thing. He doesn't really think that the numbers game is a very wicked form of gambling even though it is technically illegal, and he sees that it gives a great deal of pleasure to the poor people in his precinct. He rather likes the numbers runner and hates to arrest him. And, being an excellent rationalizer, he reflects that (a) one arrest will not stop the syndicate or even slow it down, and (b) by accepting a weekly sum from now on, he is in a way doing his bit to punish the heads of the syndicate—more than they would be punished if they came before their favorite magistrate, who is himself well paid to insure that numbers runners brought before him are turned loose with as little fuss as possible. Under the circumstances, the determinist will say, it is quite to be expected that the policeman will eventually accept the bribe, even if he can't do it until after he goes through a period of indecision and mental conflict—because his conscience does bother him a bit, and he would hate to get caught and dismissed from the force, and he knows his wife would be unhappy if she ever found out, etc.

Our aim in telling this simple tale is not to regale you with a summer television plot, but to provide one concrete case that we can refer to. Soap-opera-like or not, this sort of thing has undoubtedly happened from time to time, and it illustrates the determinist's position. Remember that he is prepared to make, in his own terms, the distinctions we touched on earlier—though these are subtle and difficult to be clear about. What is the difference between a voluntary and an involuntary action—between a shrug of the shoulders that signifies indifference and a shudder from chill or apprehension? The most important difference, perhaps, lies in the attitude that accompanies the action. A person may move his arm to deliver a blow, a quick punch, without taking thought or having any prior intention of doing so—but it is voluntary because it is done willingly: his mind (so to speak) cooperates in the action and assents to it, even if a moment later he regrets it profoundly. What is the difference between a voluntary action that is deliberate and one that is not—between choosing to take a bribe and throwing a punch without stopping to think? This last phrase points in the correct direction—the deliberate action is one that is preceded by some interval of deliberation, that is, of considering not only the action but an alternative (at least the alternative of refraining), having the experience, however momentary, of being in doubt about what to do, and having the feeling of making up one's mind to do something.

Let us consider now the other main concept of the pair that defines our present problem. Some philosophers hold that the act of choosing to do X, in the case we have described, is an act of free will. They would not say that all actions, or perhaps even all voluntary actions, are acts of free will, but they would hold that all deliberate actions in the face of a moral dilemma are acts of free will. In any case, the act of taking a bribe, performed by a person in full awareness of the nature of his act and its possible consequences, and of his duties and obligations, would be an act of free will, if any act is. But what is meant by calling it this?

Such an act is said to be one in which the agent, under the same conditions, could have refrained from acting or could have performed an alternative and incompatible action. The choice of X is an act of free will if, under precisely the same conditions Ct_n, the agent (A) could have chosen Y—in the same sense of "could" in which we say that he could choose X (which he did choose). This theory envisions a situation such as this: at time t_n, given all the antecedent psychological and physical states that are relevant, there are two different actions open to A—either X (accepting the bribe) or Y (refusing it). Ct_n is not a sufficient condition for either X or Y (though it may be a necessary condition for both); there is no law according to which X must follow Ct_n and no law according to which Y must follow Ct_n. But somehow a choice is made, and since this act of choice is in no way determined by the antecedent conditions, it is a spontaneous and (in a radical sense) free act.

In this sense, an act of free will is one that is not determined. No set of antecedent conditions causes it to happen. If Ct_n were sufficient for X, as the determinist would say, then it could not at the same time be sufficient for Y (which is opposed to X). The philosopher who believes in free will (the *libertarian*), then, is an indeterminist. He does not, of course, deny that some events are determined, but he denies that all are—and specifically he asserts that some events of a certain sort, at least deliberate acts of moral choice, are undetermined. This follows from his assertion that such acts are acts of free will, in the sense defined. Until A has chosen, says the libertarian, X and Y are equally possible; there is nothing in the nature of things to decide. The determinist holds, on the other hand, that though A of course does not know (and perhaps no one knows) which he will choose, the factors that will determine his choice have already come together decisively and are present at Ct_n.

It will be helpful to bear in mind the relationships between this free will problem and the mind-body problem which we discussed earlier in this chapter. Dualists have a choice open to them between free will and determinism. Some would take advantage of their metaphysical distinction to partition off, or demarcate, the realms of free will and determinism. They would assert that the physical realm is determined, but that some mental events, at least, are exempt from causal determination. An interactionist, for example, might agree that on the physical level all is law and order, and that many mental events are equally lawful; but he could add that mental events of a particular sort are acts of free will and capable of initiating new lines of causality. Other dualists, and especially those who accept a close connection or correlation between the mental and physical, would hold that there is determinism in the mental realm as in the physical— though the laws involved may be of a different form.

Materialists, who accept behaviorism, and critical naturalists, who may accept the identity theory, are, of course, committed to determinism for mental events, if it holds for physical events. But here again there is a choice. It is fair to say that these philosophers are generally determinists. But some have been led by twentieth-century developments in quantum physics to try to preserve a range of free will in the psychological realm by basing it on the existence of indeterminism among microphysical particles.

The complications of this issue and the amount of disagreement prevailing among experts both in physics and philosophy of science are sufficient to discourage anyone not fully at home in both fields from undertaking a thorough discussion—if he is wary. We can only touch briefly upon the matter here, as we did earlier—inviting those readers who wish to follow it up to turn to the bibliography below, which will help them get a good start on the problem. The Heisenberg uncertainty principle defines a precise limit to the predictability of individual photons, for example —where prediction would require us to know at a given moment the exact position and momentum of the photon. According to the way this principle has been interpreted by some of the greatest twentieth-century physicists (but not all), it asserts that the photon does not *have* an exact position and momentum at the same time. Then uncertainty is not a limit of knowledge, but an indeterminacy in reality. Other physicists and philosophers argue that this indeterminacy is a consequence of a particular physical theory which may be superseded—and in any case, how would it be possible in principle for a physicist to show that there cannot be *any* factors in the photon or its environment on the basis of which its motion could be predicted? Even if in practice it will always remain unpredictable, like a particular molecule of air in a blown-up balloon, that will not necessarily entail that its course is undetermined. Indeed, the statistical (noncausal) laws by which we cope with air in the mass, because that is the only manageable way to treat it, presuppose that the molecules of which it is composed are individually subject to complete determinism.

Still others have argued—and this is no doubt the point most relevant to our present problem—that the Heisenberg principle applies only to microphysical entities below the atomic and molecular level. At the higher level, which is the level we are operating on when we talk about organisms, nerve cells, muscles, and the like, determinism might still reign, whatever is true below it. So there is a question whether in fact Heisenberg's principle has anything at all to do with freedom of the will. There are two points especially to consider—and we leave them with you. First, if subatomic particles can act without any cause, would this fact support the theory that molecular particles can act without any cause? Second, if free will is identified with, or made to depend upon, causeless actions of molecular particles, can such purely random events have any significance for human life?

§ 6. • *Psychological Arguments*

The conflict between libertarianism and determinism has been stated somewhat abstractly, so that the gist of it can be clearly exposed. But its significance, and the subtleties of its ramifications, begin to emerge only when we turn to the task that will occupy us throughout the remainder of this chapter—the task of examining the main arguments that have been brought forth on both sides. These arguments can conveniently be collected under three main headings, those drawing upon physical science (which we have considered briefly), those based on psychological considerations, and those involving the notion of moral responsibility. As always in this book, our aim will be to develop possible lines of thought that philosophers have found persuasive or provocative, leaving it to you to pursue them further and to discover in what ways they may help your own thinking by connecting up with ideas that you have already thought of and partially worked out.

The psychological lines of argument against determinism must be directed to showing that it comes into conflict with some experience that is familiar and undeniable. This is difficult to do. For example, libertarians sometimes say that determinism denies that we really make choices, whereas everyone knows what it is to choose to move one hand or the other, to step forward or backward, to say yes or no. But if choosing is a special kind of action, which we are immediately aware of performing, then the determinist not only does not deny that it occurs, but must insist that it occurs. For what he says is that every choice is caused, and it would be absurd to say this if there were no such things as choices.

But perhaps determinism can be refuted by a different appeal to immediate experience. "When I move my hand freely," says the libertarian, "I introspect, and I find that no cause compels me to do it." Now this appeal to introspection is rather tricky. In the first place, what does it mean to introspect that there is no cause? "Whom did you see in front of the house as you passed by?" we might inquire of a friend, and he might reply: "I saw that there was no one." Now strictly speaking, of course, you can't see no one—you can only *not* see someone. What he saw was not the absence of anyone, but rather the *presence* of something incompatible with there being someone. He saw, for example, the whole front of the house, in unobstructed view, and he knew that if there had been someone there, that someone's body would have partially blocked his vision. An inference is involved. But in the indeterminist's appeal to introspection, there is nothing comparable. He moves his arm, and as he does so he tries to introspect a cause. This he fails to do. He cannot conclude that there is no cause, but only that if there is a cause it has eluded him—perhaps because it is unconscious.

Of course, we can often tell *which* cause prompts our actions—if (as some philosophers doubt) we can properly speak of causes when the action is a rational one. When you lift your arm, you know what your reason is: whether you are saluting the flag or hailing a taxi. "Reason" and "cause" do not mean the same thing, to be sure, and some actions that have causes do not have reasons (roughly, involuntary actions). But the determinist will say that when you act in a certain way for a certain reason, the reason can be incorporated into a causal explanation of the act: wanting to salute the flag caused you to raise your arm, or seeing the taxi activated a disposition to secure a ride.

Introspection can tell us something else, which is part of what the libertarian had in mind in his argument above. He spoke of causes as "compelling" us to act. This is a good place to make certain distinctions that are helpful—indeed, indispensable—in dealing successfully with our problem.

One thing that experience tells us is whether or not, in trying to act, we are free of external physical *restraint*. I do not know until I try it whether the door is locked, but if it is locked and I don't have the key, then the range of actions open to me is restricted. I am debarred from leaving the room; in a familiar idiom, I am not *free* to leave the room. Handcuffs, ropes, and splints are even more severely restrictive. There are also internal physical restraints, such as broken bones. The line between a restraint in the strict sense and a strong discouragement may be hard to draw precisely, but it is important. A painful sprained ankle imposes a higher price than you are willing to pay for the privilege of dancing—so you turn down the invitation and say you can't go because of your ankle. But of course you *are* making a choice here—the ankle doesn't actually prevent you from dancing, it merely takes the joy out of it. But a broken leg makes the dancing physically impossible, and takes away, as effectually as a rope, your freedom in this regard.

So let us put both the external and internal physical restraints together in one category, and let us introduce a special term to mark their absence. "A is physically free to do X," then, will mean "Nothing (physically) restrains A from doing X if he tries (or wishes, or chooses)." Anyone in sound limb is free to leave the room if the door is open—even if someone is guarding it with a gun. It will not be confusing, we believe, to let the term "restraint" cover also more active physical influences, whether internal or external. For example, a man carried through a rapids in a canoe without a paddle is physically unfree to stop moving.

But there is another kind of interference with freedom. This is *psychological compulsion.* Consider a pathological arsonist, for example, who finds himself in a deserted building, with a box of matches and a collection of kerosene-soaked rags. He feels a powerful desire to set the building afire. Now, he knows (let us say) that it is wrong, and he feels guilty about it, and he tries to put the temptation away by dropping the matches and leaving the building. He knows what it is to try, and he *does* try—but he doesn't let go of the matches. It is as though some power stronger than his will compels him, *against* his will, to light a match and set fire to the rags. The thought of the excitement he will experience when he watches the fire blaze up and the firemen trying to control it is too much for him.

If we can say of such a person that something compels him to set fires, that (without the interference or influence of others) he cannot help setting fires when the opportunity presents itself—then he, too, is unfree in an important sense. Nothing physical requires him to set the fire or prevents him from leaving the building, but he is psychologically compelled. Let us say that "A is psychologically free not to do X" then means "Nothing in A's nature compels A to do X." And again, this can be allowed to cover the positive case as well. Usually, as we said, we speak of someone's being restrained *from* doing X, but we can also speak of being restrained from *not* doing X; and usually we speak of someone's being compelled *to* do X, but we can also speak of being compelled *not* to do X (this is, for example, the sufferer from agoraphobia who simply cannot bring himself to go out of his front door and cross the street—dreadful terrors drive him back, no matter how hard he tries).

For convenience, let us group both restraints and compulsions together as *constraints,* and speak of a person as constrained to act, or not to act, in a certain way. We may then let the term *"freedom of action"* mean "freedom from constraint." Remember that this freedom always applies to a particular action. "The policeman had freedom of action in taking the bribe" means "When the policeman took the bribe, nothing constrained him to do so." Freedom of action is not to be confused with freedom of will. For, first, it is not the will that has freedom of action, but the *person*—we can speak of people as "action-free." And second, action-freedom (unlike will-freedom) is, of course, not in any way incompatible with determinism. When we say that in diving off a bridge a man was free from physical restraints, we do not imply that his action had no cause. When we say that in diving off the bridge he was free from compulsion, we say something about what kind of cause his action did *not* have, but we leave open the possibility that it had some *alternative* cause—he was deliberately seeking publicity, or something of the sort.

Whether or not an agent in a particular situation is free from a particular kind of restraint can be known to the agent, as we said, only by trying something and seeing if anything prevents him from carrying the action through. If he succeeds in carrying through the action, he knows that nothing restrained him from doing it. Whether he is free from compulsion is a harder question. In some cases, it seems, he can indeed, by introspection, discover that his urge to act in a certain way, or his inhibition from acting in a certain way, is so dominant as to take away his effective psychological freedom. This is a matter on which, no doubt, a person can be fooled. He may convince himself that he cannot control his urge to smoke, for example, though in fact if he were to try a little harder and arrange his environment more sensibly (say, by throwing the pack of cigarettes away), he could resist his desire. Perhaps it is never possible for a person to be *certain* that he is a victim of some compulsion, but he can have pretty good evidence. And so can other people. If they discover, for example, that with all the encouragement and help they can give him, with all the dire warnings and threats and rewards and promises and the most favorable and temptation-free environment that can be found, it will still always be true that if you give him one drink of whiskey he will do anything in his power to drink himself into a stupor—then they can reasonably conclude that with him the desire to drink is a compulsion, that moderate drinking is beyond his control, that he is, in short, an alcoholic.

The libertarian may readily allow all these distinctions, and even applaud them, but they leave him unsatisfied. "Granted that sometimes we have freedom of action; still, this does not exhaust our freedom, as human beings. Nor does it account for all that I know about myself as a privileged observer of my own conscious decisions. When I move my arm, I know immediately and with intuitive certainty not only that nothing constrains me to do it, but that I *could* have refrained from doing it, by a simple spontaneous act of choice."

The word "could" plays a key role in all discussions of free will, and it is a very puzzling word. Perhaps there are several subtly different senses that it can take on in various contexts, but two of these senses are especially prominent and noteworthy. Imagine someone who has just had a narrow escape—say, a large object slipped away from construction workers on a high scaffolding and he was pushed out of its way by a kindly bystander. "I could have been killed," he might say—or, "It could have killed me." It is clear what "could" means in this kind of context. Under the circumstances, we do not expect him to be articulate and precise; he is still overwhelmed by the thought of his danger. But he might equally well have said something like: "It would have killed me if it had hit me"; or, "It would have killed me if someone hadn't pushed me out of the way." Here "could have" means "would have . . . if. . . ." Let us call this the *hypothetical "could."*

The convenience of the hypothetical "could" is that we can use it in circumstances where we can't use the expression "would have . . . if . . ." because we don't know enough to complete the "if" clause. In the case of the falling object we do; in the case of a casual movement of the arm, we don't. Now, the determinist claims that propositions containing the term "could have" can be true only in the hypothetical sense—that is, they can be true only when what is meant is that something would have happened if something else had been different. In the case of the falling object, it is clear that when we say the object could have killed him, we must mean that if certain conditions had been different, it would have killed him. And the determinist says that precisely the same thing is true of the arm movement. The libertarian could have refrained from moving his arm— that is, if some condition had been different (if someone had dared him to move it, or if he had been wearier, or if he had been conditioned to salute the flag with his left hand, or if . . .), then he *would* have refrained from moving. This is so because if the conditions that existed at the moment he moved it were in fact (as the determinist claims) sufficient to cause that movement, then the movement could not have failed to occur unless the conditions had been altered.

The libertarian would again concede that this is often true: that what *could* have been, but wasn't, is what *would* have been under different conditions. But he says that the word "could" also has another sense, a libertarian one. "When I say I could have refrained from moving my arm, I mean under exactly the conditions that obtained at that moment, however fully you describe them. I could have done it even if no conditions had been different." Let us call this the *categorical "could."* Some determinists would question whether this sense of the word can really be made clear—they would profess not to understand what the indeterminist is saying. Does it make sense to say that an event that happened could have *not* happened, unless one means that something would have prevented it? The libertarian agrees that this makes no sense for events in general, but he affirms that it does make sense in the sole special case of some or all deliberate human actions. Other determinists would admit that it makes sense to say that something "could have happened" in the categorical sense, but they would deny that it is ever true.

At this point the issue is likely to be joined over the evidence. Suppose the libertarian argues this way: "Look, I'll raise my right arm for you. Watch. Now watch again; I will refrain from raising it. All right. The conditions were exactly the same; I was the same person at both times, with the same interest (namely, illustrating libertarianism): no external suggestions intervened. So I say that here is a clear-cut example of the categorical 'could.' I *prove* that I could have refrained from raising my arm the first time, under the same conditions, by actually refraining from raising my arm the second time, under the same conditions. What more do you ask by way of proof?"

But this argument, of course, cannot convince the determinist. Obviously there was one significant difference in the conditions for the two actions (counting refraining as an action): in the second case, the agent had a memory of having recently raised his arm. If he had forgotten this fact, there would have been no point in refraining; the purpose was to provide a contrast of behavior. So even the libertarian would have to admit that the two sets of conditions were not perfectly alike. And indeed, no matter how alike they seemed to be, the determinist would still not accept the conclusion. For among the conditions relevant to determining what people will do there may be all sorts of conditions that are not open to immediate inspection or introspection—unconscious impulses, memory traces, conditioned dispositions, subliminal impressions, etc. Therefore it is never possible to be sure, or even to show it to be very probable, that two different actions were performed under the same conditions. Determinism cannot be refuted that way.

If the libertarian's attack is frustrated, he may still claim an impregnable defense. Maybe determinism cannot be refuted; but can libertarianism be refuted? To deny indeterminism, is, of course, to affirm universal lawfulness in the psychological realm. Now there is no question that we often are able to understand our acquaintances well enough to predict what they will do under certain circumstances. And there is no question that psychologists have discovered certain very important generalizations about human conduct, in terms of which they can explain many of our actions. But what is the warrant for extending causality universally? The libertarian reminds us that our ability to predict behavior is limited and fallible, and that psychological generalizations are practically all less than universal. Take the most reliable one you can think of; still, it will have exceptions. Suppose someone is sitting quietly at a counter, and you go up to him, push him to the floor, spit on him, and kick him; isn't it a safe prediction that he will get mad and fight back? But not if he is trained in the techniques of nonviolence.

It seems that the psychologist can discover causes, but he cannot discover that all actions have causes. The libertarian can point out where we are ignorant of causes, but he cannot show that there are no causes to be found. If an empirical resolution of the conflict is not available, philosophers must explore other roads in search of good reasons for accepting or rejecting determinism. Some will return to arguments we were dealing with when we discussed the status of the general principle of lawfulness. Perhaps determinism is an indispensable postulate of all scientific psychology and not to be abandoned without proof of peril. Perhaps it can be regarded as a reasonable generalization from successes already achieved in the explanation of human conduct: as we learn more about behavior, we are in a better position to conclude that it is probably all subject to law. Or perhaps determinism is, after all, a synthetic a priori truth expressing a necessity of thought, which the libertarian can question verbally, but without serious effect.

If these metaphysical and epistemological inquiries fail to be decisive, there is still another road open, and we shall take it in the following sections. Perhaps an examination of the relationships between our problem and certain problems that arise in connection with moral and legal judgments will disclose some decisive considerations.

§ 7. • *Legal Responsibility*

The problem of free will and determinism is of considerable metaphysical and psychological interest in its own right. But the intensity of the philosophical concern that it arouses—and has long aroused—comes from its possible connection with ethical and legal matters of great moment. Many defenders of free will, and some determinists, have claimed that the thesis of determinism is incompatible with certain basic principles in our thinking about moral disapproval and punishment. If this claim is justified, then we still have a choice: we can either abandon determinism in order to preserve these principles, or we can maintain determinism and give them up. The stakes are high.

Our first question, of course, must be whether in fact this incompatibility really exists—and on this point a considerable number of philosophic disputes have concentrated. The central concept to be examined in this connection is that of responsibility. We shall consider first what is involved in the concept of legal responsibility, and then what is involved in moral responsibility.

Let us assume that an individual, Smith, has committed an action that violates a law: he has set fire to a building. What does it mean to say that he is legally responsible for this offense? It means that he can legally be subjected to punishment—fines, imprisonment, or whatever the law prescribes. To be sure, the process of giving a legal proof that Smith did in fact set the fire is fraught with problems of its own; but we must set these aside here. What concerns us now is that Smith may have committed the offense without being legally responsible. We must ask how the law distinguishes, among those who have committed legal offenses, between those who are responsible and those who are not. And then we must see whether the criteria for legal responsibility involve at any point the assumption of free will. If they do, then it will be necessary to choose between the idea of legal responsibility and the thesis of determinism.

There are several ways in which one who has committed an illegal action can plead that he should not be held legally responsible for it. For example, coercion is an acceptable excuse: if Smith was forced at gun point to ignite the oily rags that set off the fire, he cannot be punished for arson. Physical restraint is another ground of exemption from punishment: if Smith failed to ring the fire alarm because he was incapacitated by a blow, he is not legally responsible for his omission. Ignorance of relevant conditions of fact may also be a defense: if Smith did not know that the building he set fire to was occupied, and had every reason to believe it was not, then he cannot be held responsible for death or injury caused by his fire, though of course he might be for the destruction of property. Cases like these are comparatively easy, though plenty of bothersome borderline ones turn up in the courts. A more difficult question is whether there are psychological grounds other than ignorance for establishing lack of legal responsibility. The prevailing criterion in the courts on this point is still M'Naghten's rule, formulated in the House of Lords in 1843. According to this rule a person—free from coercion and physical restraint—is legally not responsible for an illegal action he has committed if, and only if, because of a "disease of the mind," he is unaware of the "nature and quality" of his act, and is unable to distinguish right from wrong, i.e., to know that his act is wrong.

The growth of psychological and psychiatric understanding of human behavior since the M'Naghten rule was laid down has convinced many people—even some lawyers and jurists—that it is too narrow. One of the reformulations proposed in a draft of a Model Penal Code by the American Law Institute in 1956 runs as follows:

> A person is not responsible for criminal conduct if at the time of such conduct as a result of mental disease or defect he lacks substantial capacity either to appreciate the criminality of his conduct or to conform his conduct to the requirements of law.

Some offenders who are legally responsible by the M'Naghten rule would not be legally responsible by this one. Take, for example, a compulsive pyromaniac. He may "know," in a purely intellectual sense, that his act is wrong, and be able to verbalize judgments to this effect. But he may still have a nearly total incapacity for self-control. If Jones is a pyromaniac, there are emotional and volitional factors which prevent him from being able to conform his conduct to the requirements of law, no matter how much he is punished. The M'Naghten rule was designed to mark out the class of those offenders who are unable to govern their behavior by rational considerations. But this purpose is achieved more effectively, so it is argued, by a criterion of legal responsibility like that proposed in the Model Penal Code.

We should note that the newer criterion leaves unchanged the legal responsibility of many, probably most, offenders. The ordinary driver going through a red light remains legally responsible for his action, and so does the arsonist who sets fire to a building so that he can collect the insurance. But the pyromaniac is not responsible, because his obsession is a compulsion, and his action was not free. This enlargement of the class of offenders lacking legal responsibility admittedly raises practical problems, in that it increases the number of offenders requiring therapeutic treatment rather than punitive correction. A bill incorporating the Model Penal Code's criterion for legal responsibility was passed by the Oregon state legislature in 1962—and vetoed by the governor on the ground that more state institutions would be required in order to treat the greater number of persons judged not to be legally responsible for their offenses. The practical problems created by a failure to provide therapy for offenders who need it evidently struck the governor with less force.

We began this discussion by saying that the statement that Smith is legally responsible for setting fire to a building is equivalent to saying that he can legally be subjected to punishment for this offense. Whether or not he will be punished depends in part on whether the M'Naghten rule or some other is used in the state in which Smith set the fire. This is a factual question. In most states, Smith would now be held legally responsible for setting fire to a building if he cannot show coercion or physical restraint or a disease of the mind conforming to the specifications of the M'Naghten rule.

There is nothing in the explicit formulation of these grounds for legal responsibility that refers to free will in the metaphysical sense. And if the law moves in the direction of the Model Penal Code criterion, so that psychological compulsion is recognized as a defense against legal responsibility, then the class of illegal actions for which agents are legally responsible will coincide exactly with those illegal actions in which (in our terminology) agents have freedom of action. The distinction involved here is one between two ways in which the action is caused—not a distinction between caused and uncaused actions. Even if we add the important concept of degrees of legal responsibility, based on a distinction between acts done "purposely, knowingly, recklessly, or negligently," there seems to be no explicit reference to free will.

But this way of looking at the problem of legal responsibility and free will may seem to you somewhat superficial. At least, you may feel that we have not yet tackled the problem at a very fundamental philosophical level. It is important to know the facts about whether an offender can legally be punished for a violation of law and on what grounds he is exempt from punishment. But as philosophers we want to examine more closely the basic concepts and principles underlying legal practices actually adopted or proposed. It is only by penetrating further behind the scenes of legal facts that we can hope to discover a connection between legal responsibility and free will, if such a connection exists. In more specific terms, what we must do is examine the notion of punishment.

Punishment is the infliction of pain (physical or mental) on an individual because of an offense that he is held to have committed. Questions about how punishment is to be justified arise at many levels. There are questions about justifying the particular penalty meted out to a particular offender, questions about justifying kinds of punishment inflicted for various kinds of offense, questions about deciding which offenses should be prohibited and punished by law rather than by more informal sanctions, and so on. Completely worked-out theories of punishment should provide answers to these questions. The most fundamental question here, however, is this: how can punishment *in general* be justified? Why is it *ever* right deliberately to inflict pain on a human being? Theories of punishment must come to grips with this question above all others.

Two main theories have been proposed. One maintains that punishment as an institution is justified in terms of its beneficial consequences; the infliction of punishment is justified if (and only if) there is a reasonable expectation that it will reform an offender or deter others from committing his kind of offense. This is often called the "utilitarian" theory of punishment, for reasons that will be evident in the following chapter; we shall call it the *results-theory*. The second theory maintains that punishment is justified, at least in part, by the principle that the infection of sufferin on the offender in a degree proportional to the gravity of his offense is morally right, just, or (in a special moral sense) "fitting." This is often called the "retributive"theory of punishment, which may misleadingly suggest that it identifies punishment with revenge. Since its emphasis is on the idea that punishment must be deserved by the offender, we shall call it the *deserts-theory*. This term covers any theory that appeals at any point, in the justification of punishment, to considerations other than consequences.

Theories of punishment are used to justify not only the infliction of punishment, but also the exemption of certain offenders from punishment. Thus to exempt those who are ignorant of certain facts, or who have been coerced, physically restrained, or psychologically compelled in performing their illegal actions would be justified by the results-theory on the grounds that to punish them would serve no constructive purpose of reform or deterrence. Alternatively, it would be maintained by a deserts-theory that punishment is unjust in these cases since the gravity of the offense has been so drastically reduced by the special circumstances cited.

As one might expect, most determinists have espoused a results-theory of punishment, since this theory presupposes that human behavior can be causally affected. Correspondingly, deserts-theorists have typically been libertarians. Yet there does not seem to be a logically binding relation between the two philosophical positions in either of these packages. Deviant philosophical combinations have occasionally been seen, as in the writings of W. D. Ross, a twentieth-century British moral philosopher who has defended determinism and also a modified form of deserts-theory.

There is a humaneness about the results-theory that is most attractive, but certain puzzles arise. Some philosophers have charged that, on this theory, it is difficult or impossible to distinguish punishment from other cases of inflicting pain on an individual for the good of others. If you have been exposed to smallpox, you will be forcibly vaccinated; this procedure would be regarded by most people as justified, but it would not be termed punishment. Results-theorists may at this point remind their critics that the vaccination is not punishment because an offense is not involved and insist that, for both theories of punishment, it is part of the meaning of "punishment" that it is pain inflicted because of an offense.

The critic may go on to ask what barrier there is, on the results-theory, to inflicting on an innocent man, for the sake of good consequences, exactly those same methods of causing pain or loss that are used in punishment. "Let us not quibble over a word," the critic may say. "I do not care whether or not you *call* it 'punishment' to put an innocent man in prison. The point is that when we focus our entire attention on consequences, we really undermine the purpose of insisting that the recipient of punitive treatment be guilty of an offense. Usually it won't be beneficial to put an innocent man in prison—but if it is, why not do it? A deserts-theorist, on the other hand, properly insists that it takes more than good consequences to justify the infliction of pain in punishment. The individual punished must *deserve* the suffering or loss, and this the innocent man can never do."

It may be that a more prolonged examination of this question, and especially the use of distinctions and concepts to be introduced in the following chapter, would show that some forms of result-theory can meet the objection just raised. But it is difficult to avoid the conclusion that punishment is an expression of moral disapproval, as well as an infliction of pain, and that its reforming and deterring functions are designed to operate at least in part *because of* this feature. Discussions of legal responsibility make frequent reference to such concepts as guilt and culpability. A free (unconstrained) action that is in some respect wrong is a *prima facie* ground for regarding its agent as culpable, as deserving more disapproval.

When we move from factual questions about legal responsibility to an exploration of the justification of punishment, we cross over to the territory of moral concepts. The question to be faced now is this: does the idea that people sometimes deserve moral disapproval for their actions require the assumption of free will? But this is the question of moral responsibility.

§ 8. • *Moral Responsibility*

The exact nature of moral responsibility is subject to some dispute. Many philosophers, however, would be willing to accept this equation: an individual is morally responsible for a wrong action he has committed if, and only if, to feel moral disapproval toward him for this act is justifiable. Whereas legal responsibility concerns only offenses and punishment, many philosophers would maintain that moral responsibility in its full scope concerns all those actions for which an agent would justifiably be subject to moral approval, as well as those for which he could justifiably be subject to moral disapproval. But for our present purposes only moral responsibility for wrong actions need be considered.

You will notice that we speak of "feeling moral disapproval" toward someone for his wrong action rather than of "blaming" him for it. The latter expression is natural and idiomatic, and we shall sometimes use it in what follows. It is subject to one difficulty that should be noted. We may become persuaded, through the use of this form of language, that to blame someone is essentially to perform an action, that blame is in fact a mild form of punishment. And of course to utter words to an offender expressing blame or moral disapproval may serve much the same purpose as punishment. Yet the question whether blame should be communicated to an individual offender is not the same question as whether we are justified in feeling moral disapproval toward him. We feel moral disapproval toward many agents to whom we could not express this attitude even if we wished to do so, as when we now say (or merely think), "Hitler was profoundly to blame for his crimes against the Jews." Although some philosophers have defended the view that blaming is an action, this position seems to lead to many troublesome consequences. It would seem more satisfactory to speak of *feeling* moral disapproval toward an offender, or of *judging* him morally culpable or blameworthy for a wrong action, than to regard blaming as an *action* like punishing. Punishment itself, as we have seen, is in part an expression of moral disapproval; but one may feel moral disapproval without expressing it, and one may be justified in feeling it without being justified in expressing it.

Under what conditions, then, are we justified in feeling moral disapproval of an agent for his wrong action? To a large extent, the answer here will parallel some of our earlier discussion of legal responsibility. We cannot justifiably disapprove of someone who has committed a wrong action because of constraint, i.e., the action must have been free from constraint. And we cannot justifiably disapprove of someone who committed a wrong action under certain kinds of misapprehension or ignorance as to the facts in the situation. These factors, here cited as defenses against moral disapproval, became familiar to us in the preceding section as defenses against legal punishment. But another consideration comes into play in the context of moral responsibility—the factor of motive.

A thorough discussion of the role of motives in establishing moral responsibility is impossible here, but a few of the main points can be noted. Although the rightness or wrongness of an action does not depend on the agent's motive (except insofar as a reference to this may form part of the description of the action itself), considerations of motive may be central in establishing the moral blameworthiness of the agent. Some motives, like a sincere desire to do the right thing because it is right, are very nearly water-tight defenses against moral disapproval, though the wrongness of the action is unaffected. If you think it is wrong to register as a conscientious objector but your friend, after prolonged thought, decides that he ought to do this, you will doubtless conclude that because he did what he thought was right he should not be subjected to moral disapproval for his (nevertheless, in your view) wrong action. Other motives, like a desire to hurt someone, will add to the degree of moral disapproval for a wrong action. (What "motive" means is much debated by philosophers today.)

Because motives can play such an important part in determining whether moral disapproval is justified, some philosophers would maintain that we cannot answer questions about the culpability of an agent until some information about his motives is in hand. But this may be going too far. It seems more accurate to say, as we did earlier, that if we know that a wrong action has been committed freely (without constraint) and with knowledge of relevant facts, we have *prima facie* grounds for moral disapproval, even though information about motives may turn out to eliminate, reduce, or increase the agent's moral culpability. This view of the matter has the advantage of accounting for the element of moral disapproval that seems to be part of the general concept of punishment as such. Because of the importance of uniform treatment of offenses, legal penalties must sometimes be inflicted despite the presence of an exculpating motive, but such cases do not seem to invalidate the general account of moral disapproval and punishment that has been sketched here. Often we do not know an agent's motives, and sometimes we either could not find out or are not obligated to inquire. For well-founded individualized judgments of moral disapproval, we should always try to get information about an agent's motives, but in many situations we are justified in operating only with the *prima facie* grounds for moral disapproval that are present in cases of free (unconstrained) nonignorant wrong actions.

Suppose we say, then, that there is a *prima facie* justification for moral disapproval of an agent for his wrong act if and only if the action was free from constraint and committed with knowledge of relevant facts. For some purposes, we do not need to go beyond this *prima facie* justification. These *prima facie* grounds for moral disapproval can, however, be removed if the presence of certain motives in the agent can be shown. And where a full account of the moral culpability of an agent is sought, there is an obligation on the part of the moral judge to secure as much information as possible about motives.

At last we are ready to face up to the question whether the conditions just set forth for justifiable moral disapproval are really sufficient. It is all very well to ask whether a wrong action was free from constraint, whether the agent had knowledge of relevant facts, what his motives were—but isn't all this incomplete? Don't we need to say also that the agent was exercising free will, if we are to be justified in holding him to blame for his wrong action?

Libertarians will of course answer this question in the affirmative. But the interesting thing is that we find determinists divided in their answers. Philosophers in one determinist camp, those who have come to be called "soft determinists," maintain that we do not need free will at all. Moral responsibility is quite compatible with a determinist position. In deciding whether a wrong action, say the taking of a bribe, merits moral disapproval, we need only establish certain facts about the immediate causal antecedents of the action. Beyond this we do not need to go, any more than we need to give the names of our grandparents when asked for the names of our parents. The bribe-taker merits moral disapproval because his wrong action was *his* action, in the fullest sense. It was his hand that took the bribe; it was his desire that prompted; it was his act of choice that was the immediate determinant of the action. What more can legitimately be required?

This is the account given by one group of determinists, and it is fair to say that it has enjoyed the status of a majority opinion in recent and contemporary philosophy. But it is far from being unchallenged. Let us examine two forms of challenge.

One would be offered by certain libertarians—not the more sophisticated representatives of that position. "Of course," a relatively simple-minded libertarian may reply, "we must distinguish between Smith's actions and other people's, and we do this by seeing whether in some way his will concurred, his own choice led directly to the action—we have to know this in order to decide whom to blame. But that doesn't explain why we are justified in blaming anyone at all. If all events are determined, including the agent's choices, then from the beginning of time it was settled that when the moment came he would in fact behave the way he did. Smith's action of taking the bribe, seen in this light, is exactly like the falling of a stone that happens to hurt someone—we do not blame the stone, because we realize that it couldn't help falling; why then should we blame the man, who also couldn't have done otherwise? Moral disapproval loses its justification completely in a world in which genuine alternatives are precluded by a rigid causal order."

Almost any determinist is likely to object to some of the language here; it confuses his theory with a quite different one, from which he is anxious to dissociate himself. This is *fatalism*. To say that an event is determined is to say that when certain antecedent conditions come into existence, that event will follow according to some law. Determinist predictions are thus conditional: I predict that if you run across the street in traffic you will be struck by a car. The word "fatalism" comes from *fata,* the sayings of the Roman oracles who consulted entrails and other supernatural sources of knowledge. The *fata Vergiliana* was another, later method of getting wisdom, which some people still use today, though substituting the Bible for Vergil. Ask yourself how your business deal will come out if you conclude it today, then open the book at random, put your finger down quickly, and read the sentence it points to: freely interpreted, that may be your answer. Now, to say that an event is fated is to say that it will happen no matter what antecedent conditions come into existence, and the thesis that some (or, in the same versions, all) events are fated is fatalism. Fatalistic predictions are not at all conditional, but categorical. If, as a Muslim saying has it, the day of your death is written on your forehead (where you cannot see it), that means that it doesn't matter whether you run across the street or do something else; you can neither hasten nor delay that preset date. If you are outdoors you may be struck by lightning; if you go to bed, the roof may fall in; on land, you may be the victim of earthquake; at sea, you may be drowned. In American parlance, your number is up.

If all or many important actions are fated, what becomes of the moral life? Philosophers might differ on the question whether we could still distinguish meaningfully between actions that are right and those that are wrong. In this connection it would be of interest to study certain ancient Greek tragedies, and also the moral outlook of the New England Puritans, who combined with their fatalistic theology of predestination an obsession with rigorous moral rules and laws. But, whatever is the case for concepts of morally right and wrong actions, it seems clear that concepts of morally blameworthy and praiseworthy agents could not be preserved in a fatalistic world. If a man was fated to take a bribe, it makes no sense to regard him with moral disapproval for doing so.

But the world of the determinist is not fatalistic. It is true that the future is causally determined, he says, but it is partly determined by what we decide to do now, and our decisions can be sensible or stupid, wise or careless, right or wrong. To be aware of the nature and quality of our actions, and their probable consequences, and to judge our responsibility for them, is all part of doing what we can to influence the future. For what happens tomorrow will not happen regardless of what we do; it will be causally dependent, in part, on what we choose to do today. And, if the determinist espouses what we have called the "soft determinist" view, he will resolutely maintain that it is in large part their freedom of action that makes agents legitimately subject to moral disapproval.

We must now turn to the second of the two forms of challenge hurled against the soft determinist position. Here we come to a line of thought shared, up to a point, by libertarians and by another group of determinists, called "hard determinists." It is essentially a claim that the distinction between free actions and other events is too arbitrary and fragile to bear the weight of justifying moral disapproval. Hard determinists, and libertarians of the more sophisticated sort, are not in danger of confusing determinism and fatalism. Yet they still find the soft determinist attempt to justify moral disapproval unconvincing. How do they put their challenge?

The soft determinist's opponents will invite him to examine a case in which he claims that moral disapproval of an agent for his wrong action is justified. "Let us consider, for example, the policeman who has taken a bribe, and let us assume that none of the conditions which you say would render moral disapproval unjustified is present. The policeman may still plead that he couldn't help what he did. 'I wanted the money very much,' he may say. We reply, 'But you could have helped it. If you had deliberately discouraged in yourself your intense desire for money, you would not have taken the bribe.' 'Yes, but I couldn't do that. My father always told me since I was a little kid, to get money—that comes first. And by the time I grew up I had this fixed in my mind.'

"Now"—the hard determinist argues—"one example can't illustrate all the possibilities, but we can see from this one that here is a line of argument that can be applied without exception to every single case of what you soft determinists call freedom of action. True, in your special sense, we can say he 'could have' refrained—but this means only that he would have refrained if something had been different. Maybe that something could have been different—that is, it would have been different if at some still earlier stage he had behaved differently. But if we trace the causal series back far enough, we will always get back to something outside the person himself and far beyond his conscious or voluntary control—back to his upbringing, his childhood, his genetic endowment, his sociological influences, etc., etc. So when the policeman says he couldn't help the way his father brought him up, it will follow that he couldn't help the consequences that followed from that bringing up. Therefore, it is unjust to disapprove of him morally; he is not to blame. No one, in the end, is morally responsible for his actions."

If this argument, which is certainly strong, is really conclusive, it poses a most serious dilemma. Shall we retain the thesis of determinism and give up moral responsibility, or shall we retain moral responsibility and give up determinism? And here, of course, the two groups of philosophers who agree in rejecting soft determinism come to a parting of the ways. Libertarians insist that the concept of moral responsibility must be retained, and not merely as a museum-piece but as involving an operative distinction between those who can legitimately be held to blame for their wrong acts and those who cannot. They believe that some offenders deserve moral disapproval and that if this thesis can be maintained only by assuming that their acts are acts of free will, then so be it. This appeal to what is involved in moral responsibility, and sometimes other moral concepts, has been regarded as a powerful argument for libertarianism. As we have seen, it is not the only possible argument; but it has probably been the most persuasive one. Many of those who accept it, however, have very clearly insisted that they do not believe that all human choices embody free will. One particularly influential statement (by C. A. Campbell) asserts that free will is operative only in situations of moral choice—in moral dilemmas, when an agent is struggling to do what is right.

Hard determinists, having joined forces with libertarians to oppose the soft determinist account of moral responsibility, draw a very different conclusion from that just set forth. They argue that, since determinism is better established than the concept of moral responsibility, it is the latter that must be abandoned. They would not of course claim that all concepts and principles of a normative or valuational kind must be discarded. We can still value some things and disvalue others, including some kinds of human actions and human qualities, even though we are not entitled to feel moral disapproval or approval, to blame people or to praise them for what they are or what they have done. A so-called "character trait" like cruelty should be regarded in the same light as qualities for which we have never held people "responsible," like being unattractive physically or having a low I.Q. We may take steps to change the qualities we find undesirable in people, and we may even retain "quasi-punishments" in the form of penalties for actions which we want to discourage, but the element of moral disapproval must be rooted out of the infliction of penalties.

Some hard determinists would go so far as to claim that this general way of looking at human beings, ourselves and others, would in itself lead to desirable attitudes, such as compassion, lack of envy and rivalry, and so on. Spinoza, in his *Ethics,* aimed "to show what service to our own lives a knowledge of this doctrine is." Contemporary hard determinists might charge that the impulse to punish or to feel moral disapproval is largely a primitive one, of which we ought to be ashamed and which we ought to suppress if we want to be really civilized. Read the newspaper letter-columns after a paroled sex-offender is arrested for another rape, they might say; people don't really care whether he has free will, is legally sane, or anything else—they only want to take out their own frustrations on him. But the ultimate justification for eliminating moral disapproval, for hard determinists, is not that this step will produce more desirable attitudes: it is simply that since determinism is true we must have the integrity to bring our attitudes into line with the truth. In this somewhat austere spirit, they rest their case.

Indeed, there are few philosophic issues whose impact has been felt so broadly and so deeply as the one we have been considering here. Most of those, professional philosophers or not, who grapple seriously and sincerely with this problem can feel some pull in each of the three directions we have described: soft determinism, hard determinism, and libertarianism. Possibly the issue itself needs to be conceived in a new way. There is a special challenge here, we suggest, for determinists. It may be that there is some truth, some important insight, in both the hard and soft determinist positions. Perhaps in some ultimate moral perspective, which might better be termed a religious perspective, all men are to be understood and forgiven for what they do. But still, in a more close-up view of human conduct, there is the difference between the person who is subject to constraint and the person who, because of freedom from constraint, has it within himself, by what he does now, to change his environment and himself. And when we impute responsibility to him we are not only acknowledging in him a dignity and status that we find nowhere else in nature, but demanding of him a kind of response that people must be able to give if they are to create and sustain together a society in which all can find the highest fulfillment.

CHAPTER FOUR

❧

ETHICAL JUDGMENT

A family named Green, living in a suburb of a large city, have for several years maintained their membership in a local organization known as the Sunnydale Swim Club. The club is technically a private one, but has accepted, from the beginning, any local family that applied, taking in new members according to the order of application. There have been no black members, and until a year ago there were no black applicants. But last year a black family (the Blakes), having moved into a previously all-white section of the community, applied for membership in the swim club. After a year of being on the waiting list (about the usual period) they have now been turned down by the membership committee.

The members of the club are strongly divided in their views concerning the rejection of the Blakes. A resolution supporting explicit commitment to a policy of nondiscrimination for the club is offered at a meeting of the full membership in the late spring and is defeated by a vote of 260 to 225. The Blakes have reapplied for admission, and a second black family, the Nelsons, have also applied: it is expected that these applications will be acted on next spring, a year from now.

The swim club members who oppose discrimination share a feeling of extreme disappointment over the results of the vote, and also hope that the Blakes and Nelsons will be admitted next year. But they do not agree on what should be done in the present situation. Some members plan to resign; they say that they cannot in conscience remain members of a club that practices racial discrimination. Other members maintain that they feel just as strongly about the injustice of the situation, but plan to remain in the club for the purpose of working to bring about a nondiscriminatory policy in the future.

The Greens, who have two teen-age children, have always held strong convictions opposing racial discrimination, and now find themselves very much torn, as they try to consider whether their family should resign or stay in the club. What *is* the right thing for them to do?

This example of a moral problem will enable us to bring out a number of basic concepts and principles in ethical theory. Let us first use the example to help identify the main areas in ethics.

The question most directly raised by the Greens' situation is of course the one just asked a moment ago: what ought they to do? Which course of action is right and which is wrong? Answers to questions of this kind are *judgments of moral obligation.* An answer to a concrete problem like the one facing the Greens is a particular judgment: "The Greens ought to resign now," or "It would be wrong not to stay in the club and work for a different policy." Despite the poignancy and urgency of many moral problems, ethical theory cannot long remain on the level of particular judgments of moral obligation, but must attempt to discover what good reasons can be offered for a particular judgment. Thus we move on to general judgments of moral obligation: "The Greens ought to resign because racial discrimination is wrong." *The theory of moral obligation* is the branch of ethical theory that attempts to give fundamental reasons why right actions are right and wrong actions are wrong, or what makes right actions right and wrong ones wrong. Let us notice that the expression "right actions" is sometimes used as equivalent to "actions that are not wrong," or "morally permissible actions," and sometimes as equivalent to "actions which it would be wrong not to do," or "morally obligatory actions." The context will usually indicate which meaning of "right" is intended, but it is important to be aware of the distinction.

Sometimes a question about the moral rightness or wrongness of an action is asked by the agent who is trying to decide what to do; sometimes by another person, in the role of adviser or judge. The action in question may be in the future or in the past. It is clear that questions about moral rightness and wrongness have a special urgency when asked by an agent about a possible future action of his own, but human beings can also be deeply interested in the moral standing of the actions of others, even if far away and long ago.

It would be possible and very natural to raise questions belonging to other branches of ethical theory about the Greens' problem. We could, for example, consider questions about the motives behind the actions of the Greens or other members of the club. Suppose we learned, for example, that some members who have resigned did so primarily from fear of being called bigots, whereas others resigned primarily to avoid doing what they sincerely believe to be morally wrong. This knowledge would certainly affect the extent to which we should regard these people as worthy of moral approval. Judgments of moral approval or disapproval directed towards persons for their actions, traits, or entire characters are *judgments of moral value.* They may be particular (like "John is very much to blame for disobeying his teacher" or "Ghandi was a good man") or general (like "Moral courage is a very admirable trait"). The *theory of moral value* seeks to provide fundamental reasons supporting judgments of moral value. A judgment of moral obligation (for example, that action A is wrong), along with a judgment that the agent in question is action-free (in the sense defined in the previous chapter), constitutes a *prima facie* basis for making a judgment of moral value (that the agent who committed A deserves moral disapproval). But information about the agent's motives is needed to fix the degree of disapproval, and sometimes information of this kind can remove his liability to disapproval altogether. Questions of moral value, therefore, though related to questions about the rightness and wrongness of actions, are distinguishable from the latter. The theory of moral value is significant, though somewhat underdeveloped, area of ethical theory. In connection with moral value, philosophic attention has centered, understandably, on an examination of the compatibility of the concepts of moral approval and disapproval with the metaphysical thesis of determinism. Our brief consideration of this issue, in the discussion of moral responsibility, has shown how difficult and challenging an issue it is. But it is important to remember that other questions in the theory of moral value are also very much worth working on.

A third kind of question relevant to ethics can easily be asked in connection with the Sunnydale Swim Club situation. Suppose someone in the Green family argues that to stay in the club is right because this action would make things better, would produce *better results* than resigning would. The next step would be to ask him what results he thinks it would bring about and why he thinks these are good, or better than the results of the alternative action. The argument that a given action is right or wrong because of its results is so common and familiar that we can easily see that an appraisal of results themselves will very often be called for in the course of reaching a decision on what to do in a moral dilemma. A statement asserting that an object or a state of affairs is good or bad is a *judgment of nonmoral value,* carrying with it no specifically *moral* approval or disapproval. Judgments of this kind may be particular or general and, as in the case of theories of moral obligation and moral value, the *theory of nonmoral value* seeks to provide fundamental reasons in support of judgments of nonmoral value. Questions of nonmoral value are important in ethical theory, not only in connection with questions of moral obligation about specific actions, but also because of their bearing on wide-ranging decisions about patterns of living and the "good life."

We have now identified three areas of ethical theory, but we have not yet spoken of the most fundamental dividing point for ethics. The three areas thus far described all belong to one major branch of ethical theory called *normative ethics.* In normative ethics, we usually begin with questions about particular actions, particular persons, or particular objects and try to ascertain, by asking increasingly fundamental questions, what it is that makes actions in general right or wrong, or people in general morally admirable or reprehensible, or objects in general good or bad. Yet even when we have reached the most fundamental level of reason-giving, we are still within the realm of *normative discourse*. We are still talking about actions and their rightness or objects and their goodness. But, as you will now be well prepared to understand, it is possible to go on to raise questions of quite a different kind: knowledge-questions and meaning-questions *about* ethical judgments.

Suppose Mr. Green arrives at one basic theory about what makes an action right, and a second club member arrives at quite a different one. (We shall see more concretely, in a moment, just how this might happen.) Each one has reached the end of the line in normative ethics and cannot be pushed to any more fundamental normative level. But, instead of asking Mr. Green why actions of a certain basic kind are right, we can ask him, "How do you know that actions of that kind are right?" And we can ask him, "What does the word 'right' mean?" The first is a question about the general method of justifying basic judgments of moral obligation. The second is a question about the meaning of a basic ethical term. Questions of both kinds belong to the second major branch of ethical theory— *metaethics,* sometimes called "critical ethics." Exactly how to conceive the relation between normative ethics and metaethics has been a matter of some dispute.

In this chapter we shall describe some of the main theories of moral obligation and some of the main theories of nonmoral value. We shall not enter into questions of metaethics, but questions of moral value will be touched on briefly and indirectly, in connection with the discussion of moral obligation.

Let us now return to the Sunnydale Swim Club and see, through a consideration of the viewpoints of the Greens and others, what the most significant alternative ideas about moral obligation are. We shall consider primarily how club members who oppose discrimination and voted for the resolution argue for decisions to resign or to stay in the club. But occasionally we shall also consider the views of certain club members who are in favor of the discriminatory policy.

WHAT MAKES RIGHT ACTIONS RIGHT?

As the deadline for paying dues for the new swimming season draws near, the Greens spend much time discussing their problem in family conferences and with neighbors and friends holding various points of view. Since memberships are on a family basis, the Greens seek a joint decision. Mr. Green is in favor of staying in the club. He says swimming is a pleasure and it should be enjoyed by as many people as possible. He goes on to argue in this way: "I know that admitting black members would make some people in the club unhappy. But this would be temporary. They would feel perfectly all right about it when they found out that nothing bad would happen, and some of them would even feel much better, as they lost their prejudices, than they had ever felt before. And of course the new members—the Blakes and the Nelsons and probably others later on— would be a lot happier. Besides, the example of our swim club's refusing to discriminate might lead others to follow suit, so that the same process of making more people happy (after some temporary upsets) would spread to other communities. I don't see how we can turn aside from this chance to do good. Let's stay in the club and work to change the policy!"

But Mrs. Green finds herself very much impressed by the attitude of their friends the Mortons, who plan to resign. "I can see," she admits to her husband, "that we could perhaps do some good by staying in. But, until the policy could be changed, we would be discriminating indirectly, just by belonging to a discriminatory club. We've always believed that this is wrong. I just don't think we'd be justified in staying in, and I think we should resign right now."

This difference of opinion between the Greens illustrates the main cleavage between theories of moral obligation. Mr. Green, in emphasizing the obligation to do good, to bring about as much pleasure as one can, is appealing to results. His justification for staying in the club is essentially that the results of this act would be better than the results of resigning. Any theory that holds the rightness or wrongness of an action to be determined solely by results is called a *teleological theory of moral obligation,* or, sometimes, a "result" theory. Mr. Green, at least as far as our present evidence goes, is a teleologist.

Note that it is not necessary, in order to hold a teleological theory of moral obligation, to insist on a particular kind of result. For Mr. Green, it is pleasure that should be produced as widely as possible, but some teleologists would not agree with him. Teleologists unite in believing that an action is morally right (permissible) if it maximizes good (produces at least as much net good as any other action possible in that situation); but they do not all agree on what results actually are good. The latter is of course an important question too, and we shall return to it later on, when we come to questions of nonmoral value.

Mrs. Green's approach is different. When she considers staying in the club, it is something about the action itself, rather than its results, that counts with her—namely, that it would be an act of racial discrimination. As such, it is wrong: it violates one of her moral principles. A theory that holds the rightness or wrongness of an action to be determined, at least in part, by considerations other than results, is called a *deontological theory of moral obligation,* or a "formalist" theory. Mrs. Green's ethical reasoning regarding the present problem is that of a deontologist. Some deontologists reject all consideration of results in determining the rightness or wrongness of actions. Most hold that results are relevant to this determination, but not sufficient for it.

§ 1. • *Rightness and Results*

The distinction between teleological and deontological theories of moral obligation is regarded as the most fundamental one in this branch of ethical theory. But this distinction alone cannot answer all the questions that arise concerning the basic features of right and wrong actions. If you accept a teleological theory of moral obligation, you are immediately faced with the necessity to make up your mind on certain other important points regarding which teleologists differ. For example, it is all very well to claim that the rightness and wrongness of actions depends on results only—but results for whom? Let us look at two ways of answering this question.

Mary Green, who is fourteen, agrees with her father that the family ought to stay in the swim club. But she admits (to herself at least) that her reasons for wanting to stay in are of two kinds. She is attracted by her father's argument to the effect that more people will be made happy if the club stops discriminating and that it is the Greens' duty to work for this goal. But Mary knows that she also wants to stay in the club for her own enjoyment. More than anyone else in the family, she gets pleasure from swimming. Mary's motives for wanting to remain in the club therefore are mixed, and she finds it hard to accept with equanimity the fact that most people's motives are mixed, most of the time. Mary feels guilty; but, while she is worrying about her own selfishness, she happens to hear the opinions of a neighbor, Mr. Foster, voiced in conversations with her father.

Foster says repeatedly, with considerable vigor, that he can't see what all the fuss is about. *He* certainly wouldn't give up membership in the club if he enjoyed swimming—after all, it's the only club within a radius of several miles. And he voted against the resolution condemning discrimination because Sunnydale will be more enjoyable for him if the club can avoid any awkwardness that might be caused by allowing persons of other races to join.

Mr. Green, to whom these views are anathema, charges Foster with being brutally self-centered. But to this Foster's answer is perfectly clear: "Sure I look after my own good. I think each of us ought to look after himself only, and I'm perfectly willing to have everyone else act on this principle—in fact I tell people they should." To young Mary Green (at an age when the idea of looking after oneself has a strong appeal in any case) these views seem rather admirably forthright and tough-minded.

Mr. Foster is defending the position of *ethical egoism:* the thesis that the rightness and wrongness of actions do indeed depend on results, but that the only results that should be taken into account are the results for the agent himself. Some ethical egoists believe only that it is morally permissible to maximize good for oneself; others (like Foster) hold that it is morally obligatory to do this. But ethical egoists unite in denying that anyone has a duty to consider the good of others, except as a means to his own good.

The chief defense offered for ethical egoism has been the view known as psychological egoism, a view we have already discussed in Chapter 2. You will recall that the psychological egoist claims that all actions are motivated by the desire for one's own good. It would not usually be claimed that the truth of ethical egoism (a theory about how people *ought to* behave) follows directly from psychological egoism (a theory about how people *do* behave). What the ethical egoist usually maintains is rather that the truth of psychological egoism is sufficient to invalidate all non-egoistic theories of moral obligation, since the latter theories call on us to perform actions that are psychologically impossible for us.

Opponents of ethical egoism have focused their attention to a large extent on refuting psychological egoism. We have already seen that it is often "defended" by being transformed into a tautology. But there are other questions that you will want to think seriously about in appraising the merits of ethical egoism. Here, for example, is one. It is often pointed out that the ethical egoist's theory of moral obligation places him in an awkward position when he is asked by someone else for moral advice. Suppose that Mr. Foster is asked for advice by Mary Green, who admires him. It is perfectly clear to Foster that since Mary gains so much enjoyment and benefit from swimming, she should urge her family to stay in the club, to maximize her own good. But it is equally clear to him that the club would be a pleasanter spot for *him* if Mr. Green, whom he cordially dislikes, does resign, family and all. What should he tell Mary? His general theory of ethical egoism, which states that everyone should seek his own good, may seem to point here in two directions: tell Mary to resign, and tell her not to resign. Perhaps there is a satisfactory reply that an ethical egoist can make to this kind of objection—but it might take some thought to discover it.

Most philosophers who have defended a teleological theory of moral obligation have not been egoists. They maintain, on the contrary, that in ascertaining which actions are right we must find out simply which actions will produce the most good. To the question "The most good for whom?" they answer, "The most good for anyone affected by the action in question." Good is good, and it is irrational and unjustifiable to prefer my lesser good over another's greater good, or his lesser good over my greater good. We should produce as much good as possible, letting the question of whose good settle itself, with "everyone to count for one." This kind of teleological theory is called *universalist,* and teleological theories that are universalist rather than egoist are called *utilitarian.* Mr. Green, we can now see, is a utilitarian. We noted in the preceding chapter that the name "utilitarian" is applied to what we called the "results-theory" of punishment, the theory that justifies punishment in terms of its consequences. Utilitarianism as a general theory of moral obligation has probably enjoyed more support than any other theory. The classical utilitarians, Jeremy Bentham and John Stuart Mill, were political and social reformers of notable compassion and zeal, as well as cogent and subtle thinkers on matters of ethical theory. Utilitarianism has made and continues to make a strong appeal by its theoretical simplicity and coherence and the humane and forward-looking practices to which it gives support.

One naive form of deontological theory of moral obligation is the view that we have certain simple and fixed rules that tell us what actions are right and wrong. It is right to follow, wrong to break, such rules as "Always tell the truth," "Never steal," etc. The rigidity of these rules is objectionable to many people once they have thought more than superficially about the matter: Socrates and Plato long ago pointed out that a moral rule like "Give every man his due" has exceptions. The appeal to consequences found in utilitarianism seems to provide a way of judging which exceptions to rules are justified and which are not. If to tell a lie would bring about more good than to tell the truth—if, for example, a lie would save a life—the lie should be told.

And yet many philosophers and others sympathetic to utilitarianism have felt that the place of rules in the moral life should not be dismissed quite so easily. There are some rules whose infraction seems much more difficult to justify. Consider, for example, a dilemma in which Mr. Jones, a friend of the Greens, found himself before the vote was taken on the resolution for the swim club. As a member of the club's board of directors, he was called upon to participate in the decision on how the policy question should be settled. Should a resolution be put to a vote of the entire membership? According to the club's by-laws, the board was not required to allow the members to vote on the resolution. Once the membership committee had rejected the Blakes' original application, the board had the power either to support or to overrule the committee's decision—in short, to decide the policy question by itself. It seemed to Jones (though he could not be sure) that a majority of the board favored a nondiscriminatory policy and would have overruled the committee's rejection of the Blakes. This procedure—to let the board decide—had a good chance of producing the results that Jones, like Green, thought to be very desirable. Jones felt much less sure of how the membership would vote. Yet he, along with the other board members, was in favor of letting the general membership make this important policy decision. It would have been morally wrong, he thought, to make the decision in any other way. Here was a rule—let certain kinds of decisions be made by a majority vote—that he wanted to follow even in circumstances where he believed that the results of breaking it would probably be better.

Mr. Jones was very much puzzled by his own attitude in supporting the rule of majority vote in this case and even felt that there was something vaguely inconsistent about his position. But when he discussed the matter with his niece Susan, she was able to set him straight by drawing on her college course in ethics. "You're a utilitarian, Uncle Jim," she assured him, "but you're a special kind of utilitarian called a rule-utilitarian. You judge the rightness of an action by results—only it's not the results of the action itself that you go by, it's the results of the rule under which the action falls. I ought to say, rather, that it's the results of everyone's following the rule under which the action falls. In this swim club situation, you thought the consequences of weakening the rule about majority votes on this kind of issue would be worse than the results of letting the majority vote, even though you were pretty sure they would vote wrong." Mr. Jones was grateful to Susan for her clarification and in subsequent conversations with his friend Green took satisfaction in pointing out the difference in their views: he himself, he explained, was a rule-utilitarian, while Green was an act-utilitarian.

Some philosophers have questioned whether the implications of these two theories, act-utilitarianism and rule-utilitarianism, are really different in the final analysis. But rule-utilitarians maintain that they are. Consider the question whether it would ever be right for a doctor to perform an act of euthanasia, or "mercy-killing." The rule-utilitarian claims that act-utilitarians would have to say that this would be right wherever the consequences of doing it were better than the consequences of not doing it. The rule-utilitarian, on the other hand, could argue that the results of having a *rule* that doctors should never take life are so desirable that no doctor should ever break it.

We shall speak of utilitarianism again, but now it is time to look at the other major theory of moral obligation and some of the main variations on the theme of deontologism.

§ 2. • *Rightness and Rules*

You will recall that Mrs. Green's view on whether it is morally right to stay in the swim club differs from her husband's. Mrs. Green thinks that their family should resign. However much they could contribute to the long-run happiness of others by working to change the club's policy, they would after all be participating in the discriminatory practices of the club during the period before the policy could be changed. No one seems to think this change could take place in less than a year, and Mrs. Green says she feels very badly to think of belonging to a discriminatory club for a year. She does not believe that resignation in protest would itself be very efficacious in changing the club's policy. Her belief that resigning is the right thing to do is based simply and directly on the conviction that racial discrimination is wrong and that good ends do not justify the use of wrong means to attain them.

As we noted earlier, Mrs. Green appears to be a deontologist in her general theory of moral obligation. It would be possible for someone to take the view that it is wrong to stay in the club because this would be participating in racial discrimination and as such wrong, and to go on to argue, at a more fundamental level, that racial discrimination itself is wrong because it leads to unhappiness or to other consequences regarded as undesirable. It would be possible, in other words, to give a teleological justification for resigning. But this is not Mrs. Green's position. It is because staying in the club would be, in her judgment, an action of a certain *kind,* or an action falling under a certain *rule,* that it is wrong. Mrs. Green has adopted as a moral rule an injunction against racial discrimination.

Deontologists agree that moral rightness and wrongness depend, at least in part, on something other than results (either of a particular action or of following a rule). The overwhelming majority of deontologists hold that this "something other" consists of certain features of the action itself that would make any action of the same kind also right or wrong. But there has been a considerable range of belief as to just what features of actions are the ultimate determinants of moral rightness and wrongness. Deontologists may also differ as to what moral rule or rules they regard as fundamental.

One convenient way of classifying deontological theories is to distinguish monist theories from pluralist ones. Monist deontological theories of moral obligation are those which set up one single fundamental moral rule by reference to which other rules are justified. Someone may say, "I think that we should be kind to the poor because God approves of this behavior, and it is right to do what God approves," and may also support his statements about the rightness and wrongness of other kinds of actions by reference to God's approval. It then becomes evident that he is a monist deontologist having as his single basic moral rule "Always do what God approves and only what God approves." Many philosophers have criticized this rule. They have maintained that, far from using our knowledge of God's approval as a basis for judging what is right, we must first have knowledge of what is right, and then use this to tell what God (as an all-good deity) truly approves. And they have asked the question put so memorably by Plato in his dialogue *Euthyphro:* Is what is right right because the gods approve it, or do they approve it because it is right? It is not part of our present task to examine the relation between rightness and approval by God or gods, however, but only to cite the view that we should do all and only those things of which God approves as an example of a monist deontological theory.

Suppose that someone says something like this: "If an action is legal it is morally right, and if it is illegal it is morally wrong. The only basic moral rule is: obey the laws of your society." Here again we have a monist deontological theory, of a somewhat primitive sort. The exact relationships between legal and moral concepts are difficult and interesting to work out; we saw something of the way in which they are intertwined in our earlier discussion of legal and moral responsibility. Not many who have thought about the matter with care should be satisfied to rest the whole question of an action's moral rightness on its legality. Some would argue that illegal actions may on occasion be right—as when someone drives through a red light in order to rush an injured person to the hospital. And most of us would concede that legal actions are often morally wrong.

A view related to the identification of moral rightness with legality is sometimes expressed in terms of "having a right to do something." This expression has turned up in several arguments over the swim club policy. Some club members who opposed the antidiscrimination resolution are given to saying, "Well, it's a private club, isn't it? After all, as members of a private club we have a right to exclude anyone we want to!" This comment is held, in some quarters, to carry considerable weight as a justification of a discriminatory policy. But the Greens are unimpressed by it. Mr. Green is particularly vocal on this point. "You people don't make it clear whether you are talking about a moral right or a legal one," he has often argued. "If you're talking about a legal right, no one has denied it—the club *is* private, and there's no legislation to govern the membership practices of a private club. And even if you mean you have a moral right, I'm inclined to agree with you—in the sense that other people have a duty not to interfere with what you are doing. But there are plenty of things you have a right to do that are nevertheless wrong. Having a right to do something doesn't make that something the right thing to do. I think that the club's present policy is wrong and, while I won't interfere with it's being carried out, I'm going to take other steps to try to change it!"

Monist forms of deontological theory may be rather simple and obviously vulnerable to criticism, but they need not be. A much more sophisticated and influential version of monist deontological theory can be found in Kant's views on moral obligation. Kant's position must be studied in detail and in depth to be adequately appreciated; but we can say something here very briefly about his central concept, *universalizability*. There were two key questions, Kant thought, that should be asked by anyone trying to find out whether a contemplated action is right, or in his phrase "in accordance with duty." First, you should ask what kind of action it is and what circumstances attend it. This will tell you under what "private rule" or "maxim" it falls. Second, you should ask whether that private rule (to do actions of that kind under such and such circumstances) is one that you can consistently will to become a universal rule to be acted on by *everyone* who finds himself in a similar situation. If the answer to the second question is no, the maxim is not universalizable, and the contemplated action is morally wrong. The principle incorporating this universalizability test was formulated by Kant as the first form of his celebrated Categorical Imperative: "Act only according to that maxim of which you can at the same time will that it should become a universal law." The clearest example of an action whose maxim fails to pass Kant's test would be making a promise with the mental reservation that one will break it if it becomes inconvenient to keep. For everyone to act on that maxim would make promises impossible, since no one could believe them. In this case, Kant thought, the maxim cannot be universalized because it is actually self-contradictory.

How would a Kantian justify Mrs. Green's moral rule against racial discrimination, in terms of the first version of the Categorical Imperative? One possible Kantian line of thought here would be to ask whether a maxim like "Treat others as you would treat yourself only if they are of the same race as yourself" is universalizable. A Kantian might very well argue that it is not, because the person contemplating it wants to be treated fairly by others, even when they are not of the same race as himself—that is, he would not be willing to be on the receiving end of some actions required by this rule. Such an approach to the question is essentially like that taken by Kant in what he says about the duty to help others. The maxim "Help people in trouble only if it is agreeable or convenient to do so," Kant maintained, is not universalizable, because all of us want others to give us help when *we* need it. On Kant's view maxims like the two just cited are not actually self-contradictory, like the one about promises, but they still fail to pass the all-important universalizability test because we cannot will a state of affairs in which we might find ourselves deprived of fair treatment or of help.

Perhaps you are now reflecting that the line of justification just sketched is morally not very admirable. In fairness to Kant, a word should be added about what he called a second form of the Categorical Imperative, the principle that we should always treat human beings, whether ourselves or others, as ends, never merely as means. This principle, rightly respected and of considerable influence in the history of moral thought and practice, would seem to be much more helpful as a justification of a rule forbidding racial discrimination than the first form of the Categorical Imperative. But even those who have found much to admire in each of the two forms have often been puzzled by Kant's claim that they are equivalent —merely different ways of expressing the same principle.

Returning now to the first formulation of the Categorical Imperative and the concept of universalizability, let us note one or two of the chief objections that have been brought against Kant's theory. For one thing, critics have held that it fails to deal adequately with the problem of conflicting duties. What makes the Greens' problem about the swim club so poignant is precisely that it involves a conflict of duties. One who opposed racial discrimination but thought that staying in the swim club was the right thing to do could claim that this action falls under a universalizable maxim, "Help others in distress." (In this case, the distress would consist in being victims of discrimination.) Such an individual might go on to assert that resigning from the club, since it violates the maxim of helping others in distress, is wrong on Kantian grounds. Another way of putting essentially this same criticism is to point out that actions do not come plainly labelled as exemplifying only certain maxims and not others: every action can be described in innumerable different ways and shown to fall under many different maxims. This fact—one of the hard facts of the moral life—admittedly poses difficulties for other views than Kant's, but his view may be particularly vulnerable to criticism on these grounds.

Because an action can fall under more than one maxim, we may question whether Kant's Categorical Imperative is adequate to tell us, in a complicated situation, what action is right and what action is wrong. But if we consider the principle of universalizability as a test for maxims themselves, there is a great deal to be said for it. Maxims that *cannot* be universalized are *not* acceptable as moral rules. It is important to understand just what one is committed to in saying this. A universalizable maxim becomes an exceptionless rule, holding for all moral agents in all circumstances; but this does not mean that it must be simple. One may insist on universalizability as a test for acceptable maxims without adopting simple moral rules. Instead of "Never break promises," one could say, "Never break promises except under conditions A, B, or C." The latter rule is more complex, having limitations built into it; but it is no less exceptionless and universal than the simpler one. One who accepts the second rule will regard the first one as incomplete and perhaps he might say, "Well, sometimes it's right to violate it, and sometimes it's wrong." Thus, one who regards divorce as justifiable under certain conditions must say that the maxim "Never terminate a marriage by divorce" is not universalizable, but he could hold that the maxim "Never terminate a marriage by divorce unless the couple are childless" *is* universalizable.

Thus the objection to universalizability as a condition for acceptable moral maxims on the ground that the "same action" can be sometimes right and sometimes wrong is not warranted. Where it is possible for situational differences to make some actions of a certain broad kind right and others wrong, it is necessary to formulate a maxim sufficiently complex to take care of these facts. But once the maxim is formulated, it can't be both morally acceptable and not universalizable—and this is part, at least, of what Kant maintained. Anyone who insisted that it is morally permissible for him to cheat on his income tax return but not for his neighbor to do so, without being able to cite morally relevant differences between them, would be dismissed as irresponsible and capricious. It is interesting to note that Kant, who was keenly aware of the human inclination to make exceptions in one's own favor, held that when we succumb to the temptation to do this we do not actually adopt a nonuniversalizable maxim as a moral rule or law. On this point he wrote:

> When we observe ourselves in any transgression of a duty, we find that we do not actually will that our maxim should become a universal law. That is impossible for us; rather, the contrary of this maxim should remain as a law generally, and we only take the liberty of making an exception to it for ourselves or for the sake of our inclination, and for this one occasion.[1]

[1] *Foundations of the Metaphysics of Morals,* trans. by L. W. Beck (Chicago, University of Chicago Press, 1949), p. 83.

Perhaps the major part of moral education consists in learning to rise above the temptation to make such exceptions.

Most philosophers would agree, then, that universalizability of a maxim is indeed a *necessary* condition for its acceptability as a moral rule and that Kant did a great deal to help establish this important point. It is the further claim that a maxim's universalizability is a *sufficient* condition for accepting it as a moral rule (and Kant's theory is usually interpreted as including this claim also) that seems to lead to difficulties. One who holds that the maxim "Cheat on income tax returns whenever it is possible to get away with it" is not universalizable will doubtless not say that it should become a moral rule either. But may there not be individuals who would claim that they *can* consistently will that everyone follow this maxim? If someone makes this claim and gives every indication of living up to it in his own conduct, what reply can be made on Kantian grounds? Some Americans (possibly even some members of clubs like Sunnydale) appear to believe that they can consistently will that everyone act on the maxim "Treat others fairly only if they are of your own race." They would presumably trust to their own fortunate circumstances, backed up by custom and local institutions, to insure that they themselves would never be in a position to need fair treatment from anyone of another race. A maxim may thus be universalizable—in the sense that its propounder may believe that he can consistently will that everyone act on it—without being acceptable as a moral rule. What one may regard as universalizable another may not. Some philosophers would say that Kant's position can be defended against the kind of criticism just outlined, but there is at least an apparent difficulty here. We hope that you will have an opportunity to study Kant's philosophy with some care later on—including his ideas on epistemology and metaphysics as well as ethics.

We have been considering various monist deontological theories— theories that support judgments about the rightness or wrongness of actions by reference to a single basic moral rule. In this kind of theory, it is assumed that actions are right if and only if they are approved by God, or if and only if they are legal, or if and only if their rules are universalizable. We must now look briefly at pluralist deontological theories.

Mrs. Green herself, it happens, is really a pluralist deontologist (though she did not know the name for her view until young Susan Jones thoughtfully supplied her with it). What Mrs. Green first said, when asked why racial discrimination is wrong, was that this is a foolish question. Then after a moment she added, "No, it's not really a foolish question, I guess, though there certainly isn't much I can say about it. I think racial discrimination is wrong because it is a kind of injustice. We ought to treat people equally. But what can we say beyond that? I suppose if I had studied philosophy I would know something more to say, but as it is I don't. There are a lot of things that are just wrong, and not treating people equally is one of them." Despite her apologetic tone, Mrs. Green has expressed here a view that is philosophically quite respectable. Many modern deontologists would say that the rule that people should be treated as equals, given equal consideration and equal opportunity, is indeed an ultimate, end-of-the-line moral rule. And many would agree with Mrs. Green that several moral rules have this same status. A particularly influential deontologist who has defended a pluralist position is W. D. Ross.

Ross does not believe that it is possible to find a single ultimate moral rule underlying all others. Nor does he believe that any moral rule can be said to be binding on us no matter what. Ross developed the concept of what he calls *"prima facie* duties." These are conditional rules of moral obligation, each of which tells us what we ought to do, other things being equal, or what we ought to do if there is no other *prima facie* rule to supersede it in a given situation. The possibility of a conflict of duties, which presents such a problem to Kant's more rigid theory, is accepted and even emphasized by Ross. Each of Ross's rules is, as a conditional rule, exceptionless; but as an absolute rule each would have exceptions. Two of Ross's six rules of *prima facie* duty are that promises should be kept (other things being equal) and that other persons should not be injured (other things being equal). Clearly rules like these will often conflict—as when keeping a promise to one person causes injury to another. When this happens, we must simply judge as best we can what ought to be done in the concrete situation before us. In Ross's particular form of pluralist deontological theory, there is no second-order rule to give us an order of priority for following the rules of *prima facie* duty. Every conflict of obligations, like the Greens' moral dilemma, must be resolved by weighing the respective claims of all the *prima facie* duties relevant to that particular situation.

Critics of Ross object to his theory because it cannot tell us what to do: whether, for example, the Greens should or should not resign. Ross makes a number of points in answer to this charge, especially the point that, although one could devise a simpler theory with fewer or more binding rules, such a theory would lack the "loyalty to the facts" of the moral life that his own has. His theory, he would say, can tell the Greens what basic moral questions they should raise; but only the thoughtful examination of their situation in all its concrete detail can give the answer.

There is one member of the Green household whom we have not yet heard speak his mind. This is the Greens' son, Mary's older brother Tom, who is nineteen and a college classmate of Susan Jones. Tom has given more thought to the problem than the other Greens (and, like Susan, he has had the advantage of a course in ethics). Let us see how Tom responds to the problem at hand.

Tom agrees with his mother that the central consideration in this difficult situation is one of justice, but he thinks that this very consideration leads to the conclusion that the family should stay in the club. Where he thinks his mother has made a mistake, he says, is in taking too narrow a view of what it is to treat others equally. "The rule to treat others equally,"

Tom maintains, "can't be looked at as applying only to our behavior in immediate personal relationships with others. Mother is right in insisting that it applies also to our indirect dealings with them through organizations, such as the swim club. But even this is not all that is involved. It's not enough to think of organizations and institutions as they are now constituted. The obligation to treat others equally includes an obligation to *change* patterns of social behavior in the direction of providing equal treatment. Seems to me the pro-resignation people, who are so worried about doing something discriminatory, have lost sight of this broader implication of the obligation to treat people justly. By resigning and missing out on a chance to change the policy of Sunnydale and perhaps indirectly other organizations of various kinds, those who resign are going to be guilty of a mighty big sin of omission. I think we should stay in and work, at least for a year."

This young man is strongly attracted to philosophical thinking, and he can't help reflecting on further questions about the obligation to treat people equally. It seems clear to him that this does not mean treating everyone exactly alike, but only providing equality of opportunity or giving equality of consideration, as far as the distribution of good is concerned. Tom also wonders about another problem: whether the obligation to treat people equally—the principle of distributive justice—can be supported by utilitarian reasoning. He sees that an act-utilitarian would have difficulty in defending an adherence to distributive justice, because situations can easily be imagined (and constantly arise in life) where a greater total quantity of good can be produced if the good is distributed unequally rather than equally. Suppose that the vote in the Sunnydale Club had been 400 to 85 against the open admissions policy (and Tom thinks this might easily happen in some of the suburbs near where he lives). It could then be maintained with plausibility that to admit black applicants would cause more unhappiness than to exclude them—yet Tom is convinced that exclusion would still be wrong. But could the principle of distributive justice be given a rule-utilitarian justification? Tom is inclined to believe that this would not be possible either. Adopting the principle of distributive justice would usually produce the best results for the society, no doubt; but what if it didn't? What if the general adoption of a *different* rule for distributing good would produce more good? Tom thinks that the obligation to maximize good results (the principle of utility) might point in one direction and the obligation to distribute good equally might point in another, even on a rule-utilitarian view. Accordingly, he is inclined to favor a deontological theory of moral obligation, which would include the obligation to maximize good, and the obligation to distribute it equally, and perhaps a third principle, to take care of considerations of deserts (reward and punishment). But he resolves not to make up his mind prematurely or dogmatically on these difficult fundamental questions about moral obligation —and we hope that readers of this chapter will follow his example.

Coming back to the Sunnydale Club again, we may report that the Greens have been able to reach a unanimous decision to remain members for at least a year. Mrs. Green, the only family member who had favored resigning, changed her mind after she heard Tom's argument.

But, though the Greens have finally agreed, their basic reasons continue to be different. Mr. Green remains an act-utilitarian, while Mrs. Green and Tom are deontologists. Mary finds Mr. Foster's ethical egoism less persuasive than she used to, but cannot really be said to have an explicit theory of moral obligation yet. The relations between particular moral judgments and the basic theories that support them are complex. Some general theories of obligation permit normative variations within them: for example, two people might both be pluralist deontologists but differ as to which rules have superiority in case of conflict, or as to whether there are any second-order rules at all. But the main reason why we cannot assume that those who hold the same theories of moral obligation will agree on judgments about a particular action, or vice versa, is that another extremely important variable is present: that is, the set of relevant factual beliefs held by the individual in question. For example, the Greens all believed that there was at least a reasonably good chance that a number of swim club members could be induced to change their minds about the club's policy within a year's time. Some of those who resigned, on the other hand, believed that human attitudes on such questions are rigid and unyielding. This factual belief about an empirical question played an important part in the ethical views of swim club members; and other relevant factual beliefs could be cited as well.

Emotions ran high in the Greens' community while the Sunnydale issue was being resolved. For a time there was noticeable hostility between supporters and opponents of an open admission policy, and even between those supporters of open admission who stayed in the club and those who resigned. The Greens soon saw that they could not approve or disapprove of their fellow members purely on the grounds of the action they decided on. Some of those who resigned seemed to be very much concerned with their own moral "images": the plight of the Blakes and Nelsons and other victims of discrimination seemed to be forgotten in a kind of self-conscious rectitude. It was almost as if these people were "playing a part" of a "good citizen," exhibiting what the existentialist writer Jean-Paul Sartre has so vividly described as *"mauvais foi."* On the other hand, one family who had voted for open admission but stayed in the club seemed pretty clearly to have their own interests predominantly in mind in making their decision. The Greens realized, more clearly than they had before, that questions of the rightness or wrongness of acts and questions of the moral praiseworthiness or blameworthiness of agents are different (though related) questions. This distinction showed up with particular force in connection with people who, in resigning, had done something the Greens thought wrong, but who had quite obviously acted conscientiously in so doing. "Our friends the Mortons wanted to do the right thing, and thought they were," Mrs. Green remarked, "and we can't blame people who do what they honestly believe is right." Tom Green and Susan Jones were delighted to put their ethics course to use once more. "What the Mortons did," they explained, "is in your judgment *objectively wrong.* But it was *subjectively right,* in the sense that they themselves thought it was right. Subjective rightness in an objectively wrong action protects the agent from moral disapproval." The Greens recognized also that, from the Mortons' point of view, their own action of staying in the club had been, though subjectively right, objectively wrong.

It may have seemed to you that we have not sufficiently stressed the importance of doing what one thinks is right, of following one's conscience. You may be inclined to feel that, had you been called on to advise any of the Greens, you would have said, "Just do whatever you yourself think you ought to do." But would this really have been very helpful? The morally perplexed person asking for advice is trying to figure out what is right: he doesn't know. The concept of subjective rightness has an important place in the theory of moral value; and conscientious desires, desires to do what is right just because it *is* right, are properly much admired. Kant, indeed, held that this is the only motive possessing moral value; he held that a desire to perform an action from self-interest, or for the love of another person, or even for the love of God, is lacking in moral worth. Questions concerning the grounds for moral approval and disapproval of persons and the standards used for making judgments of moral approval and disapproval are among the most interesting in ethics. They belong, however, to the theory of moral value, which we cannot discuss further here.

We hope that enough has been said to convey a sense of the complexity that characterizes many concrete moral problems and of the number of well-thought-out theories that support particular judgments of moral obligation. It is time now to turn to questions about nonmoral value and to see what the major views are in this second area of normative ethics. We shall find Sunnydale Swim Club members occasionally turning up in that discussion too.

WHAT MAKES GOOD THINGS GOOD?

At the beginning of this chapter, we saw how questions about the rightness or wrongness of actions lead naturally into questions about the goodness or badness of objects or states of affairs—the production of good results seems somehow closely tied up with the rightness of actions. Accordingly, those who adopt a teleological theory of moral obligation, whether ethical egoists or act-utilitarians or rule-utilitarians, all quickly encounter the question "What things *are* good?" And we must remember that most deontologists also hold (like Ross, but unlike Kant) that there is an obligation to produce good results, though there are other obligations as well. One who provides himself with a theory of moral obligation and does not work out a theory of nonmoral value to go with it is not going to be able to give very complete justifications for his answers to moral problems. And he will be unable to give reasons for his basic choices of life patterns.

Philosophers have distinguished a number of uses for the slippery word "good," but for our present purposes it is satisfactory to regard it as equivalent to "desirable" or "worthwhile." The question what makes good things good then becomes the question what makes desirable things desirable. This narrows its scope somewhat, but the question may still afflict you with considerable dismay. Do we have to survey the entire range of desirable things to answer it? Most philosophers would say No—that what we really want to find out is what things are desirable *for their own sake* and what makes them so. This distinction, between things that are desirable for their own sake and things that are desirable for the sake of something else to which they are means, is the distinction between things that have *intrinsic value* and things that have *instrumental value*. And a parallel distinction can be made, among undesirable things, between those that have *intrinsic disvalue* and those that have *instrumental disvalue*.

For some reason it has become customary for teachers to use a painful experience suffered in the dentist's chair as an example of something that has no intrinsic value (in fact, has intrinsic disvalue) but that has instrumental value, as a means to freedom from pain over the long run. A satisfactory example could be drawn just as well from the area of mental suffering or discomfort. What about the unpleasantness of studying under pressure for examinations? If someone asked you why you subject yourself to this sort of thing (and if the question came between examination periods, so that your perspective on the matter was in good working order), you might say, at first, that you do it to earn high grades. But why high grades? To have a better chance at a good job, or for graduate school. What's the point of graduate school? At this stage in the inquiry it becomes more difficult to predict what you would say, for answers would vary. Take, for example, our students Tom Green and Susan Jones, now sophomores, who look ahead to some sort of study after college. Susan has decided to major in sociology and plans to enter a school of social work, with a view to training for group work with underprivileged children. Why do this? To bring pleasure into their lives, she replies. But what good is pleasure? Here Susan draws a line: pleasure, she will tell you firmly, is desirable for its own sake, an intrinsic value. "And it's the *only* intrinsic value," she adds.

Tom, on the other hand, is a philosophy major, and hopes to do graduate work in philosophy. This choice on Tom's part leaves Susan somewhat impatient. "I like philosophy too," she assures him; "but I don't see why you want to spend your life doing it. What *good* is it? Once in a while you can use it to help somebody with a problem, the way I did when I told my uncle about rule-utilitarianism and act-utilitarianism, and made him feel better. But in general it really is pretty useless. I don't see how it's going to make the world a happier place." Tom is unmoved. His reply is that it doesn't *have* to make anybody happier. "I enjoy philosophy, sure, but that isn't my real reason for studying it. I just think it's important to get answers to the questions philosophers are dealing with, and I think I can help figure out some answers. Knowledge doesn't have to lead on to anything else. It's worthwhile in itself." Tom, as you see, holds that knowledge is an intrinsic value.

There are two points to notice here. One is that the difference between these two students is not merely a difference in what they *do* desire for its own sake, but a difference in what they think is *worthy* of being desired for its own sake. But, second, it is important to see exactly where the difference lies. Tom has not denied that pleasure *is* intrinsically valuable; he asserts only that it is not the *sole* intrinsic value. Knowledge, in his judgment, has the same status.

Not all philosophers have regarded the distinction between intrinsic and instrumental value as fundamental. One who has attacked this distinction is John Dewey, whose ethical theory has been called "instrumentalism," to mark the fact that Dewey holds that no values are intrinsic. In his view, the value of anything depends on its relationships to other things, its conditions and consequences. The majority view among ethical theorists, however, has been against instrumentalism. They would argue that if anything is desirable at all, that must be because something is intrinsically desirable. When we ask fundamental questions about a belief that X is desirable, the justification of this belief seems in the end to require either the statement that X is desirable for its own sake, or that it is, directly or indirectly, a means to Y, which is desirable for its own sake. Otherwise, the belief about the desirability of X is unanchored.

It is convenient to distinguish, among theories of intrinsic value, between monist theories and pluralist ones. Any theory that holds that there is only one kind of object or state of affairs having intrinsic value is monist; others are pluralist. The most important monist theory, indeed the most influential of all theories of intrinsic value, maintains that pleasure is the only intrinsic value, or, more accurately, that the quality of pleasantness is what makes anything desirable in itself. This is the position of *ethical hedonism*. Susan Jones revealed herself, by her remarks about her choice of a major in college, as an ethical hedonist.

§ 3. • *Are All Pleasures Good?*

Leading philosophers who have supported ethical hedonism include Epicurus, the third-century B.C. Greek thinker whose name has passed into our language through the word "epicurean," and the great utilitarians Bentham and Mill. Some writers define "utilitarianism" to include the thesis of ethical hedonism as one of its tenets; but it makes for greater clarity to broaden the term "utilitarianism," as we have done in this chapter, to apply to any universalist teleological theory of moral obligation, no matter what theory of value goes along with it. The position of Bentham and Mill can then be identified as hedonistic utilitarianism. We can now see that this is also the position taken by Mr. Green, who supported his view that the family should stay in the swim club and work to change its policy by saying that this would in the long run make more people happy. Although the concepts of pleasure and happiness are not identical, we may take it that they overlap sufficiently to be equated for present purposes.

We shall center our discussion of questions about intrinsic value around the theory of ethical hedonism. The strengths and weaknesses of several positions can be brought out in this way. Ethical hedonism has opponents as well as defenders, but even the opponents would doubtless agree that, in the competition among theories of nonmoral value, ethical hedonism is the one to beat.

Before we discuss this theory, however, some possible sources of confusion must be eliminated. Students sometimes say, on encountering ethical hedonism, that they do not see how any view based on something as vague and hard to pin down as pleasure can be very satisfactory. They seem to have two points in mind here. One is the fact that people find pleasure in different ways—that we vary somewhat, perhaps a great deal, in the experiences that we find pleasant. There seems to be a suspicion that this variability may rob the word "pleasure" of meaning. But the ethical hedonist does not deny that people find pleasure in different ways. He claims only that this need not prevent intersubjective communication about the experienced quality of pleasantness. Secondly, there is the charge that it is very difficult to know what someone else will find pleasant or when he is experiencing pleasure, and that any view that includes an obligation to produce pleasure for others as well as oneself will be in difficulty. Here the ethical hedonist is apt to deny that the alleged "facts" are really facts. Granted that we do not always know what others will find pleasant; still, we often know. And granted that we sometimes make mistakes in judging that another person is experiencing pleasure; we often do not. Some writers emphasize that pleasant experiences are usually experiences that we try to have continued and that unpleasant experiences are experiences that we try to end as soon as possible. Thus there can be a behavioral criterion of another person's pleasures.

Ethical hedonists say essentially three things: (1) that *all* experiences of pleasure are intrinsically desirable; (2) that *only* experiences of pleasure are intrinsically desirable; and (3) that although concrete experiences of pleasure will have other qualities as well as pleasantness, it is their pleasantness that *makes* them intrinsically desirable. Many philosophers, though not all, have held that thesis (3) entails that the amount or degree of intrinsic value of an experience depends on the amount or degree of its pleasantness.

Ethical hedonists also maintain that unpleasantness and unpleasant experiences (experiences one would seek to avoid) stand in the same relation to intrinsic disvalue as pleasantness and pleasant experiences to intrinsic value. Hedonists differ as to whether they emphasize as the goal of life the securing of the positive quality of pleasantness or the avoiding of the negative quality of unpleasantness. Unlike Bentham and Mill, Epicurus placed his emphasis on the latter: for him pain and mental turmoil were the great evils and the important thing was to avoid them. This was best accomplished, Epicurus thought, by two measures. One is to learn the truth about the world—that it is made up of atoms and the void, and that survival after death is impossible. By this knowledge the mind is freed from religious superstitions and the horrible legends of life after death. The other measure is to live very modestly, permitting oneself to develop and to satisfy only very simple desires. It is an irony of the history of thought that the term "epicureanism" in popular language should have come to stand for a way of life so different from that actually taught by this ancient apostle of moderation.

The thesis that all experiences of pleasure are, as such, intrinsically desirable is a compelling one. You may wonder whether it has ever been doubted or denied. If we consider the logical contrary of this proposition, the claim that no pleasures are intrinsically valuable, or the even stronger claim that all pleasures are intrinsically disvaluable, we shall probably look in vain for supporters. Bentham expended few words on what he called the "principle of asceticism" (the principle claiming that pleasure is something to be avoided and pain is something to be sought). He dismissed it thus:

> The principle of asceticism never was, nor ever can be, consistently pursued by any living creature. Let but one tenth part of the inhabitants of this earth pursue it consistently, and in a day's time they will have turned it into a hell.[2]

Some might argue that the spirit of Puritan morality, with its grave suspicion of pleasurable activities, did come close to turning portions of early American society into a hell. Although one cannot maintain that the Puritans held consistently to the view that pleasure is bad, there was some approximation to this; and traces of the same attitude survive today in the view that it is better for children not to enjoy the learning process in school too much. The pattern of life of the ancient Stoics also exhibited a turning away from pleasure. In one plausible interpretation of the Stoics' ethical outlook, however, their search for a state of mind impervious to whatever

---

[2] *An Introduction to the Principles of Morals and Legislation,* chap. 2; *Works* (New York, Russell and Russell, 1962), Vol. I, p. 6.

befalls was motivated by the feeling that pleasure, though desirable, is too uncertain to be counted on.

The contradictory of the first hedonist thesis—the statement that some pleasures are not intrinsically desirable—would seem to have a much better chance of being substantiated than the "principle of asceticism." Can we find any examples of pleasures that are not desirable for their own sake? It has been argued that cruel and undeserved pleasures fall into such a category. Let us see what the hedonist would reply.

Simon Legree, whipping Uncle Tom, has often been cited as the prototype of a man who cruelly enjoys the pain of another. But we need not turn to nineteenth-century fiction; twentieth-century fact will provide us with updated examples, such as brutal guards in concentration camps. The ethical hedonist repudiates any suggestion that his theory of value requires him to admire or even condone any such behavior as this. He hastens to make several points in reply. First, this behavior is wrong, because it is wrong to cause pain. Second, the trait of taking pleasure in others' pain is morally reprehensible in the highest degree. But third, the pleasure taken by Simon Legree and other sadistic individuals *is,* considered simply as pleasure, intrinsically good. It is instrumentally bad, so bad as to be undesirable, all things considered. The goodness of Legree's pleasure is a small part in a complex whose other components are sufficient to make the whole undesirable; but this consideration should not, the hedonist claims, be permitted to obscure the fact that, *as pleasure,* it is good.

Undeserved pleasures would be dealt with in essentially the same way. These are pleasures that come to agents as a result of actions for which they deserve moral disapproval. As pleasure, the glee that the unapprehended burglar feels at the sight of his loot is desirable, though we feel additional moral disapproval toward him for experiencing it. Nor would it be right, the ethical hedonist holds, to *confer* pleasure as a reward for wrong actions. (If he is a utilitarian, the hedonist will have to justify the meting out of rewards and punishments entirely on the grounds of beneficial results, which may present him with some additional problems; but these are not part of our present concern.) The occurrence of cruel or undeserved pleasures, then, does not seem to refute the hedonist—he argues that his critics have simply confused several different ethical questions: (1) whether an experience is desirable, (2) whether an action is right, and (3) whether a person, trait, or motive deserves moral approval. But above all, he says, the critics have failed to distinguish carefully between intrinsic and instrumental value. Something having intrinsic value can be a part of a complex whole that has a very high degree of instrumental disvalue, and this is the case with the alleged counterexamples.

The thesis that not all pleasures are intrinsically desirable is sometimes supported by the argument that pleasures experienced too long become tedious: we become surfeited. If pleasant experiences were really desirable for their own sake, how could it be possible to have too much of a good thing? A newspaper columnist writes, apropos of the Florida vacationland:

> There is a lot to be said for fun and comfort, but total fun and total comfort wind up by being total bores, and in the process pleasure is lost.[3]

But here again the hedonist will point out that his critic (not Mr. Baker) has mixed up intrinsic and instrumental value. What has happened when we become bored today with what brought us pleasure yesterday (say, eating shrimp salad) is just that it no longer brings us pleasure today. It is not that an experience, though still pleasant, has lost its desirability; it is that it has lost its pleasantness. And if human beings are so constituted that they need a certain amount of variety in their experiences, fine. This does not mean that variety is itself an intrinsic value; but it may be an important instrumental one.

Related to this consideration is the charge that pleasure cannot be won if pursued too directly, that it must be found as a by-product of other activities. If all pleasures are intrinsically desirable, the critic maintains, then it would seem to follow that we should seek to maximize them, that we should seek pleasure, for others of course, but at times also for ourselves. But seeking pleasure directly, for oneself at least, doesn't work out very well. If you go to a party and keep asking yourself, "Am I having a good time? Am I enjoying myself to the full?" you will have very little fun. Isn't there something strange about a goal that cannot be directly sought? This feature of the search for pleasure is called the "hedonistic paradox." Hedonists readily agree that seeking pleasure for oneself is *not* very successful if done in the style described. It is true, they admit, that pleasure is obtained best if one becomes absorbed in some other activity. But surely the wise ethical hedonist (not having been born yesterday) knows how to manage his occupations so as to combine a general strategy of seeking pleasure with tactics of forgetting about it temporarily. If certain measures are really necessary for obtaining pleasure for oneself, let them by all means be used. And of course any hedonist who is not an ethical egoist will remind us that the "hedonistic paradox" does not apply to seeking to maximize pleasure for others.

§ 4. • *Are Only Pleasures Good?*

Critics of ethical hedonism may feel that they are occupying better-fortified positions when they object to the second plank in their opponent's platform: the assertion that *only* experiences of pleasure are intrinsically valuable. Is anything *other* than an experience of pleasure desirable for its own sake? If so, the antihedonists have won the day.

[3] Russell Baker in *The New York Times,* August 9, 1964.

Before we see how a critic of hedonism might proceed to find a counterexample here, let us take note of an argument offered by many ethical hedonists in support of their position. "Don't bother to search for examples of things other than pleasant experiences that are desirable," the ethical hedonist announces. "This is a futile quest. Human beings are so constituted as to be psychologically incapable of desiring anything other than pleasure, and when they desire anything at all, it is for the sake of its pleasantness." The view that pleasure is the object of every human desire is *psychological hedonism*. It is not necessary for an ethical hedonist to claim that his view is *entailed* by psychological hedonism. He can still argue that it is *supported* by it, on the ground that there would be no point in holding something other than pleasantness to be worthy of being desired for its own sake, if it cannot be. You will notice here the similarity between the procedure of using psychological hedonism to bolster up ethical hedonism and the procedure of using psychological egoism to bolster up ethical egoism, which we discussed earlier in this chapter.

The idea of supporting ethical hedonism by psychological hedonism is an ancient one in the history of ethical theory. We find Epicurus saying,

> We call pleasure the alpha and omega of a blessed life. Pleasure is our first and kindred good. It is the starting-point of every choice and of every aversion.[4]

But the thesis of psychological hedonism itself has been repeatedly attacked. Many philosophers have sided on this issue with the eighteenth-century English bishop and philosopher Joseph Butler, whose criticisms of psychological egoism and psychological hedonism have become classics. Butler argued that each human being has many desires, including a generalized desire for his own happiness, and an enormous variety of particular desires for external objects or states of affairs. Given a desire for some external thing, a man will receive pleasure from having this desire satisfied, but without the pre-existing desire, there would be no pleasure. Thus, unless something besides pleasure is desired for its own sake, pleasure could not occur at all. Many contemporary philosophers would maintain that Butler's refutation of psychological hedonism (as well as the more general thesis of psychological egoism) can still stand.

But, even if the support offered by psychological hedonism to ethical hedonism is shaky, the challenge to produce an example of something intrinsically good other than pleasure remains. This challenge has been met in a number of different ways; in a moment we shall select one or two of these for discussion. Before that, however, we should take note of an important difference between two forms of ethical hedonism: the position of Bentham and that of Mill. Bentham defended what is usually called *quantitative hedonism*. He held that pleasantness is what makes anything intrinsi-

---

[4] From Diogenes Laertius, *Lives of Eminent Philosophers,* Book X, p. 129; trans. by R. D. Hicks (London, Heinemann, 1925), Vol. II, p. 655.

cally valuable and that quantity of pleasantness determines its degree of value. He even proposed a "hedonistic calculus," by which quantities of pleasure could be compared, in terms of intensity, duration, and other aspects. Bentham's pronouncement that, pleasure for pleasure, pushpin (a simple table game) is as good as poetry has come to be the slogan of the quantitative hedonist. If a Popeye cartoon gives a greater total quantity of pleasure than a Picasso drawing, Popeye is better, and that is all there is to it.

Mill, sensitive to the charge that the emphasis on pleasure in Bentham's version of utilitarianism rendered it a "doctrine worthy of swine," set out to rescue the view from this attack. The position that he himself set forth was still teleological and universalist in its theory of obligation, and still hedonist, so its author claimed, in its theory of value. The only difference was that Mill introduced a distinction between "higher" (mental) pleasures and "lower" (bodily) pleasures. This was spoken of by Mill as a distinction among pleasures on qualitative grounds, so that his view has come to be known as *qualitative hedonism.* And the slogan for *this* position is Mill's impassioned declaration that "it is better to be a human being dissatisfied than a pig satisfied; better to be Socrates dissatisfied than a fool satisfied."[5]

Many interesting psychological and philosophical questions are raised by Mill's qualitative hedonism and by the way in which he argued for it. The most fundamental question for us to consider here is this: is qualitative hedonism still hedonism? Many philosophers have argued that, by ranking some pleasures as more desirable than others by nonquantitative criteria, Mill was actually smuggling in one or more other standards, unspecified ones. Mill can still say, and does say, that all pleasures are intrinsically desirable and even that only pleasures are intrinsically desirable. But, if his critics are right, his so-called higher pleasures are complexes containing not only pleasantness, but something else, an unnamed ingredient that contributes to their over-all desirability. Thus Mill may not be entitled to stand on the third plank in the hedonist's platform: the thesis that it is the pleasantness of pleasures that makes them desirable. In the case of the pleasures of the intellect, something else evidently contributes to their value, and we very naturally want to know what this is. So-called "qualitative hedonism" is thus unmasked, if its critics are right, as harboring within itself the seeds of treason to a truly consistent hedonist theory. But consistency is not the only desideratum in an ethical theory; and it may be that Mill, faithful to hedonism or not, had insights that should be preserved.

We are now ready to consider theories that explicitly deny hedonism and that put forward candidates other than pleasure as having intrinsic

---

[5] *Utilitarianism,* chap. 2 (New York, Dutton Everyman's Library, 1951), p. 12.

value. Some of these alternatives to hedonism are monist, maintaining that only one thing is desirable for its own sake, such as power, or a certain relationship to God. In some ways, the most significant monist alternative to hedonism has been the theory of self-realization. Under this label, many rather loosely related positions have been grouped, all having in common the claim that the only thing desirable for its own sake is the development by a human being of his best capacities or faculties. In Aristotle's version of this view, it is the exercising of reason that is of intrinsic value. Aristotle, who made the category of purpose central in his philosophy, held that if we can determine the distinctive purpose or function of man, then we will know what man should seek as the intrinsically desirable end. An inventory of man's powers shows, Aristotle argued, that he shares the faculties of growth and nutrition with other organic beings, and sensation with other animals, but the ability to reason belongs to man alone. Since this is unique to man, it must be his true purpose or function, and rational activity is therefore the one ultimate end for human beings to pursue. It can be pursued in two ways, through the life of moral virtue and the life of intellectual virtue. The latter is higher, partly because more self-sufficient, and the supreme end for man is pure contemplation. Aristotle equates rational activity with a kind of satisfaction usually referred to as "happiness" in English translations; but he explicitly distinguishes between this and pleasure, and it would be seriously misleading to classify his view as a form of hedonism. Indeed, Aristotle's careful analysis of the strengths and weaknesses of hedonism remains unsurpassed.

No brief comments on Aristotle's position can do justice to its full power, and there is no substitute for reading his great work on ethics for yourself. But one or two questions must be raised here. The inference drawn by Aristotle from the premise that reasoning is a function *unique* to man to the conclusion that its exercise is therefore *worthy* of being desired for its own sake has often been attacked. There are obviously many activities that man alone performs, and writers have vied with each other to cite bizarre examples: laughing, doing crossword puzzles, playing baseball, mixing cocktails, etc. Such examples, it is claimed, provide a *reductio ad absurdum* of the view that uniqueness is a reliable clue to value. Critics allege that what Aristotle was really doing was like what Mill has been accused of doing—smuggling in a standard by which rational activity is judged to be of great, and intrinsic, value, but not telling us what this standard is.

We turn now to pluralist theories of nonmoral value, among which we find the most explicitly formulated alternatives to hedonism. An ethical pluralist has the advantage of being able to admit, if he wishes, that pleasure *is* intrinsically valuable, while insisting that it is not the *only* intrinsic value. What other candidates have been proposed? There have been many; but perhaps the strongest case can be made for knowledge. We have already seen that Tom Green, in the course of arguing for his decision to major in philosophy, said that he regarded knowledge as desirable for its own sake. How could this view be defended?

One method is that used by W. D. Ross, whom we have already encountered as a deontologist, and who also developed a pluralist theory of intrinsic value. Ross invites his readers to perform a mental experiment: to imagine two states of the universe equal in respect of one characteristic admitted to be intrinsically valuable, but unequal with regard to another characteristic—that is, to imagine that state 1 and state 2 of the universe are equal with respect to characteristic A, but that state 1 has more of characteristic B. If state 1 is judged better than state 2, then characteristic B has intrinsic value. Let us imagine two states of the universe in which there is an equal amount of pleasure enjoyed by the inhabitants, but an unequal amount of knowledge. In state 1 the persons have a greater scientific understanding of their surroundings and themselves than in state 2. Would we not all have to agree, Ross asks, that state 1 is better, more worthy of being desired? Therefore knowledge is itself intrinsically valuable.

Ethical hedonists will object strenuously to what they take to be the artificial conditions of this kind of experiment. They will charge that the conditions cannot hold. Knowledge, they will claim, is indeed desirable, but only as a means to the greater pleasure that it brings either to the knower or to others, or both. Where there is more knowledge, there will be more pleasure, and consequently Ross's experiment cannot be carried out, for we cannot imagine states equal in knowledge but unequal in pleasure. But the Rossian has a reply. "Even if I were to admit, as I do not," he says, "that it is impossible for there to be more knowledge without more pleasure as a consequence, this impossibility is not a *logical* one. Surely a hedonist does not *define* knowledge in terms of pleasure. And so, since anything except a logical impossibility can be envisaged or conceived, I must insist that you try my experiment. If you do, you will see that even if it were the case that knowledge always *produces* pleasure, the *value* of knowledge does not depend on the *value* of pleasure."

To the charge that knowledge is not intrinsically desirable because we sometimes think it bad for someone to know a certain fact (for a dangerously ill man to know the truth of his own condition), a philosopher like Ross has a ready answer. In cases like these, he will say, knowledge has an instrumental disvalue outweighing its positive intrinsic value. But since this circumstance does not *remove* the positive intrinsic value, the alleged counterexample fails.

In trying to make up your own mind on the question whether knowledge is intrinsically desirable, there are many matters about which you will want to think further. One is the value of your study of philosophy and of your education generally. Take the issue between W. K. Clifford, who held that it is always wrong to believe without sufficient evidence, and William

James, who held that we are sometimes justified in believing without evidence if evidence is unattainable and the consequences of believing are desirable. It might be illuminating to consider the bearing on this issue of the question whether knowledge is desirable for its own sake. Even though strict logical connections may not be present here, it is perhaps likely that one who regards knowledge as intrinsically valuable will be attracted more strongly to Clifford's position than to James's. As the noted twentieth-century British philosopher G. E. Moore (an ethical pluralist and utilitarian) wrote,

> Those . . . who have a strong respect for truth, are inclined to think that a merely poetical contemplation of the Kingdom of Heaven *would* be superior to that of the religious believer, *if* it were the case that the Kingdom of Heaven does not and will not really exist.[6]

Clifford might have wished to add a word of caution here, lest what begins as "poetic contemplation" should slip over into unwarranted belief.

We cannot discuss here the other objects or states that have been held by one or more nonhedonists to be intrinsically valuable. Some of these are, like pleasure and knowledge, states of conscious beings: love, virtue, the admiration of beautiful objects. Others are impersonal: truth, beauty, the just distribution of goods. We should note that *if* the just distribution of goods can be regarded as possessing intrinsic value, then it can be treated as a result, and a teleological theory of moral obligation can perhaps be preserved. At least, on such a view the strongest objection to utilitarianism—that it cannot account for the principle of distributive justice—would be removed. But some philosophers have argued very convincingly that only *experiences* can be said to be intrinsically good, not something impersonal like a pattern of distribution. If they are correct, the obligation to act justly remains a rule that cannot be justified by reference to results.

The choice of a theory of value, like the choice of a theory of moral obligation, is truly difficult. Certainly the theory of ethical hedonism has many highly persuasive features, not least of which are the comparative clarity with which it can be formulated and its logical simplicity. We have tried to show that there are, in addition to its genuine advantages, some difficulties. One objection often raised, however, does not seem justified. This is the charge that although quantitative hedonism requires us to estimate comparative amounts of pleasure in quantitative terms, such calculation is either extraordinarily difficult or impossible. In answer to this, two things need to be said. First, we do make implicit judgments about the comparative amount of pleasure to be gained, by ourselves or others, in innumerable choices of everyday life. And, second, other theories of value face the difficulty of having to compare amounts of whatever is taken to be intrinsically desirable. For a pluralist theory, indeed, it will presumably be

[6] *Principia Ethica* (London, Cambridge University Press, 1903), p. 195.

necessary to compare amounts of knowledge, say, with amounts of pleasure or virtue, not merely amounts of pleasure with amounts of pleasure. Some pluralists may prefer to say that each intrinsic value has a *prima facie* goodness, leaving judgments of priorities to be worked out in concrete situations for actual choices, rather than to set up any general blueprint for arbitrating between competing claims.

In concluding this discussion of theories of nonmoral value, it is in order to say something about their practical implications. As we saw in considering theories of moral obligation, the connection between a basic theory and a given judgment about a particular action is not a simple one-one correlation. The same statement can be made about theories of value. It would be possible to justify a concrete choice—say Tom Green's decision to major in philosophy—without believing that knowledge is intrinsically valuable. A hedonist, for example, who believed that knowledge has a very high instrumental value, could argue with some plausibility (you must decide for yourself how much) that the study of philosophy will contribute substantially to the sum of pleasure in the world. Factual beliefs —most especially beliefs about means-end relationships—combine with normative beliefs about intrinsic value to determine our judgments about the desirability of particular objects or states. Fundamental metaphysical beliefs about the nature of reality may also play an important part here. For example, two hedonists may make very different choices of how to spend their time if one is a naturalistic humanist and the other a theist who also believes that there is a world to come whose bliss will infinitely surpass the pleasures of this world. Finally, some theories of value permit, within their own framework, a certain amount of variation in normative judgments. Two people may both be ethical pluralists without having the same conception of value-priorities among their intrinsic values, or without agreeing that there must be rules of priority at all.

Still, our basic theories of value are an important determinant of our concrete choices, and particularly, as we suggested earlier, of those choices which affect so many other choices: decisions on vocations and policies to pursue within those vocations; decisions on whom to marry, on how to bring up children, on what kind of social goals to support. It is in these decisions that we seem to discern most clearly the effect of basic beliefs about values.

Mr. Green, whose son Tom is an ethical pluralist, is himself a hedonist, and Mr. Jones, whose niece Susan is a hedonist, is himself an ethical pluralist. Jones is particularly firm in his conviction that aesthetic experiences of certain kinds are intrinsically desirable. Both Green and Jones are television executives with some power to make policy and to choose the kinds of programs that are shown in their area, which has no educational television channel. As you might expect, Mr. Jones seeks to develop more programs that have artistic merit, though they are appreciated by relatively few viewers, while Mr. Green is impatient with this aim. The main social responsibility of their station, Green insists, is to bring as much pleasure to as many people as possible. True to the principle that equates pushpin with poetry, Mr. Green supports the choice of westerns and situation comedies over experimental dramas and operas. More pleasure will result from showing the former (also more profit, but Green says this is not for him the primary consideration and we are inclined to believe him). Thus far, Green's policy has prevailed.

Two parents who share relevant factual beliefs will set different goals for their children if one espouses quantitative hedonism while the other agrees with Mill that some pleasures are more worthwhile than others. Parents who hold that moral virtue, but not knowledge, is intrinsically desirable may adopt (perhaps for a child of either sex) the maxim so frankly set forth in a quaint old verse—"Be good, sweet maid, and let who will be clever." It is tempting to dwell on examples from child-rearing and education because here, if anywhere, we can see something of what people think about the ultimately desirable qualities of human beings and the intrinsic values that these may embody or presuppose. In bringing up children we have a chance at a vicarious fresh start, to some extent at least, and at making, for new lives, a new world.

It seems probable that, in nearly every discussion of what to do about a given ethical problem, a divergence will develop between those who think that the results of a proposed course of action are what make it the right course to follow, and those who point to some other feature of it—that it would be a violation of the rights of certain individuals, for example. And similarly for the split between those who see pleasure or happiness as the sole ultimate value, and those who hold some other conviction.

But, having uncovered such basic disagreements, must we leave matters at that? As far as this little book is concerned, the answer is yes. Yet if the nerve of philosophical thinking has been effectively exposed here, it will be clear that other questions, in some ways still more fundamental than those already discussed, lie just around the corner. Is there such a thing as truth or error in ethics, so that it makes sense to say that utilitarians or hedonists, e.g., are right, and their opponents wrong? What are we doing when we make or express a particular ethical judgment? Can we say that some such judgments are supported by better reasons than others? These questions belong to *metaethics,* a branch of ethical theory which has absorbed the attention of many able philosophers in our own century. The philosophical discussions in Chapter 2 may be seen, on reflection, to have considerable bearing on metaethics.

It is sometimes said that ethical questions are too important to be left to philosophers. Perhaps you will decide that they, along with other challenging questions in human experience and thought, are too important to be confronted without philosophy.

REFERENCES

REFERENCES

CHAPTER ONE

ON PHILOSOPHY AND ITS PROBLEMS

Broad, C. D., "Critical and Speculative Philosophy," in J. H. Muirhead, ed., *Contemporary British Philosophy,* Series 1. London, Allen & Unwin, 1924.

————, *Scientific Thought* (New York, Harcourt Brace Jovanovich, 1923), chap. 1.

Burtt, Edwin A., *In Search of Philosophic Understanding.* New York, New American Library (Mentor Books), 1965.

Hook, Sidney, "Philosophy and Human Conduct," in *Quest for Being.* New York, Dell (Delta Books), 1963.

James, William, "Philosophy and Its Critics," in *Some Problems of Philosophy* (London, Longmans, Green, 1911), chap. 1.

Johnstone, Henry W., ed., *What Is Philosophy?* New York, Macmillan (Sources in Philosophy), 1965.

Maugham, W. Somerset, *The Summing Up* (Baltimore, Penguin Books, 1946), pp. 166–219.

Murphy, Arthur E., *The Uses of Reason* (New York, Macmillan, 1943), Part IV.

Plato, *Apology.*

Russell, Bertrand, *The Problems of Philosophy* (London, Oxford University Press [Home University Library], 1912), chap. 15.

————, *Philosophy* (New York, Norton, 1927) chaps. 1, 27.

————, *Unpopular Essays* (New York, Simon and Schuster, 1950), chap. 2.

Sidgwick, Henry, *Philosophy, Its Scope and Relations.* London, Macmillan, 1902.

CHAPTER TWO

ON SCIENTIFIC METHOD

Black, Max, *Critical Thinking,* 2nd ed. Englewood Cliffs, N.J., Prentice-Hall, 1952.

————, "The Definition of Scientific Method," in *Problems of Analysis.* Ithaca, N.Y., Cornell University Press, 1954.

Cohen, Morris R., and Nagel, Ernest, *An Introduction to Logic and Scientific Method* (New York, Harcourt Brace Jovanovich, 1934), Book II.

Dewey, John, *How We Think,* rev. ed. (Boston, Heath, 1933), Part II.

Duhem, Pierre, *The Aim and Structure of Physical Theory,* trans. by Philip Wiener. Princeton University Press, 1954.

Hanson, Norwood R., "The Logic of Discovery." *Journal of Philosophy,* 55 (1958).

Hempel, Carl G., *Philosophy of Natural Science.* Englewood Cliffs, N.J., Prentice-Hall (Foundations of Philosophy Series), 1965.

Hospers, John, "What Is Explanation?" *Journal of Philosophy,* 43 (1946).

Nagel, Ernest, "The Methods of Science: What Are They? Can They Be Taught?" in Israel Scheffler, ed., *Philosophy and Education.* Boston, Allyn and Bacon, 1958.

————, *The Structure of Science* (New York, Harcourt Brace Jovanovich, 1961), chaps. 1–3.

Nidditch, P. H., ed., *The Philosophy of Science.* London, Oxford University Press (Oxford Readings in Philosophy), 1968.

Peirce, Charles S., "The Fixation of Belief." *Popular Science Monthly,* 1877.

Presley, C. F., "Laws and Theories in the Physical Sciences." *Australasian Journal of Philosophy,* 32 (1954).

Shapere, Dudley, ed., *Philosophical Problems of Natural Science.* New York, Macmillan (Sources in Philosophy), 1965.

ON SCIENCE IN GENERAL

Bronowski, J., *The Common Sense of Science* (Cambridge, Mass., Harvard University Press, 1953), chaps. 7–9.

Campbell, Norman R., *What Is Science?* New York, Dover, 1952.

Conant, James B., *On Understanding Science* (New York, New American Library [Mentor Books], 1951), chaps. 1–3.

Hildebrand, Joel H., *Science in the Making.* New York, Columbia University Press, 1957.

Nagel, Ernest, *The Structure of Science,* chap. 1.

Russell, Bertrand, "The Place of Science in a Liberal Education," in *Mysticism and Logic.* New York, Doubleday (Anchor Books), 1957.

Somerville, John, "Umbrellology." *Philosophy of Science,* 8 (1941).

ON THE LIMITATIONS OF SCIENCE

Allport, Gordon W., "Normative Compatibility in the Light of Social Science," in Abraham Maslow, ed., *New Knowledge in Human Values.* New York, Harper & Row, 1959.

Conant, James B., *Modern Science and Modern Man* (New York, Doubleday [Anchor Books], 1953), third and fourth Lectures.

Feigl, Herbert, "The Scientific Outlook: Naturalism and Humanism." *American Quarterly,* 1 (1949).

Grünbaum, Adolf, "Science and Ideology." *Scientific Monthly,* 79 (1954).

Krutch, Joseph Wood, *The Measure of Man* (New York, Bobbs-Merrill, 1954), chaps. 1–4.

Lundberg, George A., *Can Science Save Us?* (London, Longmans, Green, 1947), chap. 2.

Lunn, Arnold, *The Revolt Against Reason* (London, Sheed & Ward, 1951), chaps. 13–16.

McCarthy, Harold E., "Science and Its Critics." *The Humanist,* 12 (1952).

Murphy, Arthur E., *The Uses of Reason,* Part I.

Nagel, Ernest, "Malicious Philosophies of Science." *Partisan Review,* 10 (1943).

——, "The Perspectives of Science and the Prospects of Men." *Perspectives U.S.A.,* No. 7 (Spring, 1954).

——, *The Structure of Science,* chap. 6.

Otto, Max C., *Science and the Moral Life* (New York, New American Library [Mentor Books], 1949), chaps. 4–5.

Pollard, William Grosvenor, *Physicist and Christian: A Dialogue Between the Communities.* New York, Seabury Press, 1961.

Scriven, Michael, "The Limits of Physical Explanation," in Bernard Baumrin, ed., *Delaware Seminar in the Philosophy of Science,* Vol. II. New York, Wiley (Interscience), 1963.

Sullivan, J. W. N., *The Limitations of Science* (New York, Viking Press, 1933; New American Library [Mentor Books], 1959), chaps. 6, 7.

ON THE PRESUPPOSITIONS OF SCIENCE

Feigl, Herbert, "Scientific Method Without Metaphysical Presuppositions." *Philosophical Studies,* 5 (1954).

Margenau, Henry, "Does Physical 'Knowledge' Require *A Priori* or Undemonstrable Presuppositions?" in L. W. Friedrich, S.J., ed., *The Nature of Physical Knowledge.* Bloomington, Indiana University Press and Marquette University Press, 1960.

Poincaré, Henri, *Science and Hypothesis,* in *The Foundations of Science,* trans. by G. B. Halsted (New York, Science Press, 1913), chap. 9.

Reichenbach, Hans, *The Rise of Scientific Philosophy* (Berkeley, University of California Press, 1951), chaps. 5, 6, 14.

Russell, Bertrand, *Human Knowledge* (London, Allen & Unwin, 1948), Part VI.

Toulmin, Stephen, *The Philosophy of Science* (London, Hutchinson, 1953), chap. 5.

ON THE PROBLEM OF INDUCTION

Ambrose, Alice, "The Problem of Justifying Inductive Inference." *Journal of Philosophy,* 44 (1947).

Black, Max, *Language and Philosophy* (Ithaca, N.Y., Cornell University Press, 1949), chap. 3.

——, *Problems of Analysis* (Ithaca, N.Y., Cornell University Press, 1954), chaps. 10–12.

——, "Self-supporting Inductive Arguments." *Journal of Philosophy,* 55 (1958), pp. 718–25.

Burks, Arthur W., "The Presupposition Theory of Induction." *Philosophy of Science,* 20 (1953).

Edwards, Paul, "Bertrand Russell's Doubts about Induction." *Mind,* 58 (1949).

Feigl, Herbert, "The Logical Character of the Principle of Induction." *Philosophy of Science,* 1 (1934).

Hume, David, *An Enquiry Concerning Human Understanding* (1748), Sec. 4.

Madden, E. H., "The Riddle of Induction." *Journal of Philosophy,* 55 (1958).

Mill, John Stuart, *A System of Logic* (1843), Book III, chaps. 3, 21.

Nagel, Ernest, *The Structure of Science,* chap. 4, §§ 1, 5.

Reichenbach, Hans, *Experience and Prediction* (University of Chicago Press, 1938), chaps. 32–34, 38.

———, "The Logical Foundations of the Concept of Probability," in Herbert Feigl and May Brodbeck, eds., *Readings in the Philosophy of Science.* New York, Appleton-Century-Crofts, 1953.

———, "On the Justification of Induction." *Journal of Philosophy,* 37 (1940).

———, *The Theory of Probability,* 2nd ed., trans. by E. H. Hutton and Maria Reichenbach (Berkeley, University of California Press, 1949), Sec. 91.

Russell, Bertrand, *The Problems of Philosophy,* chap. 6.

Salmon, Wesley C., "Inductive Inference," in Bernard Baumrin, ed., *Delaware Seminar on the Philosophy of Science.* New York, Wiley (Interscience), 1963.

———, "Should We Attempt to Justify Induction?" *Philosophical Studies,* 8 (1957).

Skyrms, Brian, *Choice and Chance: An Introduction to Inductive Logic* (Belmont, Calif., Dickenson, 1966), chaps. 2, 3.

Strawson, P. F., *Introduction to Logical Theory* (New York, Wiley, 1952), chap. 9.

ON RATIONALISM

Blanshard, Brand, "Current Strictures on Reason." *Philosophical Review,* 54 (1945).

———, *Reason and Analysis* (La Salle, Ill., Open Court, 1962), chaps. 1, 2.

Descartes, René, *Rules for the Direction of the Mind.*

Ewing, A. C., *Reason and Intuition.* London, Humphrey Milford, 1942.

Locke, John, *Essay Concerning Human Understanding* (1690), Book I.

Plato, *Meno.*

———, *Phaedo.*

Reichenbach, Hans, *The Rise of Scientific Philosophy,* chap. 3.

ON SELF-EVIDENCE

Blanshard, Brand, *The Nature of Thought* (London, Allen & Unwin, 1939), pp. 237–59.

Descartes, René, *Meditations I and II.* 1641.

Frank, Philipp, "Why Do Scientists and Philosophers So Often Disagree About the Merits of a New Theory?" in *Modern Science and Its Philosophy.* Cambridge, Mass., Harvard University Press, 1949.

Stout, G. F., "Self-evidence and Matter of Fact." *Philosophy,* 9 (1934).

ON SYNTHETIC NECESSARY TRUTHS

Ayer, A. J., *Language, Truth and Logic* (London, Gollancz, 1936), chap. 4.

Blanshard, Brand, *Reason and Analysis*, chap. 6.

Broad, C. D., "Are There Synthetic *A Priori* Truths?" *Proceedings of the Aristotelian Society*, Supp. Vol. 15 (1936).

Chisholm, Roderick M., *Theory of Knowledge* (Englewood Cliffs, N.J., Prentice-Hall [Foundations of Philosophy Series], 1966), chap. 5.

Ewing, A. C., "The Linguistic Theory of *A Priori* Propositions." *Proceedings of the Aristotelian Society*, 40 (1939–40).

Kant, Immanuel, *Critique of Pure Reason* (1781), Introduction.

——, *Prolegomena To Any Future Metaphysics*, trans. by L. W. Beck (New York, Liberal Arts, 1950), Introduction and Preamble.

Lewis, C. I., *Mind and the World-Order* (New York, Scribner's, 1929), chaps. 7–9.

——, "A Pragmatic Conception of the *A Priori*." *Journal of Philosophy*, 20 (1923).

Mill, John Stuart, *A System of Logic* (1843), Book II, chaps. 5, 6.

Russell, Bertrand, *The Problems of Philosophy*, chap. 7.

Sumner, L. W., and Woods, John, eds., *Necessary Truth*. New York, Random House, 1969.

Toulmin, Stephen, "A Defense of 'Synthetic Necessary Truth.'" *Mind*, 58 (1949).

Waismann, Friedrich, *Problems of Linguistic Philosophy* (London, Macmillan, 1966), pp. 57–68.

ON THE PRINCIPLE OF LAWFULNESS

Blanshard, Brand, *Reason and Analysis*, chap. 11.

Feigl, Herbert, "De Principiis Non Disputandum . . . ?" in Max Black, ed., *Philosophical Analysis*. Ithaca, N.Y., Cornell University Press, 1950.

——, "The Logical Character of the Principle of Induction." *Philosophy of Science*, 1 (1934).

Hume, David, *An Enquiry Concerning Human Understanding*. 1748.

Lewis, C. I., *Mind and the World Order*, chap. 8.

Nagel, Ernest, "The Causal Character of Modern Physical Theory," in *Freedom and Reason*. New York, Free Press of Glencoe, 1951.

——, "Sovereign Reason," § 5, in *Sovereign Reason*. New York, Free Press of Glencoe, 1954.

——, *The Structure of Science*, chaps. 4, 10.

Reichenbach, Hans, "On the Justification of Induction." *Journal of Philosophy*, 37 (1940).

Russell, Bertrand, *The Problems of Philosophy*, chap. 6.

Schlick, Moritz, "Causality in Everyday Life and in Recent Science." *University of California Publications in Philosophy* (1932).

Warnock, G. J., " 'Every Event Has a Cause,' " in Antony Flew, ed., *Essays on Logic and Language* (2nd series). London, Blackwell, 1953.

CHAPTER THREE
ON THE MENTAL AND THE PHYSICAL

Anderson, Alan, ed., *Minds and Machines*. Englewood Cliffs, N.J., Prentice-Hall, 1964.

Chisholm, Roderick M., *Perceiving* (Ithaca, N.Y., Cornell University Press, 1957), chap. 11.

Descartes, René, *Meditations II and VI*. 1641.

Feigl, Herbert, "The 'Mental' and the 'Physical,' " in H. Feigl and others, eds., *Minnesota Studies in the Philosophy of Science*, Vol. II (Minneapolis, University of Minnesota Press, 1958), pp. 397–419.

Flew, Antony, ed., *Body, Mind, and Death*. New York, Macmillan, 1964.

Huxley, T. H., "On the Hypothesis that Animals Are Automata and its History," in *Methods and Results*. 1893.

Montague, W. P., *The Chances of Surviving Death*. Cambridge, Mass., Harvard University Press, 1934.

Morick, Harold, ed., *Introduction to the Philosophy of Mind*. Glenview, Ill., Scott, Foresman, 1970.

Quinton, A. M., "The Soul." *Journal of Philosophy*, 59 (1962).

Vesey, G. N. A., ed., *Body and Mind*. London, Allen & Unwin, 1964.

ON THE NATURE OF THE SELF

Allport, Gordon W., *Becoming*. New Haven, Yale University Press, 1955.

Ayer, A. J., *Language, Truth and Logic*, rev. ed. (New York, Dover, 1952), chap. 7.

Bergson, Henri, *Introduction to Metaphysics* (New York, Liberal Arts, 1949), pp. 24–38.

Blanshard, Brand, *The Nature of Thought*, Vol. I, chap. 14.

Broad, C. D., *The Mind and Its Place in Nature* (London, Routledge and Kegan Paul, 1925), chaps. 6, 13, 14.

Gallie, I., "Is the Self a Substance?" *Mind*, 45 (1936).

Grice, H. P., "Personal Identity." *Mind*, 50 (1941).

Hume, David, *Treatise of Human Nature* (1739–40), Book I, Part IV, §§ 5, 6; Appendix.

James, William, *Principles of Psychology* (New York, Holt, Rinehart & Winston, 1890), chaps. 9, 10.

McTaggart, J. M. E., *The Nature of Existence* (London, Cambridge University Press, 1921–27), Vol. II, chap. 36.

Mead, G. H., *Mind, Self, and Society*. University of Chicago Press, 1947.

Williams, B. A. O., "Personal Identity and Individualism." *Proceedings of the Aristotelian Society*, 57 (1957).

ON DUALISTIC THEORIES

Broad, C. D., *The Mind and Its Place in Nature*, chap. 3.

Ducasse, C. J., *Nature, Mind and Death*. La Salle, Ill., Open Court, 1951.

Hardie, W. F. R., "Bodies and Minds." *The Listener*, April 14, 1960.

Pratt, J. B., *Matter and Spirit* (New York, Macmillan, 1922), chaps. 1, 2, 4.
Shaffer, Jerome, *Philosophy of Mind.* Englewood Cliffs, N.J., Prentice-Hall (Foundations of Philosophy Series), 1968.
Taylor, Richard, *Metaphysics* (Englewood Cliffs, N.J., Prentice-Hall [Foundations of Philosophy Series], 1963), chaps. 1, 2.

ON BEHAVIORISM

Chappell, V. C., ed., *The Philosophy of Mind.* Englewood Cliffs, N.J., Prentice-Hall, 1962.
Elliott, Hugh, *Modern Science and Materialism* (London, Longmans, Green, 1919), pp. 120–31, 190–209.
Place, U. T., "Is Consciousness a Brain Process?" *British Journal of Psychology,* 47 (1956).
Ryle, Gilbert, *The Concept of Mind* (New York, Barnes & Noble, 1949), chap. 1.
Tyndall, John, "Scientific Materialism," in *Fragments of Science.* 1892.

ON THE IDENTITY THEORY

Feigl, Herbert, "The 'Mental' and the 'Physical.' "
Hook, Sidney, ed., *Dimensions of Mind* (New York University Press, 1960; New York, Collier, 1961), Part I.
Pitcher, George, "Sensations and Brain Processes." *Australasian Journal of Philosophy,* 38 (1960).
Shaffer, Jerome, "Could Mental States be Brain Processes?" *Journal of Philosophy,* 58 (1961).
———, "Mental Events and the Brain." *Journal of Philosophy,* 60 (1963).
Smart, J. J. C., "Brain Processes and Incorrigibility." *Australasian Journal of Philosophy,* 40 (1962).
———, "Further Remarks on Sensations and Brain Processes." *Philosophical Review,* 70 (1961).
———, *Philosophy and Scientific Realism.* London, Routledge and Kegan Paul, 1963.
———, "Sensations and Brain Processes." *Philosophical Review,* 68 (1959).
Strawson, P. F., "Persons," in H. Feigl and others, eds., *Minnesota Studies in the Philosophy of Science,* Vol. II. Minneapolis, University of Minnesota Press, 1958.
Taylor, Richard, *Metaphysics,* chaps. 1–3.

ON THE PROBLEM OF FREE WILL VS. DETERMINISM

Ayer, A. J., "Freedom and Necessity," in *Philosophical Essays.* London, Macmillan, 1954.
Berofsky, Bernard, ed., *Free Will and Determinism.* New York, Harper & Row, 1966.
Broad, C. D., *Determinism, Indeterminism, and Libertarianism.* New York, Macmillan, 1934.

Campbell, C. Arthur, "In Defense of Free Will," Inaugural Address, Glasgow University, 1938, in Richard B. Brandt, ed., *Value and Obligation.* New York, Harcourt Brace Jovanovich, 1961.

———, "Is 'Freewill' a Pseudo-Problem?" *Mind,* 60 (1951).

———, *On Selfhood and Godhood* (London, Allen & Unwin, 1957), Lecture IX.

Chisholm, Roderick M., *Human Freedom and the Self.* Lawrence, University of Kansas Press, 1964.

Dworkin, Gerald, ed., *Determinism, Free Will, and Moral Responsibility.* Englewood Cliffs, N.J., Prentice-Hall (Central Issues in Philosophy), 1970.

Enteman, Willard F., ed., *The Problem of Free Will.* New York, Scribner's, 1967.

Goldman, Alvin I., "Actions, Predictions, and Books of Life." *American Philosophical Quarterly,* 5 (1968).

Hampshire, S., MacLagan, W. G., and Hare, R. M., "The Freedom of the Will" (A Symposium). *Proceedings of the Aristotelian Society,* Supp. Vol. 25 (1951).

Hobart, R. E., "Free Will as Involving Determinism and Inconceivable Without It." *Mind,* 43 (1934).

Hook, Sidney, ed., *Determinism and Freedom* (New York University Press, 1958; New York, Collier, 1961), Part I.

Lamont, Corliss, *Freedom of Choice Affirmed.* New York, Horizon Press, 1967.

Lehrer, Keith, ed., *Freedom and Determinism.* New York, Random House, 1966.

Morgenbesser, Sidney, and Walsh, James, eds., *Free Will.* Englewood Cliffs, N.J., Prentice-Hall, 1962.

Pears, David F., ed., *Freedom and the Will.* New York, St. Martin's Press, 1963.

Russell, Bertrand, *Mysticism and Logic* (London, Longmans, Green, 1918), chap. 9.

———, *Our Knowledge of the External World* (New York, Norton, 1929), pp. 247–56.

Wood, Ledger, "The Free-Will Controversy." *Philosophy,* 16 (1941).

ON PSYCHOLOGICAL FREEDOM AND LAWFULNESS

Grünbaum, Adolf, "Causality and the Science of Human Behavior." *American Scientist,* 40 (1952).

———, "Science and Man." *Perspectives in Biology and Medicine,* 5 (1962).

Hampshire, Stuart, *Freedom and the Individual* (New York, Harper & Row, 1965), chap. 1.

Holbach, Paul H. D., Baron, *The System of Nature* (1770), chaps. 11, 12.

Hospers, John, "Meaning and Free Will." *Philosophy and Phenomenological Research,* 10 (1949–50).

Hume, David, *Enquiry Concerning Human Understanding* (1748), Sec. 8.

———, *Treatise of Human Nature* (1738–40), Book II, Part III, Secs. 1, 2.

Lehrer, Keith, "Can We Know That We Have Free Will by Introspection?" *Journal of Philosophy,* 57 (1960).

Mill, John Stuart, *A System of Logic* (1843), Book VI, chap. 2.

Ryle, Gilbert, *The Concept of Mind,* chap. 3.

Taylor, Richard, "I Can." *Philosophical Review,* 69 (1960).

——, *Metaphysics,* chap. 4.

ON FREE WILL AND RESPONSIBILITY

Aristotle, *Nicomachean Ethics,* Book III.

Beardsley, Elizabeth L., "Moral Worth and Moral Credit." *Philosophical Review,* 66 (1957).

——, "Determinism and Moral Perspectives." *Philosophy and Phenomenological Research,* 21 (1960–61).

Braybrook, David, "Stevenson, Voltaire, and the Case of Admiral Byng." *Journal of Philosophy,* 53 (1956). See Stevenson below.

Feinberg, Joel, "On Justifying Legal Punishment," in Carl J. Friedrich, ed., *Nomos III: Responsibility.* New York, Liberal Arts, 1960.

——, "Problematic Responsibility in Law and Morals." *Philosophical Review,* 71 (1962).

Glover, M. R., "Mr. Mabbott on Punishment." *Mind,* 48 (1939). See Mabbott below.

Hart, H. L. A., "Negligence, *Mens Rea,* and Criminal Responsibility," in A. G. Guest, ed., *Oxford Essays in Jurisprudence.* London, Oxford University Press, 1961.

Hook, Sidney, ed., *Determinism and Freedom,* Parts III, IV.

Hospers, John, "Meaning and Free Will." *Philosophy and Phenomenological Research,* 10 (1949–50).

——, *Human Conduct* (New York, Harcourt Brace Jovanovich, 1961), chap. 10.

——, "What Means This Freedom?" in Sidney Hook, ed., *Determinism and Freedom.*

James, William, "The Dilemma of Determinism," in *The Will to Believe and Other Essays.* London, Longmans, Green, 1931.

Kant, Immanuel, *The Philosophy of Law,* trans. by W. Hastie (1887), pp. 194–201.

Lewis, H. D., "Moral Freedom in Recent Ethics" and "Guilt and Freedom," in *Morals and Revelation.* London, Allen & Unwin, 1951.

Mabbott, J. D., "Punishment." *Mind,* 48 (1939).

Morris, Herbert, ed., *Freedom and Responsibility: Readings in Philosophy and Law.* Stanford, Calif., Stanford University Press, 1961.

Nowell-Smith, P. H., "Free Will and Moral Responsibility." *Mind,* 57 (1948).

——, "Psycho-analysis and Moral Language." *The Rationalist Annual* (1954).

Sartre, Jean-Paul, *Existentialism and Humanism,* trans. by Philip Mairet. London, Methuen, 1949.

Schlick, Moritz, *Problems of Ethics,* trans. by D. Rynin (Englewood Cliffs, N.J., Prentice-Hall, 1939), chap. 7.

Stevenson, Charles L., "Ethical Judgments and Avoidability." *Mind,* 47 (1938).

CHAPTER FOUR

ON TELEOLOGICAL THEORIES

Bentham, Jeremy, *An Introduction to the Principles of Morals and Legislation* (1789), chaps. 1–4.

Broad, C. D., "Egoism as a Theory of Human Motives," in *Ethics and the History of Philosophy*. London, Routledge and Kegan Paul, 1952.

———, *Five Types of Ethical Theory* (New York, Harcourt Brace Jovanovich, 1934), chap. 6.

Butler, Joseph, *Fifteen Sermons Upon Human Nature* (1726), Sermon XI.

Feinberg, Joel, "Psychological Egoism," in Joel Feinberg, ed., *Reason and Responsibility*, 2nd ed. Encino, Calif., Dickenson, 1971.

Frankena, William, *Ethics* (Englewood Cliffs, N.J., Prentice-Hall [Foundations of Philosophy Series], 1963), chap. 3.

Hobbes, Thomas, *Leviathan* (1651), Part I, chaps. 6, 11, 13–15.

———, *Philosophical Rudiments Concerning Government and Society* (1651), chap. 1.

Medlin, Brian, "Ultimate Principles and Ethical Egoism." *Australasian Journal of Philosophy*, 35 (1957).

Mill, John Stuart, *Utilitarianism*. 1863.

Moore, G. E., *Principia Ethica* (London, Cambridge University Press, 1903), chap. III, Part C, Secs. 58–65.

Nowell-Smith, P. H., *Ethics* (Baltimore, Penguin Books, 1954), chaps. 15, 16.

Rawls, John, "Two Concepts of Rules." *Philosophical Review*, 64 (1955).

Sidgwick, Henry, *The Methods of Ethics* (London, Macmillan, 1874), Book IV.

Slote, Michael A., "An Empirical Basis for Psychological Egoism." *Journal of Philosophy*, 61 (1964).

Smart, J. J. C., *An Outline of a System of Utilitarian Ethics*. Victoria, Australia, Melbourne University Press, 1961.

———, "Extreme and Restricted Utilitarianism." *Philosophical Quarterly*, 6 (1956).

Williams, Gardner, "Individual, Social, and Universal Ethics." *Journal of Philosophy*, 45 (1948).

ON DEONTOLOGICAL THEORIES

Broad, C. D., *Five Types of Ethical Theory*, chaps. 3, 5.

Butler, Joseph, *The Analogy of Religion* (1736), Dissertation II.

Ewing, A. C., *The Definition of Good* (New York, Macmillan, 1947), chap. 6.

Falk, W. D., "Morality, Self and Others," in H. N. Castaneda and G. Nakhnikian, eds., *Morality and the Language of Conduct*. Detroit, Wayne State University Press, 1963.

Frankena, William, *Ethics*, chap. 2.

Kant, Immanuel, *Foundations of the Metaphysics of Morals*. 1785.

MacKinnon, D. M., *A Study in Ethical Theory* (London, Black, 1957), chap. 3.

Paton, H. J., *The Categorical Imperative*. London, Hutchinson, 1953.
Ross, W. D., *Foundations of Ethics* (Oxford, Clarendon Press, 1939), chaps. 4–6.
———, *Kant's Ethical Theory* (Oxford, Clarendon Press, 1954), pp. 29–35.
———, *The Right and the Good* (Oxford, Clarendon Press, 1930), chap. 2.
Singer, Marcus, *Generalization in Ethics* (New York, Knopf, 1961), chaps. 8, 9.
St. Thomas Aquinas, *Summa Theologica*, Part I of Part II, Questions 90–94.

ON HEDONISM

Bentham, Jeremy. For references, see above.
Broad, C. D., *Five Types of Ethical Theory*, chap. 6.
Carritt, E. F., *Ethical and Political Thinking* (Oxford, Clarendon Press, 1947), chap. 8.
Epicurus, "Letter to Menoeceus," in Diogenes Laertius, *Lives of Eminent Philosophers*, Book X.
———, *Principal Doctrines*, trans. by Cyril Bailey. Oxford, Clarendon Press, 1926.
Frankena, William, *Ethics*, chap. 5.
Mill, John Stuart. For references, see above.
Moore, G. E., *Ethics* (London, Oxford University Press, 1912), chaps. 1, 2.
———, *Principia Ethica*, chap. 3.
Nowell-Smith, P. H., *Ethics*, chaps. 8–10.
Perry, Ralph Barton, *General Theory of Value* (London, Longmans, Green, 1926), chaps. 21, 22.
Sidgwick, Henry, *The Methods of Ethics*, Book III, chap. 14.
Taylor, A. E., *Epicurus*. London, Constable, 1911.

ON NONHEDONISTIC THEORIES OF GOOD

Aristotle, *Nicomachean Ethics*, Books I, X.
St. Augustine, "The Morals of the Catholic Church," in Whitney J. Oates, ed., *Basic Writings*. New York, Random House, 1948.
Bradley, F. H., "Ideal Morality," "My Station and Its Duties," and "Why Should I be Moral?" in *Ethical Studies*. Oxford, Clarendon Press, 1876.
Carritt, E. F., *Ethical and Political Thinking* (Oxford, Clarendon Press, 1947), chap. 7.
Moore, G. E., *Ethics* (London, Oxford University Press, 1912), chaps. 1, 2.
———, *Principia Ethica*, chap. 6.
Nietzsche, Friedrich, *Beyond Good and Evil* (1886), chap. 9.
Ross, W. D., *Foundations of Ethics*, chap. 11.
———, *The Right and the Good*, chap. 5.

INDEX

INDEX

A 1
B 2
C 3
D 4
E 5
F 6
G 7
H 8
I 9
J 0